Some Tennessee Heroes
of the
Revolution

Compiled from Pension Statements

Five Parts in One Volume

Compiled By:
Zella Armstrong

Southern Historical Press, Inc.
Greenville, South Carolina

Originally printed 1933 by:
Zella Armstrong

New Material Copyright 2022 to:
Southern Historical Press, Inc.

All rights reserved. No part of this publication may be reproduced, stored in a retrieval system or transmitted in any form or by any means without the prior permission of the publisher.

SOUTHERN HISTORICAL PRESS, INC.
PO BOX 1267
Greenville, SC 29601

ISBN #978-1-63914-089-3

Printed in the United States of America

FOREWORD

The Revolutionary Pension Lists provide an interesting source for research work. The activities of the soldiers not only during the Revolution but in after years as they sought homes in new country give information that frequently can be found no where else. The Invalid Lists of 1806 awarded pensions only to those who were disabled by reason of the War. There are three later Pension Lists, popularly known as 1818, 1832 and 1840. The requirements of the 1818 list were very rigid and comparatively few soldiers received pensions. By the time of the 1832 List it was somewhat easier to comply with Government demands as to eligibility and by the time of the 1840 List restrictions were practically removed and all who served could secure recognition. Even widows who married the quite old soldiers were allowed pension, the earlier lists having qualified only widows of early marriages. One widow received a pension although she proved that she married the soldier the day he died when he was 75 years of age!

The List of 1840 is so called because Congress authorized the Census of 1840 to include all pensioners. The list was published therefore as an appendix to the Census of that year. Soldiers and widows who applied too late to be included in the census report of 1840 are listed as of that time although they do not appear on the printed list.

The 1840 List is especially interesting to researchers as it includes many widows' applications. Widows were required to prove marriage, names of children, etc., data not demanded of soldiers who had only to prove service and eligibility. Widows' applications are, therefore, genealogical gold mines. Even those widows who could not prove marriage and consequently failed to secure pensions—there are many such papers because it was difficult to find proof of marriage which occurred sometimes sixty years earlier in a war torn land—gave data which are valuable now to descendants who can frequently in the light of later knowledge, give proof of marriage ceremony.

The soldiers' applications give proof of service, date and place of birth and residence at time of enlistment. When service was easily proved the papers contain little other information. In some cases, however, the names of parents and much other interesting data are given.

As the State of Tennessee was erected after the Revolution all soldiers who lived during the War or after it in the country now known as Tennessee are credited to other states. Those who moved to the State later are credited in the states in which they lived and served. Those who lived in the Tennessee country during the Revolution will be found on North Carolina rolls.

It should be born in mind that in addition to the pensioners thousands of soldiers whose record is thoroughly established did not apply for pensions. The names on the Pension Rolls, therefore, represent only a part of Tennessee's Heroes of the Revolution. The pension records printed herewith have not been chosen as being more important than others or more interesting. These were collected for one reason or another and are printed at the request of several historians and librarians who have expressed a desire that the information should be available. Others will be printed from time to time.

The abstracts as given include only the vital data in the pension applications. Additional biographical information when known is supplied in notes.

For the sake of uniformity where the widow drew a pension, even though the soldier did not, the paragraph is titled with the soldier's name. The original spelling in the applications has been followed.

SOME TENNESSEE HEROES

OF THE

REVOLUTION

Compiled From Pension Statements

PAMPHLET NO. I

DAN ALEXANDER,
of Marion County

Dan Alexander applied for Revolutionary pension while living in Marion County, Tenn., in April 1833. He enlisted in Mecklenburg, County, N. C., in the spring of 1781, under Lieut. Ezekial Polk, Capt. Peter Burns, Maj. Moore, Col. Wade Hampton and Gen. Sumpter. He fought in the battle of Eutaw Springs. His discharge was burned when his home was burned. He was born Feb. 15, 1764, in Mecklenburg County, N. C. and thence to Haywood County, N. C. From there he moved to Marion County, Tenn. in 1832. He died in Marion County, Oct. 1, 1839. His widow, Sarah Alexander, applied for pension while living in Dade County, Ga., Feb. 25, 1853.

DAN ALEXANDER,
of Hardeman County

Dan Alexander applied for revolutionary pension while living in Hardeman County and his name appears on the 1832 List. He was born in Mecklenburg County, N. C., 1757. He volunteered under Capt. Alexander and General Erwin. The Captain was nicknamed "Black Alexander." Col. Gates wore velvet breeches and a pale blue coat with epaulettes. He rode a bay horse.

ROBERT ALLISON

Robert Allison lived n Sullivan County, Tenn., where his widow, Martha McKinsley (?) Allison applied for pension April 22, 1844. He died March 2, 1826. He served under Capt. Paxton and was in the battles of Long Island and Fort Washington. He was taken prisoner and kept on a

British ship. He married Martha McKinsley (the name is indistinct and one can not be positive of the spelling). Her pension was not allowed as soldier's service was not on record and the widow could not prove it. Her children were: Sarah, married ———— Hodges; Elizabeth, married ————— Deery; Susannah; Joseph; John; and Martha, married ————— Gray.

ISAAC ARMSTRONG

Isaac Armstrong applied for a revolutionary pension while living in Anderson County, Tenn. He was born in Maryland, July, 1762. When he was eight years old he moved with his parents to Loudoun County, Va., and at the age of fifteen moved to Augusta County, Va., where he was living when he enlisted in 1777 or 1778 under Col. Robert Craven. He enlisted again and moved to Botetourt County where he enlisted again. He moved to Greenbriar County, Va., and thence to Powell's Valley, now Tennessee. He settled in Anderson County about the year 1812. In 1837 he was transferred to Indiana as he moved to that state.

THOMAS ARMSTRONG

Thomas Armstrong applied for revolutionary pension while living in Lincoln County, Tenn. in October, 1832. He was born July 20, 1755 in York County, Pa. While a resident of Guilford County, N. C. he enlisted in April, 1777 and served three months as a private in Capt. John Davis' and Capt. George Pierce's Companies in Col. McDowell's North Carolina Regiment. He had previously enlisted while a resident of York County, Pa., the date not being given. He served two months under Capt. Arbison and Maj. John Aidy. He was engaged in guarding prisoners, said prisoners having been taken when Burgoyne surrendered. He then served two months with Pennsylvania troops and was engaged in capturing escaped prisoners. He served several short tours. After the close of the Revolution he moved with his father, the name not being given, to York District, S. C., where he married, name of wife not being given. He moved to Lincoln County, Tenn.

CARTER BARNETT

Carter Barnett applied for revolutionary pension while living in Roane County, Tenn. He enlisted as a marine at Newberne, N. C. in 1780 under Capt. Tatum. Pete Ferbish was mate. He was taken prisoner while on his way to St. Thomas and carried to Kingston, Jamaica where he was held as a prisoner until Peace was declared. He moved to Roane County, Tenn.

SPENCES BENSON

Spencer Benson applied for revolutionary pension while living in Rhea County, Tenn. He enlisted in Sussex County, Del., April 1, 1776 under Col. Simon Kollick, Maj. John Mitchell, Capt. Robert Houston, Lieut. John Craton and Ensign James Bronton. He served three months and volunteered again in August for the purpose of guarding Sussex and adjoining counties from acts of depredation and incursions by British seamen on the Chesapeake Bay. He volunteered again. He was born Dec. 4, 1755, in Sussex County, Del. After the War he removed to Raleigh, N. C., to Sevier County, Tenn. and to Rhea County, Tenn.

CHRISTOPHER BOSTON

Christopher Boston applied for revolutionary pension while living in Claiborne County, Tenn. in 1825. He enlisted in 1781 in a North Carolina regiment under Capt. Alerander Brevard and Major Blount. He was in the battles of Eutaw Springs and Ninety-six. His wife, Rebecca, was about 56 in 1824, so born about 1769. He died in Monroe County, June 9, 1849. His first wife, Rebecca, died in Buncombe County, N. C. in 1824. He married Elizabeth Masters Blount, Nov. 15, 1834, Justice Hooper officiating. The second wife died in Macon County, N. C.

WILLIAM BRADFORD

William Bradford applied for revolutionary pension while living in Sumner County, Tenn. in August 1828. He was born in Virginia. He enlisted in August 1777 in Capt. John Chilton's company, Col. Thomas Marshall's Regiment. He was discharged in Fauquier County, Va. After the Revolution he moved to Tennessee.

WILLIAM BRAGG

William Bragg applied for revolutionary pension while living in Cocke County, Tenn. in August 1832. He was born at Alexandria, Va. May 18, 1765. He was living in Maryland when he first enlisted. In Sept. 1781 he went to Loudon County, Va., where he enlisted as a substitute for William Alford. He enlisted again under Capt. Lewis and Col. West. He was present at the surrender of Cornwallis. He guarded British prisoners. He left the service in October, 1781. In 1782 he enlisted again as a substitute for Jonathan Sparrow. He received his honorable discharge in writing which he sold to a merchant for five pounds in Maryland currency, payable in drygoods. He moved some years after the War to Cocke County, Tenn. His widow also drew a pension.

THOMAS BRANNON

Thomas Brannon applied for revolutionary pension while living in Bledsoe County, Aug. 25, 1818. He enlisted in 1777 in Capt. Anthony Sharp's Company, Ninth North Carolina Regiment. He was in the battles of Eutaw Springs, Monmouth and Stoney Point. He was discharged in 1780 having served four full years. He moved after the War to Bledsoe County. Tenn. where he died March 22, 1828. It is said that he was 100 and some years of age and the oldest man who ever lived in the County.

STEPHEN BROWN

Stephen Brown applied for revolutionary pension while living in Bledsoe County, Tenn. in February, 1832. He was born in Cumberland County, Va. in 1756. He was living in Buckingham County, Va. when he enlisted in the Virginia troops under Capt. Redd. He was employed in guarding British prisoners. He declared that he could prove his service by Charles Thurman, a citizen of Bledsoe County, who served in the same regiment with him. He was stationed for a time near Albermarle and served near Guilford Court House before the battle. He moved to Bledsoe County, Tenn. about thirty years after the War. His discharge was burned when his house was burned about 1813.

DANIEL BROYLES

Daniel Broyles applied for revolutionary pension while living in McMinn County, Tenn. He was born n Culpepper County, Va., May 1, 1763. He enlisted in Culpeper County under Col. John Barbour and Major Roebuck. He entered service again under Capt. William Rice and Lieut. William Dickens. He moved to Rhea County where he drew pension on the 1840 list. After his death his children drew the arrears of his pension.

JAMES BUTLER

James Butler applied for revolutionary pention in Rhea County, N. C. in 1777. He moved to South Carolina and enlisted in South Carolina troops under Gen. Francis Marion. He was born in Culpeper County, Va. in 1749. Mrs. Phoebe Butler Ford declares that she is the eldest child of James Butler who died Jan. 12, 1836, leaving a widow, Agnes Butler, whose marriage to the soldier took place in 1785. The widow died March 1, 1846. Phoebe Butler Ford was 57 years of age, Feb. 10, 1852. Her husband Edmund Ford, was also 57 in 1852.

ZACHARIAH BUTLER of Maury County

Zachariah Butler applied for revolutionary pension while living in Maury County, Tenn., Sept. 22, 1832. He was born in Amelia County, Va., Nov. 15, 1764. He enlisted in Virginia as a substitute for John Foster of Amelia County and was in the Siege of Yorktown. He married Elizabeth Noble, Dec. 6, 1787, in Amelia County, the ceremony being performed by Rev. John Noble. Sarah Pillow of Maury County stated that she was present at the marriage. Zachariah Butler died in Maury County, April 8, 1842. His widow, Elizabeth Butler, applied for a pension which was granted. She states that her oldest child was born Sept. 23, 1788 and that a son was born in 1789. Some years after the Revolution Zachariah Butler moved to Maury County, Tennessee.

ZACHARIAH BUTLER of Sullivan County

Zachariah Butler applied for revolutionary pension while living in Sullivan County, Tenn., Aug. 21, 1832. He was born June 28, 1756. He enlisted in Maryland and served in the Maryland Militia. Several years after the Revolution he moved to Sullivan County, Tenn. His widow, Elizabeth Butler, maiden name not given, applied for a widow's pension which for some reason was not granted.

Note:—Two revolutionary soldiers by the name of Zachariah Butler drew pension in Tennessee. It is a coincidence that both their wives were named Elizabeth. One drew a widow's pension and one failed to obtain a pension.

GEORGE CALDWELL

George Caldwell applied for revolutionary pension while living in Blount County, Tenn. He was born in Prince Edward County, Va., Feb. 15, 1760. He enlisted in Capt. Butler's Company. He enlisted again under Capt. Isaac Hampton and Col. Campbell and again under Capt. James Newell and Col. William Preston. He was in active service three years, chiefly as a scout.

JAMES CAMPBELL

James Campbell applied for revolutionary pension while living in Knox County, Tenn., Oct. 5, 1832. He was born Feb. 15, 1759, in Augusta County, Va. He enlisted while a resident of Washington County, N. C. in May 1870 and served six months as a private in Capt. James Gibson's company, Col John Sevier's North Carolina regiment. He enlisted again in June and served six months as a private in Capt. James Gibson's and Capt. Nathaniel Davis' Company, Col. John Sevier's regiment after which he immediately volunteered and served two months as Orderly Sergeant under Col. John Sevier against the Cherokee Indians. He died April 8, 1844 in Knox County. He married Oct. 6, 1779, in Washington County, Gennett (also spelled Gennat and Ganatt) Allison. She was allowed a widow's pension on her application executed April 13, 1844, while a resident of Knox County, aged eighty-six years, so born 1758. They had children but the names are not given.

JAMES CAMPBELL

James Campbell applied for revolutionary pension while living in Carter County, Tenn., Aug. 13, 1833. He was born in Moore County, N. C. in Oct., 1756. He enlisted in Moore County in February, 1780, and served under Capt. Cage and Lieut. Nicholas Hall in a North Carolina regiment. He was in the Siege of Charleston where he was captured and held prisoner eight days. He was released on parole after which, in the fall of 1780 at Santee, South Carolina, while on his way home he volunteered and served two months under Col. Wayde against the Tories. He again enlisted in 1780 and served two months as a private in Capt. Jacob Duck's company, Col. Philip Alston's North Carolina regiment. He volunteered early in the fall of 1781 and served three months under Capt. Henry Gaston in North Carolina troops and was in an engagement at Cross Creek in Cumberland County, N. C.

JEREMIAH CAMPBELL

Jeremiah Campbell applied for revolutionary pension while living in Carter County, Tenn., Aug. 14, 1832. He was born Dec. 15, 1762, but does not give his birth place. He enlisted Oct. 1, 1780 in Washington County, N. C. and served three months as a Private in Capt. Valentine Sevier's company, under Colonels John Sevier and Campbell in North Carolina troops. He was in the battle of King's Mountain. He enlisted again early in September 1781, serving four months in Capt. Landon Carter's company, Col. John Sevier's regiment and was in the engagement on the Ashley River. He died in Carter County, Oct. 4, 1843.

ROBERT CAMPBELL

Robert Campbell applied for revolutionary pension while living in Carter's Valley, Hawkins County. Tenn., Aug. 27, 1833. He was born Jan. 3, 1759 in Prince Edward County, Va. In the fall of 1776 he moved to North Carolina, that section which was later Tennessee, where he volunteered immediately and served two months on scouting parties in Hawkins County against the Indians. He volunteered again in 1779 and served three months as a private in Capt. Christie's company, Col. Evan Shelby's regiment and was in the Chickamauga Expedition. He again volunteered in the latter part of 1779 or early in 1780 and served two months in Capt. John Looney's company, Col. Arthur Campbell's regiment against the Cherokee Indians. He also served as a scout under Capt. Kyle.

Note—He married Oct. 15, 1785, Mary Young, born in Rockbridge County, Va., Feb. 12, 1765. Her mother was Elizabeth Long Young, born Oct. 28, 1744, died 1835, who remembered seeing Washington and Braddock pass her father's house on the ill-fated Braddock Expedition. Mary Young Campbell died April 1. 1841, and is buried beside her husband on the home place 17 miles from Rogersville. They had 13 children: James Young, born 1786; Andrew, born 1787; Alexander, born 1789; Joseph, born 1791, died 1867, married Frances Vermillion; Robert, born 1793; Mary, born 1795, married Isaac Carmack; Jane, born 1797, married Samuel Curry; Elizabeth, born 1799, married John McNeal; Anna, born 1800, married Manson Merriman; Nelson, born 1802, died 1806; Anderson, born 1802 (twin to Nelson); Nelson (a second child by the name) born 1806; Phoebe, born 1809.

WILLIAM CARROLL

William Carroll applied for revolutionary pension while living in Roane County, Oct. 2, 1832. He was then aged about 77 years, and was therefore born in 1755. He enlisted in the North Carolina troops as a substitute for George Carroll.

LANDON CARTER

Landon Carter's widow, Elizabeth Carter, applied for revolutionary pension while residing in Carter County, Dec. 8, 1838. She was born July 9, 1765 Landon Carter was a Captain in the Revolution. He served under Col. John Sevier and Col. Arthur Campbell in 1780 and 1781. He married Feb. 26, 1784 and died June 5, 1800. Jeremiah Campbell testifies that Landon Carter served as stated and that he, Jeremiah Campbell, was in Capt. Carter's company and was in the South Carolina Campaign. Isaac Taylor also testifies that he was in Capt. Carter's Company. They were in the battle of Boyd's Creek and in an expedition against the Cherokee Indians.

Note:— Capt. Landon Carter was the son of Col. John Carter and Elizabeth Taylor Carter and was born in Virginia Jan. 29, 1760. He was educated at Liberty Hall, now Davidson College, N. C. He signed the Watauga Petition to have the settlement annexed to North Carolina and he was an active leader in all affairs of the upper East Tennessee country. Carter County, Tenn., was named for him and its County seat, Elizabethton, was named for his wife. He was a strong supporter of the State of Franklin and was Secretary of the first Franklin Convention. He married Elizabeth McLin. Their children were: Alfred Moore, born 1784, died 1850; John McLin, born 1786, died young; Sarah Stuart, born 1789, died 1879; William Blount, born 1792; George Washington, born 1794; Eliza M., born 1797; and Mary (Polly) C., born 1799.

RICHARD COOPER

Richard Cooper applied for revolutionary pension while living in Rhea County. He enlisted in Essex County, Va., under Lieut. Mosely and served nine months. He was transferred to Col. Proctor's Artillery and was in the battles of Brandywine, Monmouth, Guilford Court House and Eutaw Springs. He moved to Rhea County in 1807.

JOHN CRAWFORD

John Crawford applied for revolutionary pension while living in Hamilton County, Tenn. He was born Oct. 29, 1762, seven miles below Staunton, Va. He moved with his father to Surry County, N. C. where he resided during the Revolution. He enlisted three times, first in Surrey County in 1778; the second time in 1780 under Capt. Gibson Woodridge and Maj. Joel Lewis; the third time in 1781 under Capt. Edmund Hickman and Col. Rutherford. He was in the battles of Eutaw Springs, Briar Creek and others. After the War he moved to Washington County, N. C. (now Tennessee), and then to Greene, Knox, Anderson, Bledsoe and Hamilton Counties, Tenn. He seems to have lived for a time in Rhea County also. The arrears of his pension were paid to his children.

Note:—He also served in the War of 1812, enlisting in the Washington County Infantry. While he lived in Washington County he was a member of the Constitutional Convention of Tennessee and a member of the General Assembly of Tennessee. His descendants lived in the Graysville section of Hamilton County, Tenn., although it is said in the family records that he died in Ross's Landing. He died after 1840 as he is on the 1840 Pension List, but by that time the village of Ross's Landing had been renamed Chattanooga. He married Mary Vernon, daughter of Alexander and Margaret Chesnee Vernon. She was born in 1767 and the marriage tookplace in Spartanburg, S. C. about 1782. They had at least three children and possibly others. The oldest son, William Ayres Crawford. Another son, John Crawford, junior, born in Washington County, Dec. 16, 1809, entered the Confederate Army and died a prisoner at Camp Morton, Ind., April 10, 1762. Polly, a daughter of John Crawford and Margaret Chesnee Crawford married ———— White, (probably Silas White.)

WILLIAM CRYE

William Crye applied for revolutionary pension while he was living in McMinn County, Tenn. where he drew a pension on the 1832 list. As he was 80 years old when he made his application he was born about 1752. He was a native of the Isle of Mann but came to America when he was a child and was reared in Chester, Pa. He moved to North Carolina and was volunteered under Capt. Hagan in Mecklenburg County, N. C. He volunteered again under Capt. Drummond in Greenville, S. C., other officers under whom he served being Col. Neel. and Col. Ezekial Polk. In 1780 he served under Gen. Gates. After leaving North Carolina he lived in South Carolina, in Hale County, Ga. and in Tennessee. He died Aug. 30, 1835. He married Sarah Hagan, April 8, 1779. She died Feb. 8, 1844. She drew pension in Bradley County. A page from their Bible was enclosed in her application showing the marriage date and the marriage of their son, William Crye, Jr., to Elizabeth Barker. Aug. 11, 1822 and that the children of William Crye, Jr. were Sarah, born June 4, 1823 and Mary, born Nov. 7, 1825. William Crye, Sr., had a brother, John Crye.

JOHN CUNNINGHAM

John Cunningham applied for revolutionary pension while living in Warren County, Tenn., April 6, 1833. He was born February 10, 1784, in Lunenburg County, Va. He enlisted in Lunenburg County, in April, 1776, in Capt. Robert Dixon's company, Col. Dangerfield's regiment and served five months as private. He enlisted Feb. 15, 1781, and served about two months as a private in Capt. James Hollaway's company, Col. Nathaniel Cocke's regiment. He was in the battle of Guilford Court House. In 1833 a grandson, John Cunningham, junior was living in Warren County, Tennessee.

VALENTINE CUNNINGHAM

Valentine Cunningham applied for revolutionary pension while living in Roane County, Tenn. He enlisted Feb. 19, 1778 in Virginia in Capt. William Cunningham's company, Col. Richard Parker's regiment. He married a widow, Frances Lahow, who was born 1784. She had children by her first marriage to West Lahow. Valentine Cunningham and Frances had a son, Martin Cunningham, aged one year at the time the pension application was made. The name of the soldier's first wife is not given.

JAMES DAVIS

James Davis applied for revolutionary pension while living in Hamilton County, Tenn., Aug. 28, 1832. He was born in Faupuier County, Va., the date not given but he was seventy-one in 1832, therefore born in 1761. He was living in Wilkes County, N. C., when he enlisted in Capt. John Key's company in which he served three months; he also served five months in Capt. Smith's company, six weeks in Col. Cleveland's regiment and three months in Capt. Gordon's company, Col. Malbury's regiment and was in the battle of Eutaw Springs. He also served six weeks in Capt. Pendleton Isbell's company. He moved after the Revolution to Greene County, Tenn., then to Campbell and White Counties, Tenn., then to Jackson County, Ala., then to Marion County, Tenn., then to Hamilton County, Tenn., where he died Dec. 9, 1843. He married Mary, her surname not being given, in 1782, when she was sixteen years of age, so born 1766. She survived him and died in Hamilton County, after 1844 when the record states that she was living and before April 19, 1845. They had several children who were then residents of Hamilton County.

Note: The graves of James and Mary Davis are in that section of Hamilton County which became Sequatchie County, Tenn.

NICHOLAS DAVIS

Nicholas Davis applied for revolutionary pension while living in Jefferson County, Tenn., June 10, 1818. He served during the Revolution in the Virginia troops. He died in Jefferson County, June 16, 1829. He married Mary Hays, Aug. 15, 1781 or 1782. She applied for widow's pension while living in Jefferson County. Feb. 4, 1839. Their children were: Sarah Peggy, Aley (Alexander?), Polly, Betsy, Nicholas H., Samuel, Nelly, Mahala and James. (He had a brother Snead Davis who went to Alabama to reside.)

ROBERT DAVIS

Robert Davis applied for revolutionary pension Nov. 21, 1832 while living in Marion County, Tenn. He was about 82 years of age and therefore born about 1750. He enlisted in 1781 in the 10th Regt., North Carolina Continental Line. he then resided in Caswell County, N. C., where he enlisted. His widow, Lucinda Malone Davis applied for a pension while living in Dade County, Ga., June 8, 1853, when she was 73 years old. therefore born 1780. She says that she married Robert Davis in Guilford County, N. C., Nov. 25 1808 and that Robert Davis died in Marion County, Tenn., July 8, 1835.

Note: As there was a difference of 30 years in the ages of Robert Davis and Lucinda Malone Davis it is possible that she was a second wife.

SAMUEL DAVIS

Samuel Davis applied for revolutionary pension while living in Warren County, Tenn., Nov. 8, 1819. He was born in Craven County, S. C., Sept. 1757. He moved to North Carolina about 1772 or 1773 and enlisted in Bute County, N. C. in April 1776 in Capt. Turner's company, Col. Sumner's regiment, 3rd North Carolina Continental Line. He was discharged Oct. 1778. He re-enlisted in the South Carolina Militia and served six months. He resided in North Carolina until 1801 when he moved to Chester District, S. C. and resided there until 1818 when he moved to Tennessee. He lived for a time in Dickson County, Tenn. and he had a grant of land in Madison County but returned to Warren County where he died between Jan. 1836 and 1840. He married Lucinda R. Munsey, born in North Carolina in 1760. She survived him and lived with her daughter Rachel in Washington County, Tenn. where she died after 1850 being over ninety years of age. Their children were Benjamin Munsey, born N. C., 1785; Samuel, Jr., born 1787, married 1819, Jane Richardson; James U., born 1789; David, born 1791; Lucinda, born 1794; Frances, born 1797; Joseph H., born 1801; Rachel, born 1802; Marcy C., born Chester District. S. C. 1806, died unmarried; and William, born 1809.

GUILFORD DUDLEY

Guilford Dudley applied for revolutionary pension while living in Franklin, Williamson County, Tenn., Oct. 12, 1832. He was the son of Christopher Dudley and was born April 17, 1756 on the Rappahannock River, Caroline County, Va. He enlisted in North Carolina troops in July, 1775 and in February, 1776 under Christopher Dudley and in June, 1780 under Samuel Lockhart. He was a private in his first three enlistments. March 22, 1781 he was entered the service again as Major of his regiment and March 30 was commissioned Lieut.-Col.; May 22, 1781 he was Colonel of the Regiment of Light Horse. He was in the battles of Camden and Hobkirk Hill. He resided during the War in Halifax County,

N. C. He moved to Tennessee and died in Franklin, Feb. 3, 1833. He married May 23, 1784 in Halifax County, N. C. Anna Eaton, born Dec. 21, 1763. She was the daughter of Thomas and Anna Eaton. She survived her husband and applied for pension while living in Franklin, Tenn., March 19, 1839. Their children were Frances Elizabeth, born 1785; Frances Bland, born June 30, 1786, married 1815, Dr. Samuel Crockett; Julia Ann Eaton, born 1788, married, 1810, Dr. Elliott Hickman; Thomas Eaton, born 1792; Elizabeth Helen, born 1794; Sarah Bland, born 1796; Guilford, Jr., born 1799; Judith Randolph, born 1800, married 1822, Nicholas I. Long; Carolina, born 1802; Virginia, married 1830, Thomas Woodson Cash, and Mary Matilda Pugh married 1830, James C. Hill.

CHARLES DYCHE

Charles Dyche applied for revolutionary pension while living in Greene County. He drew pension on the 1832 List and was born about 1760. He enlisted in Rockingham County, Va. and served in a Virginia Regiment commanded by Col. George Riddle. He was in the battle of Jamestown and at the Surrender of Cornwallis. He served under Gen. Benjamin Harrison in one of his enlistments and again under Capt. George Houston. He states that he was well acquainted with Gen. Morgan and Gen. George Washington. Michael Roark testifies that he knew Charles Dyche well and served in the same regiment with him for six months.

GEORGE FULLER

George Fuller applied for revolutionary pension while he was living in Roane County, Tenn., March 15, 1825. He enlisted May 2, 1781 in Caswell County, N. C. in Capt. Tilman Dixon's company, Col. Henry Dixon's regiment. He was in the battle of Eutaw Springs. His wife was 63 or 64 years of age in 1825, therefore born about 1762. A letter enclosed in the application from William Hill, Secretary of State for North Carolina, states that George Fuller served in the 10th Regiment, North Carolina Troops.

AMBROSE GAINES

Ambrose Gaines applied for revolutionary pension while living in Sullivan County. He was born in Amelia County, Va. He enlisted in Virginia troops as a substitute for his father, Robert Gaines, and served in Capt. John Oliver's company Col. William Campbell's regiment. He was in the battle of Guilford Court House and the Siege of Yorktown. He died in Sullivan County, Jan. 12, 1840 and his widow, Mary Moore Gaines, whom he married in Stokes County, N. C., June 9, 1792, applied for widow's pension while living in Sullivan County, April 10, 1844. She was born 1771.

Note:—Among their children were Elizabeth, born 1798 married William F. Butler, son of Zachariah T. Butler; Matthew Moore, born 1809, died 1893, married No. 11, 1830, Margaret Luttrell, born 1816, died 1892, daughter of James Churchwell Luttrell I, and Margaret Armstrong Luttrell, Samuel D., born Oct. 19, 1811; Sara E., born Dec. 2, 1813; and Francis Henry. Ambrose Gaines, the revolutionary soldier was the son of Robert Gaines and Mildred Bohanan Gaines.

HARRIS GAMMON

Harris Gammon applied for revolutionary pension while living in Knox County, Aug. 24, 1830. He was born in Pittsylvaria County, Va., Sept. 25, 1757. He moved with his parents when he was an infant to Goochland County, Va. and later moved back to Pittsylvania where he lived until 1796 when he moved to Knox County, Tenn. Alexander Norton testified that he served in the Revolution with Harris Gammon. In 1840 Harris Gammon was living in Knox County with Lewis Gammon. He married ———Brawner. Among their children were Dozier Brawner Gammon, who married Letitia Turbeville; and Lewis.

THOMAS GANN

Thomas Gann applied for revolutionary pension while living in Hamilton County in February, 1833. He was born in Virginia, March 17, 1764. He moved to Washington County, N. C., now Tennessee while he was young. He enlisted under Capt. William Trimble and Col. John Sevier. The company was sent to Santee in South Carolina and joined the army under Gen. Greene, marched from Santee to Gen. Marion's Headquarters above Charleston and there discharged. Later he served in a lighthorse company. He served "off and on" as a ranger until the close of the War. He was in many skirmishes, one in the vicinity of King's Mountain. He served under Col. Sevier in the Cherokee War and was in engagements at Coosa and "Hightown." He considered himself in the service of the United States or the State of North Carolina about six years. He was paid in continental money. He had a brother, Carter Gann, who lived in Washington County. He lived in Washington County 20 to 25 years and then moved to Rhea County where he lived for 8 years. He then moved to Hamilton County about 1823. His application gives the names of Justices of Hamilton County in 1833 and this is the only surviving record of some of them as county officials.

RICHARD GRANTHAM

Richard Grantham applied for revolutionary pension while living in Grainger County, Aug. 21, 1832. He was born March 16, 1754 and was the son of John and Ann Grantham. He enlisted while living in Dobbs County, N. C. in Col. Charles Coatsworthy Pinckney's 1st South Carolina Regiment. After the Revolution he moved to Hawkins County, N. C., now Tennessee and subsequently lived in Grainger County. He died in Grainger County, June 22, 1846. His widow. Frances Amis Grantham, applied for pension Oct. 14, 1846. Her brother was Lincoln Amis. She says they were married in Hawkins County, by Thomas Murrell, a minister, April 14, 1785. Frances Amis, daughter of Thomas and Alice Amis, was born April 16, 1765. Enclosed in her application is the original Bible page with the foregoing birth dates and the following information. Children: Penelopy, born 1786; Mary, born 1788, died 1820, married George Saunders, 1805; Ann, born 1789, died 1814, married Hezekiah Robertson, 1807; Amis (a son), born 1791, married Margaret Williams, 1815; Tabitha, born 1793, married Hezekiah Robertson (as his second wife) 1816; Rachel, born 1795, married James Dobson, 1817; Rhoda, born 1797, married James Moore 1817; Lincoln, born 1798; John Thomas, born 1800, married Margaret Littleton, 1824; James, born 1801; Alice Gale, born 1803, married Hughes W. Taylor, 1823.

Note:—The wife of Thomas Amis was Alice Gale.

GEORGE GREGORY

George Gregory served in the Revolution and his widow, Sarah Gregory, applied for pension while living in Hamilton County, Sept. 1, 1844. She was then living in the home of her son-in-law. George Gregory lived in Cocke County and was 75 years of age in November 1832, therefore born about 1757. He was a native of Germany. He enlisted in Meckenburg County, N. C. He died in Cocke County, Feb. 20, 1837. The marriage took place in South Carolina in 1792.

An original page of the Family Bible is enclosed in her application giving the children as follows: Catherine, born 1792; Richard, born 1795; Margaret, born 1801; Sarah, born 1805; Thomas, born 1812; Lncinda, born 1815.

AMON HALE

Amon Hale applied for revolutionary pension while living in Washington County, April 17, 1833. He was born in North Carolina, June, 16, 1759, but when he was an infant his father took him to Baltimore County, Md. He entered the service in Baltimore County under Joshua Stephenson. He died in Washington County, Dec. 4, 1843. His widow, Mary Hale applied for pension while living in Washington County, Dec. 18, 1843, and was then 79 years old. She was therefore born 1764. She died Jan. 29, 1849, leaving eight living children, two children having predeceased her The original Bible pages are enclosed in application showing that Amon Hale was born June 16, 1759, that the marriage took place Sept. 30, 1785, that their children were: Elizabeth, born 1786; Martha, born 1788; Jessie, born 1791; Macajah B., born 1793; Robert G., born 1795; Mary, born 1797; Joshua, born 1800; Priese (the name begins clearly with P, the rest uncertain) born 1802; Amon C., born 1805; and Ruth, born 1807.

JOHN HALE

John Hale applied for Revolutionary pension in 1833 while living in Bledsoe County, Tenn. He was born in Bedford County, Va. in 1753 or 1754. He enlisted in Bedford County, Va., in 1776. He volunteered in Capt. Harry Bluford's Company, Lieut. John Frields, Ensign Abram Sharp. They marched to the Cherokee Country and were in the battle of Long Island. He was discharged and returned home. He went to school and re-enlisted under Capt. Charles Watkins. He had 24 months' service in all. His discharge was burned in Blount County in 1803. After the War he moved to Wythe County, Va., then to Greene County, Tenn., to Washington County, Tenn., to Blount County, Tenn. and then to Bledsoe County about 1813.

NATHAN HALE

Nathan Hale applied for pension while living in Giles County, Tenn., in November 1832. He was born in North Carolina in 1857 and when he was a child his father moved to Baltimore County, Md. He enlisted while he was residing in Baltimore County in Col. Joshua Stephenson's Maryland regiment. Richard Hale of Giles County also desposes that he was in the Revolution. Nathan Hale says that his father moved after the Revolution to Tennessee. They lived first in Washington County, Tenn. and then Nathan Hale moved to Giles County.

Note:—It is evident that Amon Hale, see above, and Nathan Hale were brothers and that possibly Richard Hale was also a brother.

NICHOLAS HALE

Nicholas Hale applied for revolutionary pension while living in Davidson County, Oct. 27, 1832. He was then nearly 70 years of age, therefore born about 1762. He entered the service while living in Washington County, N. C., now Tennessee, in 1780, in a company commanded by Capt. Sevier, Col. Robertson's regiment. He moved after the Revolution to Davidson County.

Note:—Capt. Sevier's company was Capt. Robert Sevier's company.

FRANCIS HUGHES

Francis Hughes applied for revolutionary pension while living in Bledsoe County, Tenn., July 21, 1833. He was born in Augusta County. Va., in 1759 and was the son of Francis Hughes. He resided in Burke County, N. C. in June 1776 when he enlisted in the 3rd North Carolina Regiment. He moved to the Tennessee Country and volunteered in 1777 under Col. John Sevier. He volunteered again in the fall of 1780 and was in Capt. Samuel Williams' company in the Battle of King's Mountain. He volunteered again under Col. John Sevier for the Cherokee Expedition. Nathan Gann swears in the pension application, that Francis Hughes was a soldier of the Revolution and Felix Earnest also testifies to his revolutionary record. Francis Hughes states that he has **children but does not give their names.** In 1840 he was living with Margaret Hughes, possibly a daughter.

Note:—Francis Hughes had a brother John Hughes, whose record is given below. Descendants of Francis Hughes live on Walden's Ridge near Chattanooga.

JOHN HUGHES

John Hughes applied for revolutionary pension while living in McMinn County, Tennessee, Sept. 5, 1832. He was born in 1752. He served in the Revolution. enlisting first in Burke County, N. C. Later he enlisted again in Capt. Sevier's North Carolina Company and was in a battle on the Watauga River. Later he served in Capt. Jacob Tipton's Company under St. Clair and was in the battle of St. Clair's Defeat. He moved from Burke County, N. C. to what is now East Tennessee and settled in Blount County. From Blount County he moved to McMinn County where he died.

Note:—John Hughes was a brother of Francis Hughes whose record is given above. He was the son of Francis Hughes of Augusta County, Virginia. the family moving to that point from Lancaster County, Pa. John Hughes had a son Francis Hughes. The well known East Tennessee family of Hughes comes from this line.

DARLING JONES

Darling Jones applied for revolutionary pension while living in Washington County in July 1834. He was born in Wake County, N. C. in 1764. His father moved from Wake County to what is now upper East Tennessee at a very early period and Darling Jones enlisted in Capt. Landon Carter's company, Col. Shelby's regiment in Washington County, N. C., now Tennessee. They joined Gen. Francis Marion. He volunteered again and was in the battle of King's Mountain. He died Oct. 9, 1848. His widow, Nancy Jones, applied for pension March 28, 1848. She was born in 1813 and married Darling Jones in March 1833. She was Nancy Huff before her marriage. They were married by William Blount Carter. Samuel Huff states that the marriage took place in his home. The children of Darling Jones were Alfred and James.

Note:—Darling Jones was married twice, the name of his first wife is not known to the compiler of these notes but their daughter, Rebecca, married David Stevens who was born 1787 and died 1860. The children of the second marriage were Alfred, who was born 1833 and died in Johnson City, Tennessee in 1927, and James, who was born 1836.

JAMES JONES

James Jones applied for revolutionary pension while living in Marion County, Aug. 22, 1832. He was then 77 years old and therefore born in 1755. He enlisted in 1776 or 1777 with Peter Horry and was attached to Capt. Snipe's company, South Carolina Line. He served in the battles of Camden and Eutaw Springs.

WILLIAM KELLY

William Kelly applied for revolutionary pension while living in McMinn County, Tenn., June 6, 1833. He was born July 11, 1758, in Union County, S. C. While a resident of that county he enlisted in the spring of 1775 and served six months as a private in Capt. James Stein's company, Col. John Thomas' South Carolina regiment. He enlisted again in the spring of 1779 and served in Capt. James Stein's company. He was in the battle of Stono. He moved to Rutherford County, N. C. where he enlisted in the fall of 1781, serving three months in Capt. Jacob Vinsant's company, Col. Porter's North Carolina regiment. He moved to McMinn County, Tenn. after the Revolution and he died in Georgia, Dec. 27, 1837. He married Nov. 1, 1782, Elizabeth, who survived him. She applied for pension while living in Smith County, Tenn., April 28, 1843, when she was 79 years of age, therefore born 1764. She died in Smith County, Aug. 22, 1850. Their children were: Joshua, born 1783; Rachel, born 1785; Nancy, born 1787; Easter, born 178-; Jane, born 1791; Judah, born 1793; Dinah, born 1796; Daniel, born 1798; William, born 1802; Ricrard, born 1805; Elizabeth, born 1807; Alcy or Alsey, born 18--; John, aged 38 in 1832; and Samuel, age not given. Grandchildren are mentioned as Luice or Lewis Kelly, born 1831 and Emmeline Kelly, born 1834.

WILLIAM KEY

William Key applied for revolutionary pension while living in Sumner County, Tenn., in November, 1832. He was born in Chesterfield County, Va., Oct. 14, 1751. He entered the service under Capt. William Lewis in Dinwiddie County, Va. He married in Halifax County, N. C., in 1793, Elizabeth who was born 1770, died July 28, 1844. She applied for widow's pension in Sumner County. William Key died Jan. 18, 1834. James Key states in the widow's application that he is their son.

JOHN LEONARD

John Leonard applied for revolutionary pension while living in Hawkins County, Tenn., Nov. 27, 1823. He was born April 7, 1754 in Germany. He was raised in Germany and sold into British service to fight against the Americans. At the first opportunity he deserted the British and enlisted in the American Army in Shenandoah County, Va., in September or October 1781 and served two years as a private in Capt. Kirkpatrick's company, Col. Hawes' regiment. He died in Hawkins County, Oct. 7, 1841. His widow Edy Leonard, applied for pension, March 27, 1850, while residing in Hawkins County. She states that their marriage took place in Greenbriar County, Va. in the latter part of June, 1796. She was born Feb. 22, 1771. Their children were: David, born 1797; Elizabeth, born 1799; John Leonard, Jr. born 1801, William, born 1803; Agnes, born 1805; Jacob, born 1807; and Edy, born 1811.

EDMUND LOVE

Edmund Love applied for revolutionary pension while living in Rhea County, Tenn., May 31, 1833. He was born June 1, 1760 in Pasquantunk County, N. C. He entered the service in Currituck County, N. C. about Oct. 15, 1775, under Capt. James Blount. He served in the battles of Trenton, Brandywine, Schulkill and Monmouth, all under the command of Gen. Washington. He knew personally Generals Washington, Wayne, Morgan, Stephens and Howe. He moved before the War to Currituck County, N. C., then to Moore County, N. C., then to Union District, S. C., then to Barren County, Ky., and then to Rhea County, Tenn., about 1830. He died there before July 13, 1838 and was survived by his widow for several years.

ABEL LANHAM

Abel Lanham applied for revolutionary pension while living in Claiborne County, Tenn., Feb. 6, 1837. He was then 75 years old, therefore born 1762. He says he would not apply for pension while affluent but is now forced to do so as he has lost his property. He enlisted March 1, 1778 in Rutherford County, N. C. He moved during the War, Feb. 1, 1782, to Washington County, N. C., now Tennessee. and enlisted again under Col. John Sevier and Capt. Samuel Williams in the Indian Campaign of that year. "We were marched against the Cherokee Nation of Indians. We started from Big Island on the French Broad River and marched on the Tennessee River and crossed the same at an Indian town called Echota. From there we went to Hiwassee River, passed Bullstown and crossed Coosee River to an Indian town, called Estanolee; from there we went to Little Shoemaker Plains and from there to Hiwassee Town. In this campaign we destroyed the Indian crops and fourteen towns and returned home, Dec. 1, 1782." Abel Lanham died in Claiborne County, Aug. 25, 1837. The widow, Sarah Lanham, applied for widow's pension while a resident of Laurel County, Ky., March 17, 1853, aged 66 years, therefore born 1787. She says that she was married to Abel Lanham about 1814.

Note:—Sarah Lanham was possibly a second wife.

HEZEKIAH LOVE

Hezekiah Love applied for revolutionary pension while living in Roane County, Tenn., March 12, 1832. He was born Oct. 10, 1852. He enlisted in March 1776 in South Carolina troops under Capt. Eli Cashion, Lieut. Col. Mason and Col. Thompson. He was in the battle of Fort Moultrie, and also in the battles of Hanging Rock, Columbia, Eutaw Springs, Sumpter's Defeat, Fish Dam Ford and King's Mountain. He had a discharge but it was lost when a party of Tories attacked and pillaged the home of his brother, James Love. Edward Eskridge testifies that he knows that Hezekiah Love served in the Revolution.

JOSEPH LANE

Joseph Lane applied for revolutionary pension while living in Roane County, Tenn. He enlisted in Amherst County, Va. He died in Roane County in March, 1846. His widow, Rebecca Lane, applied for pension while living in Bradley County, Tenn. in 1846 being then 96 years old, therefore born in 1750. They married in Amherst County, Va. in 1775. Among their children were John Lane and Joseph Lane, Jr. Joseph Lane, Jr. married Patsey Wright in Amherst County, Sept. 25, 1795.

JAMES MILLER

James Miller applied for revolutionary pension while living in Claiborne County, Tenn., April 21, 1834. He was born Aug. 12, 1748, in Baltimore County, Md. He lived in Shenandoah County, Va., when he enlisted in October or

November 1780 in Capt. Jacob Rinker's company, Col. Butler's Virginia regiment. He was in the battle of Guilford Court House. He enlisted again in May 1781 in Capt. William Reagan's company, Virginia Militia. He died Aug. 26, 1841, leaving a widow. Her name is not stated nor is it stated whether they had children.

JOHN H. MILLER

John H. Miller applied for revolutionary pension while living in Knox County, Tenn., Aug. 21, 1832. He was born in Bucks County, Amity Township, Pa., in 1735. He enlisted in the service in Henrico County, Va., in July or August 1778.

MARTIN MILLER

Martin Miller applied for revolutionary pension while he was living in Claiborne County, Tenn., Sept. 17, 1832. He was born about 1760. He was living in Granville County, N. C., when he enlisted Dec. 22, 1776, as a private and a musician in Capt. Cook's company of the Ninth North Carolina regiment. He was discharged Jan. 27, 1780. He was in the battle of Germantown. He married Feb. 5, 1798, in Wilkes County, N. C., Elizabeth Giddens. She applied for widow's pension Sept. 2, 1850 while living in Claiborne County, Tenn., aged 70 years, therefore born 1780.

SAMUEL MILLER

Samuel Miler drew a pension while living in Hamilton County Tenn. He served in the 39th United States Infantry and was placed on the pension roll July 9, 1814. He died and is buried in Chattanooga, Tenn. His head stone in the National Cemetery has on it the words, "S. Miller, Soldier of the Revolution".

JAMES MITCHELL

James Mitchell applied for revolutionary pension while living in Maury County, Tenn. He was born in Orange County, N. C. in 1765 and died in Maury County, Tenn., 1843. He served as a private in North Carolina Militia until the close of the War.

SOLOMON MITCHELL
of Hawkins County

Solomon Mitchell applied for revolutionary pension while living in Hawkins County, Tenn., Sept. 7, 1833. He was the son of Robert and Jane or Tanee Mitchell and was born in Abbeville District, S. C., in 1759. He served in the South Carolina troops. He moved to Hawkins County, Tenn. and died there Jan. 27, 1839. He married in Abbeville District, S. C. in May 1787, Nancy, who survived him and applied for widow's pension while residing in Hawkins County, July 9, 1845 when she was 83 years old, therefore born in 1762. Their children were: Stephen, who died young; Rebecca; Lewis; Greenberry; Jesse; Polly or Mary; Robert; Morris; Nancy; Richard; Susannah or Susan; and Elizabeth.

Note:—Solomon Mitchell's will in Hawkins County, Tenn. names a son John, who does not appear in the above list. It is possible that he died before the widow applied for pension. *William and Mary Quarterly*, Vol. X, pages 112, 113, says that Solomon Mitchell served in Capt. Thomas Hall's company, Lieut. Col. Francis Marion's South Carolina regiment. As Solomon and Nancy Mitchell named sons, Lewis and Morris it is possible that her maiden name was one of these.

SOLOMON MITCHELL
of Sumner County

Solomon Mitchell applied for revolutionary pension while living in Sumner County, Tenn., Nov. 12, 1832. He was born in Dorchester County, Md. in 1769. While a resident of Dorchester County he enlisted in 1777 and served as a Minute Man in Capt. Joseph Robertson's company, Col. Bartholomew Ewelds' Maryland Regiment. In 1781, when he had moved to Guilford County, N. C., he enlisted and served as a Minute Man in Capt. Andrew Wilson's North Carolina company.

CHAPMAN POINDEXTER

Chapman Poindexter made application for revolutionary pension while living in Grainger County, Tennessee. He was born in 1759. He entered the army in Louisa County,

Va., under Captain John Saunders. He served in the battle of Guilford Court House and in an engagement at Camden. He was taken prisoner in the Siege of Charleston and was wounded in the body, arm and thigh. He was parolled by the British commander, Col. Samuel Conger, July 9, 1791. He moved to the Tennessee country after the revolution and drew pension in Grainger County where he died May 21, 1851. His widow, Elizabeth Poindexter, applied for pension in Grainger County. Her pension was granted, suspended, restored and increased. She lived after the War Between the States and was obliged to prove her loyalty to the United States during that period. Her marriage to Chapman Poindexter took place July 1815 but she may have been a second wife as he was then 56 years old. Their children were: Talton, born 1816; Sarah, born 1817; John M., born 1819; and William, born 1823.

JAMES RANGE

James Range lived in Carter County, Tenn. He was a soldier of the Revolution serving in the 8th Virginia Volunteer Regiment. He enlisted April 1775 and was discharged Jan. 29, 1778. He served under Capt. William Darke and Col. Peter Muhlenburg. He married Oct. 30, 1787 in Washington County, N. C., now Tennessee, Barbara Hammer. He died in July 26, 1825 in Carter County and the widow, Barbara Hammer Range, died in the same county, April 2, 1843. Their children were Mary, born 1788, married Thomas Buck 1786; John, born 1790, died 1803; Elizabeth, born 1793 and died 1812; James, born 1795; Margaret born 1798; Jacob born 1801; and Jonathan, born 1803. These facts are in the pension application of Jonathan Range, son of James Range and Barbara Hammer Range, July 5, 1843.

Note:—James Range was one of the early Adventurers on the Big Harpeth River in Tennessee in 1779. His name is not signed to the Cumberland Compact as it is found in the Tennessee histories, but his petition to the General Assembly of Tennessee, Aug. 30, 1813, states that in the year 1779 he made a small improvement on the Waters of Big Harpeth consistent with the laws of North Carolina and petitions for grant to said land. It was granted. Two brothers of James Range also served in the Revolution. John Range was a Lieutenant in York County, Penn. and Peter Range is thought to have belonged also to the 8th Virginia Regiment. The roll of this regiment, frequently called the German Regiment, has never been found. It was recruited by Col. Peter Muhlenburg in the Northern Neck of Virginia, the southern or southeastern counties of Pennsylvania and the western counties of Maryland. Peter Range owned and operated a Mill and as a miller his services might have been valuable to the cause of Liberty but all family records state that he served in the Revolution. He died in Washington County, Tenn. about 1817. His will is on record in Jonesboro, the county seat. (This Note is contributed by Nancy Jones Stickley).

ALEXANDER RITCHIE

Alexander Ritchie applied for revolutionary pension while living in Claiborne County, Tenn., April 21, 1835. He was then 71 years old, therefore born 1764. He entered the service in 1776 when he was residing in Montgomery County, now Scott County, Va. He served as an Indian spy under Capt. James Gibson. After the War he served again against the Indians. This was in 1786. Some years after the Revolution he moved to Powell's Valley, near Cumberland Gap, and from there moved to the place in Claiborne County where he resided at the time he applied for his pension. A letter enclosed in the application says that Mary Noel, widow of Richard Noel, applied for a pension.

EDMUND ROBERTS

Edmund Roberts applied for revolutionary pension in McMinn County, Tenn. He was born 1856. He enlisted in 1775 in Ca8swell County, N. C. in North Carolina troops under Capt. Alfred Moore, Col. Francis Nash and Lieut. Lawrence Thompson. He was in the battle of Guilford Court House. He died in McMinn County in 1848.

WILLIAM ROBERTS

William Roberts applied for revolutionary application while living in Hamilton County, Tenn., Sept. 25, 1832. He was then 71 years of age. He was born in Johnston County, N. C. He volunteered in Wilkes County, N. C. in North Carolina troops under Capt. John Cleveland. He volunteered again under Maj. Lewis and volunteered again under Capt. Robert Cleveland and served in all eighteen months. He was in the battle of Giulford Court House He moved to Tennessee and lived in Grainger, Knox, Anderson and Hamilton Counties. He was transferred to Green County, Missouri.

JEREMIAH ROGERS

Jeremiah Rogers applied for revolutionary pension while living in Marion County, Tenn., in August 1832. He enlisted in 1780 in Virginia troops, Col. Joseph Crockett's regiment.

JOSEPH ROGERS

Joseph Rogers applied for revolutionary pension while living in Bedford County, Tenn., Jan. 21, 1832. He was born in Amelia County. Va., Sept. 17, 1750. He enlisted while living in Fairfield County, N. C in 1780 in North Carolina troops under Capt. Eleazer Mobley and Col. John Winn. He enlisted for a second tour of service. After the close of the Revolution he moved to Fayette County, Ky. and from there to Georgia, thence to Rutherford County, Tenn., and then to Bedford County, Tenn.

WILLIAM ROGERS

William Rogers applied for revolutionary pension while living in Hamilton County, Tenn., in March 1832. He was born in Bedford County, Va. in 1740. He entered the service in Bedford County, Va. under Capt. John Arwin and Col. Callaway. He moved from Bedford County to Washington County, Ga. about two years after the Revolution. He then moved to Buncombe County, N. C. to Perry County, Ky. and from there to Hamilton County, Tenn.

MICHAEL ROARK

Michael Roark applied for pension while living in Hawkins County, Tenn. He was born in Bucks County, Pa., Sept. 29, 1746. He lived in Rockingham County, Va. when he volunteered in Virginia troops. He states that he was well acquainted with Gen. George Washington. He died in Hawkins County, Jan. 9, 1839. His widow, Letitia Roark applied for widow's pension in Hawkins County in 1840 being 93 years of age, therefore born in 1747. The name is spelled in several ways, Rork, Rorak, Roreck and Roark.

JAMES SEVIER

James Sevier appilied for revolutionary pension while living in Washington County, Tenn. Dec. 11, 1832. He was born in Virginia in 1764. He enlisted in North Carolina troops while living in that part of North Carolina which became Tennessee in 1780 in his uncle Capt. Robert Sevier's company and was in the battle of King's Mountain where Capt. Robert Sevier was mortally wounded. Other officers were Col. John Sevier, Maj. Jesse Walton and Maj. Jonathan Tipton. He enlisted again in Capt. Landon Carter's company and was in the battle of Boyd's Creek. He enlisted for the South Carolina campaign and his officers were Col. John Sevier, Lieut. Col. Charles Robertson, Maj. Valentine Sevier and Maj. Jonathan Tipton. They joined Gen. Greene and were sent on to join Gen. Francis Marion. He was with a party that captured 100 British soldiers near Monk's Corner. He enlisted again in 1782 in Col. John Sevier's Cherokee Indian Campaign, serving in Capt. Alexander Moore's Company. Other Captians in this campaign were Capt. Samuel Wear and Capt. Robert Bean.

Note:—James Sevier was the second son of Gov. John Sevier and his first wife, Sarah Hawkins Sevier. He married Nancy Conway, daughter of Col. Henry Conway. See *Notable Southern Families, Vol. IV., The Sevier Family.*

COL. JOHN SEVIER

Col. John Sevier's children applied for revolutionary pension and the certificate was issued May, 31, 1839. He served as Commissiary and Colonel during the Revolution and was one of the Colonels in command in the battle of King's Mountain. He conducted two campaigns against the Cherokee Indians. He was the first Militia General of the State of Tennessee and the first Governor of the State. He died near Fort Decatur, Ala., Sept. 24. 1815. He married his second wife, Catherine Sherrill, in Tennessee in 1780 and she died in Russellville, Ala., Oct. 2, 1836, aged 80 years. therefore born 1756. James Sevier testifies to his father's services.

Note:—The Sevier family was large and a full sketch of Gov. John Sevier would require much space. For detail of the family history see Notable Southern Families, Volume IV, The Sevier Family, Lookout Publishing Company.

MAJOR VALENTINE SEVIER

Valentine Sevier's widow, Naomi Douglass Sevier, applied for and drew a pension until her death, July 17, 1845. Her daughter, Rebecca Sevier applied for increase of her moth-

er's pension while living in Greene County, Tenn. on July 17, 1851. Valentine Sevier served as a Major in the Army of the Revolution. She states that at that time of her mother's death (1845) she had only two living children, James Sevier and Rebecca Sevier Rector and that Valentine Sevier died some fifty years ago.
Note:—For information of Major Valentine Sevier see Notable Southern Families, Volume IV, The Sevier Family.

GEORGE SHELTON

George Shelton applied for revolutionary pension while living in Fentress County, Tenn., Jan. 6, 1834. He was born " on the James River in Virginia" date and name of county not given, but as he was 72 years of age in 1834, he was born in 1762. He was reared in Buncombe County, N. C. where he resided when he enlisted in the winter of 1777 in Capt. Gray's North Carolina company in an expedition against the Cherokee Indians. He enlisted again in the spring of 1777 and served again in Capt. Gray's company, marching against the Cherokee Indians. He enlisted again and served in Capt. Mucklehaney's company (the name also appears as Mclehaney), North Carolina troops and was in the battles of King's Mountain and Eutaw Springs. After the Revolution he lived in Buncombe County, N. C. for many years. He then moved to Rutherford County, Tenn. to Knox County, Tenn., where he lived ten years, to Anderson County, Tenn., and then to Fentress County about 1823.

RANSOME SMITH

Ransome Smith applied for revolutionary pension while living in Marion County, Tenn. in October, 1833. He was born in Hanover County. Va., April 11, 1761. He volunteered in Granville County. N. C. where he then resided, under Capt. Howell Lewis. After the Revolution he moved to what is now Claiborne County, Tenn., to Campbell County and then to Marion County in 1831.

LIEUT. ROBERT SMITH

Robert Smith applied for revolutionary pension while living in Hawkins County, Tenn., 1818. He was born April 18, 1750. He enlisted under Capt. John Walker in the 1st South Carolina Regiment in Johnson County, S. C. in 1775. He served as a Litutenant. His widow, Elizabeth Smith, applied for pension in Hawkins County, Nov. 17, 1838. She was born in February 1761. She married Lieut. Robert Smith in 1779 in Johnson County, S. C. Robert Smith died in Hawkins County, Tenn., Jan. 3, 1838. She died Jan. 6, 1842. Their children were: Susannah, married, 1808, Grinefield Taylor, son of Daniel and Jane Rowland Taylor; Elizabeth married John Lee; Allen; Redden; Claiborne; Zilphia, married John Draper; Anna; Edith; and Ferraby who married John Monney.

EZEKIAL STONE

Ezekial Stone applied for revolutionary pension while living in Marion County, Tenn., Aug. 3, 1832. He was born in Fauquier County, Va., Nov. 24, 1756. He entered the service in Surrey County, N. C. under Major Joseph Winston and Capt. Richard Good. He also served under Capt. William Bostick and Capt. Humphries. He moved to Surrey County, N. C. before the Revolution and was living there when he enlisted. After the Revolution he moved to Sevier County, now Tennessee, about 1795 and moved in 1815 to Bledsoe County, Tenn. and then to Marion County in 1819.

NOTE:—Ezekial Stone was the son of David and Elizabeth Jenifer Stone and the family records say that he was born in Charles County, Md., although the pension record says Fauquier County, Va. It is probable that his parents moved from Maryland to Virginia when he was an infant. He died in Marion County when he was nearly one hundred years old. He married Jane Wood. Their children were: William, who married Mary Randall; Richard W.; Thomas; Mary; Hannah; Rebecca; Elizabeth; and Mary. For further information concerning this family see *Notable Southern Families. Vol. I,* the Stone Family.

SOLOMON STONE

Solomon Stone applied for revolutionary pension while living in Marion County, Tenn. in 1832. He was born in Prince Edward County, Va., Dec. 3, 1752. He moved to Surrey County, N. C. before the Revolution and was living there when he enlisted in 1776 in North Carolina troops under Capt. Richard Gold and Col. Joseph Williams. He was in the Long Island Campaign under Gen. Christian. After the Revolution he moved to Georgia, then to South Carolina, then to Tennessee, then to Alabama and then to Marion County about 1829.

CAPT. JAMES TAYLOR

James Taylor applied for revolutionary pension while living in Blount County, Tenn. He was born in Culpepper County, Va., Jan. 30, 1760. He enlisted in the 3rd North Carolina, serving as a substitute for Joseph Myers in Capt. Martin's company. He enlisted again and served under Capt. Gibson Woolridge. He was captured by British forces but escaped. He served in a battle near Shallow Ford. When the officers of the company were missing after an engagement he was elected Captain. He volunteered again in 1781 and was elected Ensign. He died in Blount County in 1841.

NOTE:—James Taylor's will was drawn in Blount County, Jan. 24, 1839 and probated in 1841.

DANIEL SUTHERLAND

Daniel Sutherland applied for revolutionary pension while living in Bledsoe County in 1833. He enlisted while residing in Rowan County, N. C. and served under Capt. Pendleton Isbell. He moved to Wilkes County, N. C. and enlisted again under Capt. Pendleton Isbell. He moved to the Tennessee country and settled in Bledsoe County. Late in life he transferred his pension to Madison County, Ark., as he had gone there to live with a daughter who married John Holdeman and moved to that State and County.

CAPT. CHRISTOPHER TAYLOR

Christopher Taylor applied for revolutionary pension while living in Washington County, Tenn. He states that he resided in the country which was afterwards Washington County, Tenn., before 1776 and that he enlisted under Col. Christian at Long Island. He volunteered in the Expedition that Col. John Sevier made against the Indians in the Chickamauga towns. He was in the battle of King's Mountain. He had five "constant years of service." He died in Washington County, Sept. 10, 1833. His widow, Mary Edwards Taylor, applied for widow's pension while living in Washington County. She died March 29, 1837. Their children were: Henry; James; Arty (name indistinct, but evidently a daughter), married ————, Wyley; Matthew; Greenbury; Stephen; and Sarah who married ————Maclin and died January 3, 1849.

NOTE:—Capt. Christopher and Mary Edwards Taylor are buried in Washington County, on their farm.

CAPT. LEROY TAYLOR

LeRoy Taylor applied for revolutionary pension while living in Washington County, Tenn., Sept. 14, 1832. He entered the service while living in Burke County, N. C. He moved to Tennessee country which was then North Carolina, in the spring of 1789. His last pension payment was made to his grand daughter, Margaret Irwin. He died March 24, 1834.

NOTE:—LeRoy Taylor is called Colonel Taylor because of service after the Revolution in the Militia. He and his brother Parmenas, moved to the Tennessee country. They were sons of William Taylor of Prince County, Virginia. William Taylor's wife was Sarah Bradford. He was born in Prince William County, Va. and moved to Burke County, N. C. in his youth with his mother and step father, Hosea Rose. He was born July 25, 1758. He died March 24, 1834 in Leesburg, Washington County, Va. He married twice. His first wife was Susan Sherrill, sister of Catherine Sherrill who married Col. John Sevier. The second wife was Mary Bradford, a kinswoman of his mother. His children were Nellie; William; Robert; Joseph; Sallie or Sarah who married John Campbell; Levi (first child by the second wife) married Mary Houston Rogers; Malinda married Patrick Irwin; Jacob married Polly Keys; LeRoy, Jr., married Jean Inman; Peggy married Young Kibbler; Betsey married Henry Haire; Ruth married Hiram Swaney; It is believed there were five other children, twenty-four in all.

CAPT. JOHN TEDFORD

Capt. John Tedford applied for revolutionary pension while living in Blount County, Tenn., where he lived for 45 years. He was born in Augusta County, Va., afterwards Rockbridge County, and was living there when he enlisted in Virginia troops and was appointed Ensign. He was afterwards promoted to Captain. He was in the battle of Guilford Court House where his brother, Capt. Alexander Tedford, commanding a company of Rockbridge militia, was killed. Robert Tedford, who drew a pension in Blount County was also his brother. Capt. John Tedford's widow was Jane Tedford.

LIEUT. JONATHAN TIPTON

Lieut. Jonathan Tipton applied for revolutionary pension while living in Wilson County, Tenn., Sept. 25, 1832. He was born April 15, 1753, fifteen miles from Baltimore, Md. He enlisted in 1779, or 1780. He was a Lieutenant in Maryland Troops under Capt. Maury, Col. Thomas Guess and Col. Frederick Decker.

WILLIAM TIPTON

William Tipton applied for Revolutionary pension while living in Blount County, Tenn, July 9, 1834. He was born in Shenandoah Valley, Va., Feb. 13, 1761. He enlisted in the Virginia troops in 1778 and first drew pension on the invalid list in Virginia in 1803. He lived in the Shenandoah Valley for 23 years and states that his father was a member of the Virginia Legislature. He lived in Greene County, Tenn., Knox County, Tenn. where he lived 25 years and then moved to Blount County.

JACOB TROXAL

Jacob Troxal applied for revolutionary pension while living in Marion County, Tenn. in 1759. He moved to Loudon County, Va., before the Revolution and enlisted in Virginia troops while living in that County. After the Revolution he moved back to Maryland and from thence to Sullivan County, Tenn. then to Pulaski County, Ky., and thence to Marion County. He died in DeKalb County, Ala. July 1, 1843. His widow, Elizabeth Troxal, applied for widow's pension while living in Winchester, Tenn.

GEORGE TURNLEY

George Turnley applied for revolutionary pension while living in Jefferson County, Tenn. He was born in Bedford County. Va., Aug. 30, 1762. He moved with his father to Botetourt County, Va. and lived there until he was 16 years of age, when he moved to Henry County, Va. He enlisted while a resident of Henry County under Capt. John Fountain in June 1780. Col. Patrick Henry was instrumental in getting up the organization and in giving council and advice but he did not command. Other officers were Capt. John Clark, Col. Williams and Maj. John McNeal. George Turnley was discharged at Old Stone on Smith River in September, 1780. In November he moved to Watauga where an expedition was about to march against the Cherokees and he enlisted under Capt. David McNabb and Col. John Sevier. The place of rendezvous was Grassy Cove on Nollichuckey River in Washington County. Major John McNabb, Capt. Davis and Lieut. Bond were killed on this expedition. He volunteered again in 1782 on an expedition against the Cherokees on the Tennessee River, the chief of which was the Chuckamoguh. 300 men were in the expedition. He was discharged in Jonesboro in November 1782. He served two campaigns against the Cherokee Indians under Col. Parmenas Taylor after the Revolution. He also served in the War of 1812 against the Creek Indians in 1813 in Capt. Zacheus Copeland's 2nd Tennessee Militia. Other officers in this War were Col. William Lillard and General John Cocke. He died Sept. 3, 1848 in Jefferson County.

NOTE: He married Charlotte Cunnyngham, daughter of James and Arabella Goode Cunnyngham. Their children were: John, Mary, Elizabeth Jane. James Alexander, Polly, William Henderson, Rachel, Hugh Lorenzo, Mathew Jacob, who married Miriam Isbell, George Washington, Greenbury Madison, Andrew Jackson, and Julia Ann.

JAMES WEIR

James Weir's widow, Margaret Weir applied for revolutionary pension while living in Blount County, March 7, 1845. She was born Dec. 22, 1763. James Weir enlisted in the Army of the Revolution in Washington County, Va., and was in the Battle of King's Mountain under Capt. Edmondson and in the battle of Guilford Court House. She married James Weir in Augusta Co., Va., Feb. 19, 1783. James Weir died March 11, 1820. The original Bible pages are with the application giving the children's names as follows: Anny, born 1784, also spelled Anna, married September 6, 1803; Hugh born 1786 married Peggy———Dec. 18, 1810: John S., born 1787; William, born 1790; Betsy, born 1795; James Preston, born 1797; Patsey born 1799; and Lusina Porter Weir, born Jan. 21, 18—(paper torn).

NOTE:—Margaret Weir, widow of James Weir, was the daughter of John Sharp. She died in September, 1848. The daughter, Anna Weir, married James Berry.

BENJAMIN WILLIAMS

Benjamin Williams applied for revolutionary pension while living in Knox County, Tenn., Oct. 16, 1833. He was born 1742. He enlisted July 20, 1776, while residing six miles from Abingdon, Va. and served in Capt. Benjamin Gray's company, Col. Christie's Virginia regiment. He moved to North Carolina (that part which is now Tennessee) "to the waters of the Nolachuckey River" where he enlisted in Capt. John Clark's company, Col. John Sevier's regiment. He died in Knox County, June 5, 1835. He married, Dec. 9, 1829 in Knox County, Nancy Israel. She applied for pension while residing in Knox County, Sept. 5, 1853 when she was 50 years of age.

NOTE: Benjamin Williams was married twice. His second wife, who applied for pension, was Nancy Israel. The name of his first wife is not positively known but among her children was Elizabeth Williams who married David Key, and became the ancestress through her son, Rev. John Key, of a long and distinguished line, including many Chattanoogans. Mrs. Sarah Key Patten, Mrs. S. R. Read (Katherine Key), Mrs. Garnett Andrews (Elizabeth Key), Bessie Key Johnston, Miss Margaret Key and others.

TURNER WOOTEN

Turner Wooten applied for revolutionary pension while living in Jefferson County, Tenn., Sept. 13, 1832. He was born 1757. He enlisted while a resident of Buckingham Co., Va., in Capt. Tabb's company, Col. Charles Dabney's Virginia regiment and was in the Siege of Yorktown after which he was detailed under Capt. Ewell, serving twelve months in all. He died in Jefferson County, Nov. 22, 1833. He married Jan. 2, 1792 or Oct. 26, 1794, in Chesterfield Co., Va., Nancy Roper, who was born Jan. 25, 1773. She died in Bradley Co., Tenn., June 28, 1851. They had the following children: Nancy, Jack, Sally, Polly, Rhodey, Josiah, John R., William H., George W., Elizabeth who married Henry Price, James S. and Robert W.

SOME TENNESSEE HEROES

OF THE

REVOLUTION

Compiled From Pension Statements

PAMPHLET NO. II

TENNESSEE HEROES OF THE REVOLUTION
SOME PENSIONERS WHO LIVED IN THE VOLUNTEER STATE

JOHN ADAIR

John Adair applied for revolutionary pension while living in Wayne County, Ky., in September 1832. He was born in County Antrim, Ireland, in 1754. His father and family came to America, landing in Baltimore when he was about 18 years old or a little before. They lived in Maryland one year, moved to Pennsylvania, where they lived a year and moved to Sullivan County, now Sullivan County, Tenn. John Adair lived there during the Revolution and enlisted in companies serving against the Indians who were commanded by Chief Logan. He enlisted again in 1777 or 1778 in Capt. George Brooks' company. He volunteered the following spring under Capt. James Elliott and in the following spring, when his father was drafted, substituted for him in Capt. Samuel Brashear's company. In 1791 he moved to what is now Knox County, Tenn. He lived fourteen years in the Tennessee country, before removing to Kentucky.

---o---

ENSIGN JOSEPH CAMPBELL

Ensign Joseph Campbell applied for revolutionary pension while living in Hamilton County, Tenn., Nov. 27, 1832. He was born in Culpepper County, Va., in 1762. He enlisted in Albemarle County, Va., and served three months as a private in Capt. Bradley's company. His father, Joseph Campbell, Sr., moved about this time from Albemarle County, to Washington County, Va., where Joseph Campbell, Jr., enlisted in the summer of 1789, serving three months as a private in Capt. Robert Edmondson's company, Col. William Campbell's regiment and was in an engagement with Indians on the Holston River. He next substituted for his father, serving three months in Capt. Edmondson's company and was in the battle of King's Mountain. Shortly after this date he was appointed Ensign in Capt. Black's Virginia company, receiving his commission from Gov. Patrick Henry, and for three months was engaged in cutting out the Kentucky Road. He died Jan. 9, 1841, in Bradley County, Tennessee.

Note: He went to Bradley County to visit a daughter who lived near Calhoun and died in her home. His widow, Christiana Campbell, received the arrears of his pension. She was probably an Anderson before her marriage as a close connection with the East Tennessee Anderson family is indicated. The children of Ensign and Christiana Anderson Campbell, were: William, who married Rebecca Shahan, George, John and James.

LIEUTENANT SAMUEL CARTER

Samuel Carter resided in Albemarle County, Virginia, when he enlisted immediately after the capture of Burgoyne. He served in Captain John Martin's Company, Colonel Fountain's Regiment. About Nov. 1, 1778, he moved to Fairfield District, S. C., and soon after enlisted in Captain Robert Frost's Company, Colonel David Hopkins' Regiment. Shortly after his enlistment he was elected Lieutenant and served in Colonel Richard Winn's Regiment. He served two months in command of a company against Tories on the South Edisto River. He was in the battle of Eutaw Springs. He moved from Fairfield District, S. C., to Rutherford County, N. C., and lived there until 1810, when he moved to Haywood County, N. C. In 1813 he moved to Sevier County, Tenn., after which he moved to Blount and Monroe Counties, Tenn. He was allowed pension on his application September 21, 1832, while he was living in Monroe County and he was then 78 years of age, which places his birth in 1754. He drew pension in Polk County in 1840.

JOHN CHESTER

John Chester applied for revolutionary pension in Sullivan County, May 29, 1829, aged 74, which places his birth in 1745. He served in the battles of Germantown, Stony Point, Monmouth and Brandywine. He was discharged from service in Trenton, N. J. His daughter, Elizabeth Chester, states that he died Feb. 4, 1841, and that he left a widow, Mary Birdwell Chester, who died Oct., 17, 1852, born 1766. At her death the surviving children were Elizabeth, Obadiah and Jane who married a Patterson. The original page of the Family Bible is enclosed with the widow's application giving the following information: John Chester married Mary Birdwell, March 21, 1781. Their children were: Elizabeth, born Sunday, Dec. 25, 1787; Robert, born Wednesday, Dec., 9, 1789; John, born Thursday, Oct., 20, 1791; Mark, born Friday, Sept., 13, 1793; Jane born Wednesday, Jan., 6, 1796; Ezra, born Wednesday, Dec., 20, 1797; Mary, born Dec., 3, 1800; George, born Feb., 6, 1802; Obadiah, born Sunday, June 17, 1805; Nancy, born Friday, July 14, 1811. The following marriages are recorded on the Bible page: Robert Chester married Feb., 1810; John Chester married Dec., 15, 1814; Ezra Chester married June 25, 1818; Obadiah Chester married Feb., 11, 1835. (The names of the women whom they married are not given).

WILLIAM CLARK

William Clark applied for revolutionary pension while living in Pickens District, S. C., Oct. 5, 1835. He was born April 7, 1757, in Shenandoah County, Va. He enlisted when he was a resident of Washington County, N. C., (now Tennessee) in 1777, as a private and served six months in Capt. Thomas Price's company, Col. John Sevier's regiment. In 1778 he enlisted and served one month and thirteen days in Capt. Valentine Sevier's company. In the fall of 1780 he enlisted in Capt. Asher's company. In the fall of 1771 he served three months in Capt. Samuel Williams' company, Col. John Sevier's regiment and was in the battle of Monk's Corner. In 1782 he enlisted and served one month in Capt. Alexander Moore's company, Col. John Sevier's regiment and was engaged in the battles with the Cherokee Indians. He died June 4, 1843 in Hall County, Ga. He married Feb. 14, 1792, in Franklin County, Ga., Ruth Gordon, born May 14, 1767. She applied for widow's pension April 2, 1844, while residing in Hall County, Ga. Their children were: John, born Nov. 5, 1792; Oliver, born Oct. 9, 1794; Sevier, born Sept. 11, 1794 and Sabra, born March 3, 1799.

WILLIAM CLAY

William Clay applied for revolutionary pension while living in Grainger County, Tennessee, in 1832. He was born in Chesterfield County, Va., in 1760. He enlisted in Chesterfield County, in 1776, at the age of sixteen. He moved to Amelia County, Va., where he again enlisted in 1781. He served in the Seige of Yorktown. A few years after the Revolution he moved to Halifax County, Va., where he lived until 1793 when he moved to Washington County, Va., and from thence in 1794 to Grainger County, Tenn., where he resided until his death Aug., 4, 1841. His widow, Rebecca Clay, applied for pension in August 1843, while living in Anderson County, Tenn. She states that she was married to William Clay in Halifax County, Va., Dec., 30, 1788, in her father's house and that her name was Rebecca Comer. Her father was Samuel Comer. She states that her son, Hon Clement Comer Clay of Alabama, was born Dec., 17, 1792; Nancy, born Sept., 18, 1794; William, born July 18, 1794; Cynthia, born Dec., 15, 1789; Maacha, born June 18, 1802, and Samuel Anderson, born March 29, 1805.

JOHN CURTIS

John Curtis applied for revolutionary pension while living in Bledsoe County, Tenn., in November 1832. He was born in Dinwiddie County or Sussex County, Va., in 1759 or 1760. His father died when he was very young. He was living in Dinwiddie County when he enlisted and served in Virginia troops. He moved to Orange County, N. C., and then to Chatham County, N. C. He then moved to Giles County, Tenn., Sumner County, Tenn., White County, Tenn., and to Bledsoe County. He died August 7, 1844 in Bledsoe County. He married Dolly Huneycut, Oct., 10, 1793. She survived him and applied for widow's pension while living in McMinn County, Tenn., in 1848, being then 78 years old, therefore born 1770. Their oldest child the name not being given in the application, was born in 1796.

JOHN DALTON

John Dalton applied for revolutionary pension in Feb., 1833, while living in Bledsoe County, Tenn. He was born Oct., 3, 1758 in Albemarle County, Va. He enlisted in the spring of 1778 in Albemarle

County, his company officers being Capt. William Sims, Lieut. William Flint and Ensign William Dowell. He enlisted again in 1779 under the same officers and again in 1781 under the same officers He married a daughter of Capt. William Simms. His uncle was William Grant, two members of whose family were killed by Indians in North Carolina in 1781. After the war John Dalton moved to Rutherford County, N. C., and to Bledsoe County, Tenn., about the year 1817. His widow, ———— Sims Dalton, survived him.

Note: His pension does not state that he was a minister, but in signing an application for a friend's pension he wrote his name, John Dalton, D. D.

ANDREW DAVIS

Andrew Davis applied for revolutionary pension while living in Bledsoe County. He was born Dec. 21, 1750 in the Waxsaw settlement of South Carolina. He was living there when he enlisted Nov. 1, 1775, under Capt. John Barkley, Col. Richardson and Gen. Sumpter, serving two months. He enlisted again and was in Charleston during the battle of Sullivan's Island but was not in the battle. In 1777 he served under Capt. James Pettigrew, Col. Samuel Jack and Col William Terrell in a regiment which was called the Minute Troops. He served in 1779 under Capt. Robert Davis. He volunteered in a cavalry company in Lincoln County, N. C., under Capt. Samuel Martin. His papers were lost when his house was burned. He knew Andrew Jackson as a boy. He moved from South Carolina to Iredell County, N. C., during the Revolution and subsequently he moved to Rutherford County, Tenn., to Warren County, Tenn., and to Bledsoe County. He then moved to Benton County, Ala., and applied to have his pension transferred to that county.

JOHN DAY

John Day applied for revolutionary pension while living in Jefferson County, Tenn., July 7, 1833. He was accompanied to make his declaration by John Day, Jr. He was born June 39, 1742, in Bucks County, Pa. He served as an Ensign in Botetourt County, Va., in 1776 and 1777. He resided in Botetourt County on the Greenbriar River. He received his Ensign's commission from the Virginia Committee of Safety. He served under Capt. Paxton and was appointed a spy under Capt. Cook. About four years after Cornwallis surrendered he moved to what is now Jefferson County, Tenn., then Greene County, N. C. John Day, Jr., swore that he was a small boy during the Revolution andthat he knew that his father served. John Day, Jr., says that he was about 65 years of age in January, 1833 The pension was granted for service as an Ensign for three months and as a private for eighteen months.

Note: He married, 1758, Polly Susan ————. Among their children was John Day, Jr., born in Virginia, 1760, died 1837, married Rebecca Hall.

JOHN DOSS

John Doss applied for revolutionary pension while living in Marion County, October, 1826, when he was 86 years old, therefore born 1840. He enlisted March 17 1777 in Pittsylvania County, Va., under Capt. Thomas Dillard, Col. Morgan and others. He says that he marched through the wilderness 600 miles across the Mississippi to Illinois town and back to Virginia. He was honorably discharged after two years service, but while moving down the River the boat sank and all his papers were lost. He moved to Marion County, Tenn.

JOHN DYER

John Dyer was born May 7, 1760, in Braintree Norfolk County, Mass. He enlisted in the Revolutionary Army in 1775, while residing in Braintree, Norfolk County, Mass., and served nine weeks as fifer in Capt. Nathan Alden's Massachusetts' Company. He enlisted again in 1776 and served six months in Capt. Alden's and Capt. Nathan Snow's Companies, Col. Jeremiah Hall's Massachusetts Regiment. He enlisted again in the spring of 1778 and served nine months as drum and rifle major under Lieut. Zachariah Watkins in Cols.. Woods and Bailey's Massachusetts Regiment. He enlisted again in the spring of 1781 and served under Capt. Mark Packard. He was in the skirmish at Morrisania and at the capture of Cornwallis. After the Revolution he moved to Halifax County, N. C., thence to Edgefield District. S. C., thence to Hancock County, Ga., thence to Cocke County, Tenn., thence to that part of Rhea County, which was later Meigs County, Tenn., where he died. He applied for pension while living in Meigs County, May 3 1836. There is no information in the pension applicaton concerning his family.

JOHN DYSART, SR.

John Dysart, Sr., applied for revolutionary pension while living in Bedford County, Tennessee., August 2, 1832. He was born in Chester County, Pa., Dec., 25, 1849. He enlisted while residing on Muddy Creek, Burke County, N. C., in 1776, 1777, 1779, 1780 and 1781. He served under the following officers: Captains, William Moore, Robert Patton and Samuel Woods, Col. McDowell. He was in the battle of King's Mountain. He was referred to as John Dysart, Sr. His father, James Dysart, and his brother, William Dysart, were killed on the Yadkin River when Gen. Davidson was killed. He died in Bedford County, Tenn., Sept., 10, 1842.

Note: John Dysart, Sr., married twice. He first married in 1733, Martha Patton. His second wife was ———— Woods. It would seem that both his wives were daughters of or otherwise closely related to his revolutionary officers, Capt. Robert Patton and Capt. Samuel Woods. The children by the first marriage were: James, born 1799, died 1852, married 1797, Martha Cowden; Robert, William, Frank, Andrew and a daughter. Children by the second marriage were Davis and John Dysart. Jr.

WILLIAM ELLIOTT

William Elliott applied for revolutionary pension while living in Marion County, Tenn., Aug., 17, 1833. He enlisted in Mecklenburg County, N. C., where he then resided, in February, 1731. He moved from Mecklenburg County to Wilkes County, Ga., where he lived two years. He then moved to Jefferson County, Tenn., to Bledsoe County, Tenn., and to Marion County. He married Miriam Leith, June 22, 1790. He died in Marion County, June 27, 1834. Miriam Leith Elliott survived him and applied for widow's pension. August, 1842. Enclosed in pension application are pages from the family Bible with the following information: Marriages: William Elliott to Miriam Leith, June 22, 1790. She was 22 years old and was born Oct. 12, 1768; Jenne (?) H. Elliott married Henry Baird, Oct., 31, 1809; Susanna Elliott married Thomas Walker, April 4, 1816; Betsy Elliott married Risden,(?) Robertson, June 27, 1816; Nancy Elliott married Jesse Howard, July 28, 1818; Joshua L. Elliott married Caty Moore, April 12, 1826; Benjamin Elliott married, (word married appears but no name and no date); (?) Elliott married John Bowen, May 5, 1825; Malinda Elliott married Thomas Payne, Jan., 1828; William E. Elliott married Margaret W. Austin. No births of children are given but presumably the list refers to the children of William and Miriam Elliott. On the back of the Bible page are births of several children in the Roberts family but no connection is shown with the Elliotts or Leiths.

JOHN ESTES

John Estes applied for revolutionary pension while living in Grainger County, April, 1834. He was born in Louisa County, Va., October 41, 1751, and moved to Halifax County, Va., while he was a boy. He enlisted in Halifax County, Feb., 9, 1776, in the 7th Regiment, Virginia Troops. He was in the battle of Brandywine. He had a brother, Thomas Estes. The widow of John Estes drew his arrears of pension but her name is not given.

JOHN ETHERIDGE

John Etheridge applied for revolutionary pension while living in Blount County, Aug., 4, 1820. He was born August 4, 1836. He enlisted in the 1st Regiment North Carolina Troops and served three years under Capt. Henry Dixon; he served one year under Capt. James Reid and served the balance of his seven years' service under Capt. Peter Becoff (?). He served seven years lacking two months when he was honorably discharged. He moved in 1825 to Davidson County and was transferred to that point. His widow, Mary Etheridge was aged 83 years April 3, 1843, when she applied for pension in Davidson County. She was born, 1860. She says that she was married to John Etheridge, March 7, 1780, in Halifax County, N. C., at the house of Col. Bradford, who was a justice of the peace. John Etheridge was then in service and received permission from his captain to stay at home for ten days after his marriage. He was taken prisoner at Charleston and was wounded twice during the War, once in the arm and once above the right eye. He died Dec., 12, 1839.

ANDREW EVANS

Andrew Evans applied for revolutionary pension while living in Rhea County, Tenn., Sept., 24, 1832. He was born April 4, 1763, in Frederick County, Va. He was living in Washington County, Va., when he substituted for his father, Samuel Evans, who was drafted in that county, in April, 1779. In September, 1780 he substituted for his brother, Joseph Evans, who was drafted in Washington County, He served under Lieut. Robert Campbell, Capt. Andrew Colville and Lieut. Col. William Campbell and was in the battle of King's Mountain. He had moved to Washington County, Va., before the War and after the War he moved to Knox County, Tenn., then to Grainger County, Tenn., then to Sevier County, and then to Rhea County, where he died.

JOSEPH EVANS

Joseph Evans applied for revolutionary pension while living in Claiborne County, Tenn., Nov., 14, 1820, when he was 61 years old, therefore born 1759. He served in the 7th Virginia Regiment in Capt. Joseph Crockett's company and was in the battles of Morristown, Monmouth, Brunswick, Edgefield and at the taking of Burgoyne. His pension was transferred to Montgomery County, Ill., where his children lived as he wanted to be with them.

SAMUEL EVANS

Samuel Evans applied for revolutionary pension while living in Roane County, July 12, 1717. He was born in 1863. He enlisted in a North Carolina Regiment commanded by Col. William Washington. His Captain was Capt. Guinn. He served five years or during the period of the War and continued to serve after the surrender of Cornwallis. He was in the battles of Eutaw Springs, Guilford Court House and Cowpens. He lost his right leg as it was amputated because of a wound. He says that five children, the oldest a boy of 13, are living with him. His widow, Peggy Evans, applied for pension in 1854. She lived until after 1869, when Rufus Wilson was appointed her guardian. She was a second wife. She married him Oct., 1829, in Monroe County, when he was 68 years old. She was Peggy Stoyles (?) before her marriage. Samuel Evans died Aug., 26, 1851. His children were: Samuel, Jr., born 1805, died after 1851; Harris; Nancy married ——— Mitzell; Esther married ——— Davis.

WILLIAM EVERETT

William Everett applied for revolutionary pension while living in Marion County, Tenn., April 9, 1833. He was born May 24, 1863, in Richmond County, Va. His father died in Halifax County, Va., about 1803. William had a brother, John Everett, who lived in Caswell County, N. C. A few years after the Revolution, William Everett moved to Bedford County, Va. After four years he moved to Caswell County, N. C. He then moved to Hawkins County, N. C., now Tennessee and lived their eighteen years. He moved to Knox County, Tenn., and lived there fifteen years. He moved to Marion County, eighteen months before he applied for pension. His widow's name is not given and a son, Duissett (?) applied Nov., 27, 1838, for final payment of his father's pension.

LIEUT. ALEXANDER EWING

Lieut. Alexander Ewing's son made application in Davidson County, Tenn., for pension for Mrs. Sally Ewing, deceased widow of Alexander Ewing, as the son and administrator. Alexander Ewing was a Lieutenant in the 14th Regiment of Virginia Continental troops in the Revolutionary War. He was commissioned Sept., 3, 1777. He served until Jan., 1, 1782 when he resigned his commission. Later he received a North Carolina Military warrant in consideration of his services. After Alexander Ewing quit the service he moved to what is now Tennessee where in Davidson County, (then N. C.,) he married in 1788, Sally Smith. Alexander Ewing died April 9, 1822, leaving his widow, Sally Smith Ewing, who died June 15, 1840. She was born August 12, 1861. Alexander Ewing was born March 10, 1752. Alexander Ewing was wounded in the leg. Several papers concerning his service are included in his record with the signatures of John Jay, Brig. Gens. Muhlenberg and "Steuben," Major Gen. Commanding etc. The children of Alexander Ewing and Sally Smith Ewing were: John Love, born 1789; James, born 1790; Lucinda, born 1792; William, born 1799; Oscar Smith, born 1801, and Louisa

EBENEZER FAIN

Ebenezer Fain resided in Georgia when he applied for revolutionary pension, but he lived in Washington County, N. C., now Tennessee, when he served. His pension record shows that he enlisted in the service when he was only fourteen years of age and that he was born August 27, 1762 in Chester County, Penn. He enlisted in June, 1776, and served three months under Capt. James Montgomery and Col. William Christian of Virginia. He served three months under Capt. William Trimble and Capt Cunningham and Capt. Charles Robertson in North Carolina. He also served three months in Georgia under Col. Clash. He enlisted Sept. 15, 1780, for three months under Capt. Christopher Taylor, Col. John Sevier, of North Carolina. In 1781 he served three months under Colonel John Sevier, Col. Carter and Capt. Christopher Cunningham. He was in the battles of Musgroves Mills, Woffords Iron Works and King's Mountain where he was wounded in the leg.

Note: Ebenezer Fain was the son of Nicholas and Elizabeth Taylor Fain and was one of five brothers who served in the Revolution with their father, who also served. The six were in the battle of King's Mountain. Another brother was killed by Indians during the Revolutionary period and the seventh brother of the group is believed to have served although documentary proof has not been found. Ebenezer Fain married Mary Mercer, June, 1781. She died February 11, 1846. Their children were: David, John, Elizabeth, Margaret, Sarah, Mercer, Mary Ann, Rebecca and Polly Ann Fain.

JOHN FORD

John Ford applied for revolutionary pension while living in Bledsoe County in February, 1833. He was born in Albemarle County, Va., Nov., 13, 1764. He enlisted in Fluvanna County, Va., in Capt. Thomas Thurman's Company. After the Revolution he moved to Roane County, Tenn., where he lived eight years. About 1817 he moved to Bledsoe County, where he died. He received a Bounty land warrant. He died in Bledsoe County, August 5, 1844. He married April 12, 1785, in Fluvanna County, Va., Elizabeth England, who survived him. She applied for pension August 21, 1844, when she was 80 years of age, naming six children: Jane, born 1786, married ——— Mathis; Sarah, born 1789, married ——— Bristoe; John Ford, Jr., born 1796; Nancy, born 1798, married ——— Loden; Mary, born, 1803, married ——— Renfroe; and Reuben, born 1806. She died September 30, 1845.

HENRY GOODMAN

Henry Goodman applied for revolutionary pension while living in Anderson County, Tenn., Aug. 28, 1832. He was born Dec. 18, 1758, in Georgetown District, South Carolina. He resided in Cheraw, S. C., when he enlisted in hte South Carolina troops as follows: from 1775 or 1776, three months as a private in Capt. Henry Arrington's company, Col. George Hicks' regiment; during the next spring or summer, three months in Capt. Arrington's company, Col. Thomas Loyd's regiment; and for the next summer six months in Capt. Arrington's company under Major Robert Horry and Col Horry. For the spring of 1779 he served six months as orderly sergeant in Capt. Henry Council's company, under Col. Thomas Loyd and Col. Lawrence and he was wounded in the right thigh in the battle of Stono. From March or April, 1780, he was orderly sergeant in Capt. Morris Murphey's company under Maj. Robert Loyd and was in the Siege of Charlestown where he was taken prisoner. He was paroled and was at home until summer when he was called out by Col. Abel Culp against the British Tories. He was out at various times under Col. Culp, Col. Lemuel Benton and was in the battle of Eutaw Springs under Gen. Francis Marion. All of his services from 1775 of 1776 to a date after the battle of Uutaw Springs amounted in all to about three years. He married in 1780 Catherine Smithhart. He died June 11, 1833. She died Sept. 30, 1836. The following children were alive in 1852: Esther Massengale, Catherine Stout, and John L. Goodman, who was then 54 years of age.

DAVID GOODWIN

David Goodwin applied for revolutionary pension while living in White County, Tenn., April 9, 1833. He was born Feb. 24, 1763 in St. David's Parish, South Carolina. He entered the service when he was 17 years of age when he resided in St. David's Parish, S. C. The State was afterwards laid out in Districts and St. David's Parish was called Darlington District. He served under Capt. William Standard, who was in Col. Abel Culp's regiment under Gen. Francis Marion. He enlisted again as a substitute for his step-father, John

Flowers. He moved after the war to Marlborough District, S. C., where he lived for four months and then moved to Chesterfield, then to the hills of Santee, in Sumpter District, S. C. In 1827 he moved to White County, Tenn., where he died Nov. 23, 1838. His widow, Nancy Goodwin, aged 81 in 1853, so born 1772, applied for widow's pension. She was married March 6, 1800 in Darlington District, S. C., by Rev. Coleman, a baptist minister.

Note: His widow, Nancy, was Nancy Carter before her marriage. She was David Goodwin's second wife. Among the children by the second wife was William, born Dec., 1809, died Jan., 1885, married Charity Linville, born 1802, died 1854.

WILLIAM GRAHAM

William Graham applied for revolutionary pension while living in Anderson County, Tenn., Oct. 10, 1832. He was born May 25, 1749, in Loudoun County, Va. He moved to Brunswick County, Va., and while a resident there he enlisted in April, 1779, and served three months in Capt. Benjamin Jones' company, Col. Frederick McLin's Virginia regiment. While a resident of Caswell County, N. C., he enlisted in March, 1781, and served three months in Captain Aaron Horrell's Company, Colonel Wadkins' North Carolina Regiment. He enlisted again in October, 1782, and served five months in Captain Swan Ironton's Company, under Major Bennet Crafton in North Carolina aroops. After the Revolution he moved to Tennessee. He died in Anderson County.

WILLIAM HALE

William Hale applied for revolutionary pension while living in McMinn County, Tenn., July, 1833. He was then about 75 years old. He enlisted in 1775 when he was 16 years of age, in Hillsboro, Orange County, N. C., with Alfred Moon. He served in a regiment which was commanded by Col. Francis Nash. Other officers were Alfred Moon and Lawrence Thompson. He enlisted for six months and was discharged in March, 1776, at Wilmington, N. C. He moved to the Tennessee country and settled in McMinn County, where he died.

BENJAMIN HARRIS

Benjamin Harris applied for revolutionary pension while living in White County, Tenn., in 1832. He was born in 1762 in Southampton County, Va. He lived in Brunswick County, Va., when he entered the service, his regiment being commanded by Col. Lucas. The regiment was stationed in the Isle of Wight County, Va. After the War he moved to Rutherford County, N. C., then to Greeneville District, S. C., and from thence to White County, Tenn. He died in White County, May 21, 1834. His widow, Ruth Harris, moved to Illinois where she died before 1853. They had a daughter, Mary Ann Harris Courland.

SAMUEL HAWKINS

Samuel Hawkins applied for revolutionary pension while living in Hamilton County, in February, 1833. He was born May 18, 1735. He entered the service in Boston, Mass., under Capt. Lemuel Stewart and Col. James Easton, in Williamston, Mass., in the first year of the War and was marched to Albany, N. Y., where the company joined other companies under Gen. Schuyler. He received a written discharge. He knew personally, Gen. Washington, Gen. Schuyler, Gen. Putnam, Gen. Gates. Gen. Sullivan, Gen. Nixon, Gen. LaFayette, Gen. Arnold, Gen. Montgomery and many other officers. After the War he moved to Caswell County, N. C., and to Hawkins County, Tenn., where he lived 30 years. He moved to Hamilton County, Tenn., in 1831. His pension application was signed by Congressman John Blair. He died in Hamilton County, May 6, 1836. His widow, Pharaba Hawkins, made application for pension while living in Greene County, Tenn., July 29, 1848, aged 67 years, therefore born 1781. She states that she was married to Samuel B. Hawkins in Hawkins County, at her father, Samuel Spears' house by William Paine, Justice of the Peace, for Hawkins County, in August, 1797. Mrs. Nancy Pruitt (Mrs. Charles Pruitt) says that she was an attendant at the wedding and says that she herself was married in the same house a few years later.

FRANCIS HAWLEY

Francis Hawley applied for revolutionary pension while living in Sullivan County, Tenn., Sept. 25, 1832. He was born Dec. 12, 1762. He lived in Stafford County when he enlisted in 1779. He states that his father and mother moved from Virvinia to Sullivan County, Tenn., about 1806 or 1807 and that they both died. Francis Hawkins died in Sullivan County, Feb. 21, 1840. His wife, Sarah Hawley, was born April 11, 1762, and died Jan. 26, 1844. The names of their children are on the original Family Bible page as follows: James, born 1781; Ansey, born 1783; Francis Hodgeman (?) 1785; William, born 1787; Millenda, born 1789; Sanford Rodney, born 1791; William Augustus, born 1794; John Barbin, born 1796; Thomas Carroll, born 1798; Matilda, born 1801, married John Foust; Addison, born 1803; and Percy (a daughter) born 1805, married ——— Ford.

MESHACK HENDERSON

Meshack Henderson applied for revolutionary pension while living in Roane County, Tenn., March 1, 1834. He was born in Culpepper County, Va., in 1756. He lived in Rowan County, N. C., when he enlisted in 1778 under Capt. Wynn. After the Revolution he moved to Roane County, Tenn. His only heir was a daughter, Margaret.

REUBEN HERNDEN

Reuben Hernden's widow, Frances Hernden, applied for a widow's revolutionary pension while living in Hamilton County, Dec. 8, 1843. Reuben Hernden died in Franklin County, now Coffee County, Tenn., in March 1813. He had a younger brother, James Hernden, who also served in the Revolution and drew pension in Rutherford County, according to the statement of his son, Jacob Hernden, who testifies in Frances Hernden's application. He says that his father, James Hernden, died in Rutherford County, Oct. 1, 1843, that James Hernden married about 1781 and had six children. That Reuben and James were sons of Jacob Hernden, Sr., and that Reuben enlisted when he was 19 years of age and was taken prisoner in Col. Buford's defeat at or near Lunenburg Court House, Va., and that James Hernden was serving in the same company and was also taken prisoner. Frances Kenneda was born June 6, 1765 and was married in Charlotte County, Va., on Twitty Creek in the Mossyford Meeting House by John Williams, a Baptist Preacher. Her name is spelled three ways in the application, Kenneda, Canada and Kennedy. After she secured her pension she moved to Dekalb County, Ala. The children of Reuben and Frances Hernden were: Sarah, born 1791; James, born 1792; William, born 1795; John, born 1779; Elijah, born 1799; Jacob, born 1801; Reuben Jr., born 1804; Enoch, born 1806, and Jane, born 1809, who married William George.

ENNIS HOOPER

Ennis Hooper applied for revolutionary pension while living in Marion County, Tenn., Aug. 21, 1832. He was born 1750. He enlisted in Guilford County, N. C., in 1777, and again, the second enlistment being under Capt. William Armstrong. He was in the battles of Guilford Court House, Briar Creek, Stone River, Gates Defeat and Eutaw Springs. He was given a land warrant by the State of North Carolina. After the Revolution he moved to Marion County, Tenn.

HOWELL HORTON

Howell Horton applied for a new pension certificate while living in Hamilton County, March 16, 1825, stating that the original had been destroyed by his children about sixteen years previously near Warrenton, North Carolina. The names of his children are not given. He served under Col. Thomas Eaton and was transferred from the Invalid Pension Roll of North Carolina, to the East Tennessee Roll. The dates of his enlistment and discharge, length of service, war in which he served and the nature of his disability are not matters of record, because the pension papers filed prior to 1814 were destroyed when the British burned Washington in 1814. Howell Horton died May 24, 1832.

ENSIGN JAMES HOUSTON

Ensign James Houston applied for revolutionary pension while living in Blount County, Tenn., Aug. 10, 1832. He was born Nov. 12, 1757, in Augusta County, Va. He enlisted in the spring of 1776 under Capt. William Buchanan and then resided in Augusta County. He served in the battle of Long Island and in the Chickamauga Expedition under Col. Shelby. He volunteered again under Capt. Nathaniel Henderson and was in the battle of King's Mountain. He moved in 1782 from Washington County, Va., to Greene County, N.

C., now Tennessee, and about 1792 to what is now Blount County, Tenn. He was a member of the Convention of 1796 from Blount County, and was also a member of the First General Assembly of Tennessee. He was an Ensign in the battle of King's Mountain as he was promoted to that office at the death of Lieut. Edmundson.

PETER HUGHES

Peter Hughes enlisted while living on Beaver Creek in the Holston Country, then North Carolina and now Tennessee in 1777 and served two months as a ranger against the Cherokee Indians as a ranger in Capt. Robert Craig's Company of Virginia troops. He enlisted again August 20, 1778 and served as a private in Capt. Archibald Taylor's Company against the Shawnees and Delawares in the Ohio Country and marched to Fort McIntosh. He served eight months. He enlisted again in September 1780 and served three months as a private in Capt. Craig's Company, Col. Campbell's Virginia regiment and was in the battle of King's Mountain and later against the Indians. In September, 1781, he enlisted again and served two months in Col. Lynch's Virginia regiment. He was allowed a pension for which he applied Aug. 29, 1832, while living in Sullivan County, Tenn. In 1847 he had moved to Virginia where his grandson had built a house for him and his daughter, the names not being given in the pension record. He died in Washington County, Va., May 22, 1849. He married sometime in March, April 8, or May 8, 1787, (all three dates are given) in Sullivan County, Lucy Blevins. She applied for pension August 26, 1850, while she was living in Washington County, Va., and 88 years (so born in 1762). She died Nov. 15, 1855. They had a large family of children, the names given being: David, the oldest son Nancy, married ——— Starling, and William, Lucy Blevins Hughes, the widow had a sister, Nancy Girtman.

LIEUT. SAMUEL JACKSON

Lieut. Samuel Jackson applied for revolutionary pension while living in Washington County, Tenn., July 13, 1829. He was born Sept. 16, 1755. He enlisted in the fall of 1775 and served until he resigned in 1778. He served in Georgia troops under Capt. Joseph Lane and Col. Stark. He was in the battle of Ogeechee River where he was shot in the hip. He died in Washington County, May 2, 1836. His widow, Elizabeth Woodrow Jackson, born Dec. 22, 1764, died Jan. 8, 1844, applied for widow's pension Nov. 6, 1839, while living in Washington County. She was married in Philadelphia, Pa., April 20, 1780. Her children were: Harry, born 1789; Tamey, born 1783, died 1783; Charles, born 1785, died 1786; William, born 1787, died 1787; Susan, born 1788; Mary Ann, born 1790, died 1810: Tamey, born 1793; Julia Adelaide Eliza, born 1797, died 1817; Caroline, born 1799; Harriet, born 1803, and Alfred Eugene, born 1807.

Note: Samuel D. Jackson was the son of Philip Jackson. He was born in Carlisle, Pa. He was a merchant in Philadelphia in 1801. He purchased 39,000 acres in Middle Tennessee from Gov. Blount. He moved to Middle Tennessee for a time but returned to East Tennessee, and located on the Nolachukey River. In a wager with Gen.

Andrew Jackson he lost 10,000 acres and fought a duel with Jackson in which Jackson ran him through the body with his sword. The historian very quaintly says that this caused a coolness between them. His wife was an intimate friend of Dolly Madison and was a bridesmaid in her first marriage. Concerning her children given in the pension application: Susan W., married Thomas G. Watkins; Julia Adelaide Eliza, married David Anderson Deaderick; Caroline married John A. Aiken; Harriet, married Oliver B. Ross; Alfred Eugene, married Serephina Taylor, daughter of Gen. Nathaniel Taylor.

WILLIAM JACKSON

William Jackson applied for revolutionary pension while living in Blount County, July 10, 1818, when he was 64 years of age, therefore born, about 1754. He served in Maryland, Pennsylvania and Virginia troops. He lived in Pennsylvania when he enlisted in 1776 under Capt. Armstrong. He enlisted in other states later. After the War, in 1784, having married he went to housekeeping in Rockingham County, Va., and later moved to Blount County. He was given a land warrant for 100 acres for service as a private in Virginia troops. In 1837 he wrote from Lauderdale County, Ala., requesting that his pension be transferred to that county.

WILLIAM JENNINGS

William Jenkins applied for revolutionary pension while living in Lincoln County, Tenn. He was born Feb. 26, 1761. He lived in Prince Edward County, Va., in April 1777, when he entered the service. He served under Capt. Henry Walker, Col. Mason, Lieut. Richard Holland and Ensign John Black. In the summer of 1781 he enlisted in Prince Edward Co., under Capt. Cunningham. He was at the surrender of ornwallis. In 1836 he asked for a transfer of his pension to Shelby County, Ala. He died July 17, 1840. His widow Polly Jennings said that she was married Jan. 18, 1787, her name before marriage being Polly Kidd. She was born Nov. 4, 1771. Their children were: Martin, born 1787; Nancy, born 1789; Elizabeth, born 1792; Allen, born 1796; William Kidd, born 1789; Sally, born 1801; Webb, born 1802; William Calvin, born 1803; Robert, born 1808; Lucrecy, born 1810; Sophy, born 1812; James W., born 1813.

WILLIAM LONGLEY

William Longley was born in the state of New Jersey in the year of 1861. While he resided in Loudoun County, Va., he enlisted in Oct. 1789 and served in Captain Thomas Humphries Company, under Major Armisted, Col. Niswonger, Col. George Eskridge and Col. Summers. He was in the battle of Burrell's Ferry, Williamsburg and at the Siege of Yorktown. He was discharged in February, 1782. After the Revolution he lived a short time in Loudon ounty, and then moved to Shenandoah, Rockbridge and Washington Counties, Virginia, and in 1800 to Sevier County, Tennessee. He was allowed pension on his application, June 3, 1833, and was then a resident of McMinn County. He moved to Polk County and resided there when he drew pension in 1840. He died there Nov. 7, 1841. He married Sept. 1, 1784 in Loudon County, Va., Mary, her name not being given in his pension application. She died June 7, or 9, 1844, in Polk County and she was then about seventy years of age. The following children survived their mother; Jonathan, born 1788; Joel, born Sept. 1, 1791; James, Mercy, Sarah and Abigail, their ages not shown, and John C., born 1806. John C. Longley was living in Polk County at the time of his mother's death and he stated that he was the youngest child of his parents. Abigail and her husband, William T. Patterson, were living in Catoosa County, Ga. Mrs. Etha Burk, sister of the widow, Mary Longley, was living in Catoosa County, Ga., in 1854, and was at that time 73 years of age.

JOHN MALABY

John Malaby applied for revolutionary pension while living in Bledsoe County, in February, 1833. He enlisted in Dobbs County, N. C. under Capt. Bryant, Col. Caswell, Col. Adam Shepherd, Maj. John Shepherd, Gen Butler, Col. Collier and others.

LIEUT. ROBERT MARTIN

Robert Martin applied for revolutionary pension while living in Marion County, Tenn., in August 1832. He was born in Lancaster County, Pa., April 10, 1755 and died in Hamilton County, Tenn., in 1844. He enlisted in the summer of 1775 in North Carolina troops in Mecklenburg County, N. C., under Capt. Caleb Fifer and Col. John Fifer. He served as a Lieutenant under Col. John Fyfer and Gen. Rutherford, when he volunteered again in February, 1776 in Mecklenburg County. He enlisted again in 1781 under Lieut. William Ross and Col. Caleb Fyfer and made cartridge boxes for the army. He lived in Mecklenburg County about 40 years. He moved to Marion County, Tenn., in 1821. He moved to Hamilton County later and his pension was transferred. In Hamilton County he lived with his son, Alexander Martin.

WILLIAM MAY

William May was born May 3, 1764, in Essex County Virginia. While residing in Henry County, Virginia, he enlisted in the fall of 1779 or 1780 in Captain Hamby's Company, Colonel Abram Penn's Virginia Regiment. Later he enlisted in Captain Dillard's Company Colonel Penn's Regiment. At the time of the battle of Guilford Court House he enlisted in Captain Peter Hasting of Haston's Company. In 1781 he enlisted in Captain Hiram Crite or Cryte's Company, Colonel Stephens' Regiment. He was in the Siege of Yorktown. He was discharged October 20, 1781. About eight years after the War he moved from Henry County, Va., to Union County, S. C.. and six years later he moved to Buncomb County, N. C., and then to Blount County, Tenn., to a site on the Hiwassee River then in the Cherokee Nation. He then moved to the Chattahoochee River and later to what became Murray County, Georgia. He was allowed pension while living in Murray County, Ga., August 2, 1833, but his application was executed in McMinn County, Tennessee. He died

March 4, 1844, in Polk County. He married in July 1783 Rhoda ———
———, her maiden name not being given in the pension application. She was allowed pension May 6, 1844, while living in Polk County, Tenn., but in 1849 she was living in DeKalb County, Ga., for two years. The children of William and Rhoda May were: Orpha, born May 6, 1784; John, born January 11, 1786; Daniel born April 16, 1788; William May, Jr., born January 11, 1790; Ruth, born October 8, 1792; Mary Ann, born February 8, 1795; Asa, born October 29, 1797; (in the pension application lines are drawn through his name and the date of his birth), and James May, born April 29, 1800.

ANDREW McDONOUGH

Andrew McDonough applied for revolutionary pension while living in Bledsoe ounty, Tenn., in 1833. He was born in Beaufort County, N. C., Nov. 30, 1759. He enlisted in Beaufort County in North Carolina troops in 1771, substituting for John Burrow. He enlisted a second and third time.

ELI McVEY

Eli McVey applied for revolutionary pension while living in Hawkins County, Tenn., in Nov. 1820. He was born about 1763. He enlisted in Orange County, N. C., in Capt. Dickinson's regiment in Continental Line in May, 1781 for the duration of the War. He was in the battle of Eutaw Springs. He resided in Hawkins and Grainger Counties, Tenn., for twenty years. He stated that his wife is aged 48 years and that he had two sons, one aged 10 and one aged 7 years. Mildred McVey, his widow, stated that he died Sept. 30, 1830. She said that she was married to Ely McVey in Prince Edward County, Va., in 1787. She died April 18, 1850. Daniel B. McVey stated April 24, 1844, that he was the only surviving child and that he was 44 years old. However, in February 1839 Daniel and James McVey applied for and received a warrant for 100 acres of land on account of their father's military service, declaring themselves the only heirs at law.

WILLIAM METCALF

William Metcalf applied for revolutionary pension while living in Marion County, Tenn., in 1832. He was born in Virginia in 1764. He served under Col. Jack, who commanded a regiment of North Carolina Minute Men. (His officers were Capt. James Taylor, Lieut. Grier and Lieut. Anthony Metcalf, who was the father of William Metcalf. He enlisted in Rutherford County, N. C., when he was about 15 years of age. Three of his brothers joined the same regiment. He stated that (in 1832) his father was dead and his oldest brother and that two brothers were living in Rutherford County, N. C. He moved with his father fom Virginia to Rutherford County, N. C., before the Revolution. After the Revolution he moved to Jefferson County, Tenn., to Knox County, Tenn., to Claiborne County, Tenn., to White County, Tenn., and to Marion County, Tenn., about 1824.

MICHAEL MILES

Michael Miles' widow, Mary Miles, applied for revolutionary pension while living in Washington County, Tenn., Jan. 3, 1840. She states that she was married to Michael Miles in Kentucky County, Va., near where the city of Louisville now stands, in the home of Squire Hansbury, at Col. Floyd's Station on Bear Grass (Creek?) in the latter part of 1781 or the first part of 1782. She remembers that the ground was covered with snow. Michael Miles was then an officer of the Revolution under Gen. Rogers Clark. She was 14 years old, therefore born about 1768. She was escorted by a guard of soldiers from the home of her father, Thomas Harrison, at the Post at the Falls of the Ohio to the house where the marriage took place. She had only one child who died at the age of two months. Her husband, Michael Miles she says in her application, "died about 45 years ago on the French Broad River." This places his death about 1795.

ADAM MILLER

Adam Miller applied for pension while living in Roane County, Tenn., in 1833. He was born in Cumberland County, Pa., June 8, 1769. He lived in Mechlenburgh County, N. C., when he enlisted in North Carolina troops in 1781 under Capt. Peter Burns. He served in the First Regiment of Dragoons, commanded by Col. Wade Hampton. He was in the battle of Eutaw Springs. He married in 1786. He had seven children. He died in Roane County, July 5, 1848.

THOMAS MOORE

Thomas Moore applied for revolutionary pension while living in Rhea county, Tenn., Feb. 15, 1833. He was then 103 years old, therefore born 1730. He served in North Carolina toops as a substitute for William Deale. He was then living in Granville County, N. C. He served in the battles of Cowpens, Gate's Defeat, Guilford Court House, Eutaw Springs and King's Mountain. He lost a thumb in the battle of Cowpens.

JAMES MORGAN

James Morgan applied for revolutionary pension while living in Marion County, N. C. He enlisted in the spring of 1777 or 1778 in North Carolina troops under Captains William Polk, Charles Polk, Vestal, Walker and Colonels Thomas Polk, Rhodes, Crump, Ledbetter and Locke. He was in the battles of Ramsour's Mill, where he received a slight wound on the right wrist, Shallow Ford, Siege of Ninety-six, and Lindley's Mill, where he was again wounded on the wrist and on the head. He was taken to the garrison on Hickory Mountain to recover from his wounds and remained there six or eight months. He rejoined the army and was again wounded in a skirmish near Cross Creek. He returned to Hickory Mountain,

MICHAEL MILES

Michael Miles' widow, Mary Miles, applied for revolutionary pension while living in Washington County, Tenn., Jan. 3, 1840. She states that she was married to Michael Miles in Kentucky County, Va., near where the city of Louisville now stands, in the home of Squire Hansbury, at Col. Floyd's Station on Bear Grass (Creek?) in the latter part of 1781 or the first part of 1782. She remembers that the ground was covered with snow. Michael Miles was then an officer of the Revolution under Gen. Rogers Clark. She was 14 years old, therefore born about 1768. She was escorted by a guard of soldiers from the home of her father, Thomas Harrison, at the Post at the Falls of the Ohio to the house where the marriage took place. She had only one child who died at the age of two months. Her husband, Michael Miles she says in her application. "died about 45 years ago on the French Broad River." This places his death about 1795.

ADAM MILLER

Adam Miller applied for pension while living in Roane County, Tenn., in 1833. He was born in Cumberland County, Pa., June 8, 1769. He lived in Mechlenburgh County, N. C., when he enlisted in North Carolina troops in 1781 undtr Capt. Peter Burns. He served in the First Regiment of Dragoons, commanded by Col. Wade Hampton. He was in the battle of Eutaw Springs. He married in 1786. He had seven children. He died in Roane County, July 5, 1848.

THOMAS MOORE

Thomas Moore applied for revolutionary pension while living in Rhea oounty, Tenn., Feb. 15, 1833. He was then 103 years old, therefore born 1730. He served in North Carolina toops as a substitute for William Deale. He was then living in Granville County, N. C. He served in the battles of Cowpens, Gate's Defeat, Guilford Court House, Eutaw Springs and King's Mountain. He lost a thumb in the battle of Cowpens.

JAMES MORGAN

James Morgan applied for revolutionary pension while living in Marion County, N. C. He enlisted in the spring of 1777 or 1778 in North Carolina troops under Captains William Polk, Charles Polk, Vestal, Walker and Colonels Thomas Polk, Rhodes, Crump, Ledbetter and Locke. He was in the battles of Ramsour's Mill, where he received a slight wound on the right wrist, Shallow Ford, Siege of Ninety-six, and Lindley's Mill, where he was again wounded on the wrist and on the head. He was taken to the garrison on Hickory Mountain to recover from his wounds and remained there six or eight months. He rejoined the army and was again wounded in a skirmish near Cross Creek. He returned to Hickory Mountain,

THOMAS PALMER

Thomas Palmer applied for revolutionary pension while living in Cocke County, Tenn., Nov 28, 1832. He was born in 1760 in Loudon County, Va., and resided in that county when he enlisted in Virginia troops. He served in the battles of Valley Forge, Cowpens and Yorktown. After the Revolution he moved to Bedford County, Va., then to Greene County, Tenn., to Cocke County, Tenn., and then to Hamilton County. He had a brother, John Palmer.

Note: Thomas Palmer is buried at Birchwood, near Chattanooga, Tenn. He married in Winchester, Va., Emily Atkins. Their children were: Thomas Palmer, Jr., who married Lydia Doughty; William Palmer; John Palmer, and Maria Palmer. It is said that he told his children he stood very near Gen. Washington when Cornwallis surrendered.

ROBERT PATTERSON

Robert Patterson was born March 5, 1757, in Pennsylvania and moved to South Carolina when he was a child. He enlisted while living in York County, S. C., and served about ninteen months in all. His officers were Capt. McMullen, Capt. Moffit, Col. William Hill and Col. Neal and Gen. Sumpter. He was in battles of Reedy River, Hill's Iron Works, Williams' Lane, Rocky Mount and Blackstock. After the War he moved to North Carolina and after a number of years moved to Rutherford County, Tenn. He applied for revolutionary pension in 1832 while living in Giles County, Tenn., having moved there in 1830. He was still living in 1843 and at that time his wife and two single daughters were living.

ABEL PEARSON

Abel Pearson applied for revolutionary pension while living in White County, Tenn. He was born May 2, 1764 in Carroll Tract, Pa., and had moved before the War to the Tennessee Country, then North Carolina. He entered the army under Col. John Sevier and Maj. Jesse Walton and was in the battle of Boyd's Creek. He enlisted again under Capt. Jacob Brown and served in the battle of King's Mountain. He enlisted again under Capt. Luke Boyer. He states that his father's family Bible was then in the possession of a daughter who lived in Bledsoe County, Tenn. Thomas Gist testifies that he served at the same time and was under Capt. George Doherty.

Note: The printed pension list of White County says that Abel Pearson served in Virginia troops but this is an error. He had a son, Abel Pearson, who was born in North Carolina, now Tennessee, in 1787, and died in Hamilton County, Tenn., in 1856.

JESSE PERRY

Jesse Perry applied for revolutionary pension while living in Knox County. He was born March 15, 1755 in Granville County, N.

C. While a resident of Fairfield District, S. C., he enlisted and served in the South Carolna troops three months in Capt. William Lang's Company, Col. Robert Goodwin's Regiment—this service was in the "Snow Campaign;" three months in Capt. John Smith's Company, Col. Robert Goodwin's Regiment, during which service he was on an expedition to capture the Tory Colonel Fletchell; three months in Capt. John Taylor's Company, Col. Joseph Kirkland's Regiment; three months in Capt. James Craig's Company, Col. Henry Hunter's Regiment; three months in 1781 in Capt James Craig's Company, Col. Thomas Taylor's Regiment; and one year in Capt. John Cook's Company, Col. Arthur Middleton's Regiment; udring which time he was active against the Tories and was in a skirmish at Juniper Springs. A short time after this service while he was at home he was taken prisoner by a company of Tories under Col. Thompson and was taken by them to Camden and was later released on parole. After his release by the enemy he went about twenty miles above King's Mountain where he remained with friends until the termination of the War. He resided in Fairfield District, S. C., until the year 1806 when he moved to Duck River, Tennessee, and remained there until 1812. He then moved to Knox County, Tenn. He applied for pension August 18, 1832. In his application he states that at the time he volunteered for the year's service he moved his wife to the home of his mother three miles distant. In 1832 he refers to a brother-in-law but gives no family names.

YOUNG PAUGH

Young Paugh applied for revolutionary pension while living in Marion County, Tenn., in December 1833. He was born in Campbell County, Va., Jan. 1, 1754. He was living in Charlotte County, Va., when he enlisted in Virginia troops. After the War he moved to Greene County. Tenn., where he resided 34 years. He then moved to Blount County, Ala., and Macon County, N. C. He then moved to Marion County, Tenn.

CHATTEN D. POLLARD

Chatten D. Pollard applied for revolutionary pension while living in Franklin County, Va., in January 1833. He was born in Culpepper County, Va., moved to Frederick County, Va., then to Franklin County Va., and from that county, after he had secured his pension, to Bledsoe County, Tenn., where he died, Oct. 3, 1843. He stated that all of his children had moved to Bledsoe County. He enlisted in the army in 1780 and guarded prisoners. He was in the Siege of Yorktown and aided in the capture of Cornwallis. His widow, Mary Greer Pollard, applied for widow's pension while living in Bledsoe County, in 1843. She states that their marriage took place in Franklin County, Va.. Sept. 16, 1790. Her brother, John F. Greer, was Justice of the Peace in Bledsoe County, in 1843. The widow mentions a son, Chatten Pollard and other children whose names she does not list.

MITCHELL PORTER

Mitchell Porter applied for revolutionary pension while living in Sevier County, Tenn. He was born about 1760. He enlisted in Winchester, Va., in Virginia Troops, in 1777. He moved in 1780 to Botetourt County, Va., and after the War moved to the Tennessee Country. He died in Sevier County, April 3, 1836. His widow, Penelope Porter, applied for pension in Sevier County, Feb. 4, 1839, aged about 74 therefore born about 1765. They were married in 1785 in Virginia. The original pages of the Family Bible are enclosed showing their children's names: Alexander born 1786; William, born 1787; Elizabeth, born 1790; Ester, born 1791; John W., born 1793; Mary, born 1795; Mitchell, Jr., born 1796; Joshua Mc., born 179⁻, died 1803; Nancy, born 1801; Sally R., born 1802; James Douthett, born 1805, and Mc (Kindree?) born 1807.

AMOS RICHARDSON

Amos Richardson applied for revolutionary pension while living in Campbell County. He was born in Bedford County, Va., in 1762. He entered the service in North Carolina troops in Burke County N. C. He married Fanny Farmer, who survived him and applied for widow's pension some years after his death.

LOVETT REED

Lovett Reed applied for revolutionary pension while living in Bledsoe County, in February 1833. He was born in North Carolina, October 14, 1754. His aunt was Nancy Hays, wife of Henry Hays. He enlisted in North Carolina troops under Capt. Nelson, Lieut. Charles Hughes and Ensign McBride. He lived in Guilford County, N. C., at the beginning of the Revolution and moved to Caswell County during the War. After the War he lived in many places, principally in Sullivan, Roane and Bledsoe Counties, Tenn. He moved to Bledsoe County 1818. He died in Bledsoe County in November, 1834. His widow, Libby Reed, applied in 1840 for widow's pension. She was then living in Bledsoe oCunty. She lived until after 1851. She was married on the border between Guilford and Caswell Counties, N. C., in June 1779, in the home of Henry Hays. Her oldest son, George Reed, was born March 16, 1781. She was within hearing of the guns of the battle of Guilford Court House. The second child was born June 13, 1784. Other children were: James, born 1787; Peggy, born 1789; Henry, born 1792; Polly, born 1795, married David Brown of Morgan County, Tenn., and Libby, born 1795. The widow stated that her son, Henry Reed, had two children, David and William.

MATHEW PRYOR

Matthew Pryor applied for revolutionary pension while living in Marion ounty, Tenn. He was born in Granville, County, N. C., March 15, 1759. He volunteered under Capt. Douglass, Lieut. Thomas Healy, Ensign Burness and Col. James Williams in Caswell County, N. C.

He served in the battle of King's Mountain when Col. Williams was mortally wounded. Mathew Pryor enclosed his discharge with his pension application. He enlisted again and served under Col. Yancy and Gen. Greene. He lost his horse in the battle of King's Mountain. He moved to Richmond County, Ga., to Granville County, N. C., to Washington County, Va., returned to North Carolina and then moved to Roane County, Tenn., and to Marion County, Tenn.

CAPT. JOHN RAINS

John Rains applied for revolutionary pension while living in Bledsoe County in 1831. He was born Aug. 2, 1759, near Fredricksburg, Va. When he was a boy he moved with his father to Randolph County, N. C. He enlisted in Randolph County in 1779 under Capt. James Robertson, Lieut. William Arnett and Ensign William Rainey. He was appointed Captain. He commanded a company of Rangers under Col. Colyar and Major Dugan. He remained in service until 1783. After the War he returned to Virginia and there married Letitia ————. March 8, 1787. He moved to Sevier County, Tenn., where he lived twenty-two years. He died in Bledsoe County, Jan. 28, 1835. His widow, Letitia Rains, lived after 1843. Among their children was Samuel Rains.

WILLIAM PORTER REID

William Porter Reid applied for pension while residing in Hamilton County, Tenn. He was born Dec. 10, 1762, in Caswell County, N. C. He enlisted Jan. 1, 1777 under Capt. Waddy Tate, Lieut. Davis, Pieut. Patton and Col. Shepherd. He volunteered again May 1, 1780 but hired a substitute, Thomas Thaxton. He volunteered again and was made sergeant of a company commanded by Capt. John Graves and Lieut. Hammond. He volunteered again under Maj. Elijah Moore and again under Capt. John Oldham. After the Revolution he resided in Pendleton District, S. C., until 1800 when he moved to Jackson County, Ga.; from there he moved to Hall County, Ga.; from there to Cherokee County, Ga.; and from there to Hamilton County, Tenn., where he died Jan. 15, 1843. His widow, Violette Reid, applied for widow's pension in Hamilton County in 1844, when she was 76 years old, therefore born in 1768. She states that at one time during her absence from Hamilton County, William Reid was induced to marry but the marriage was not recorded and was proved illegal. She says that she was married to William Reid Jan. 4, 1789 and that she was Violette Brown before her marriage. She died in Hamilton County in 1861 or 1862. Bible pages enclosed in her application give the names of children as follows: Clayton, born 1789; Cynthia, born 1791; Alfred, born 1794; Elizabeth Brown, born 1796; William Porter, Jr., born 1801 and Edey Shotwell, born 1804. Nancy Reid Adams, a sister of William Porter Reid, was living in Habersham County, Ga., in 1836, aged 71 years and was declared to be "an old lady of note and usefulness in her neighborhood."

JAMES SIMS

James Sims applied for revolutionary pension while living in Blount County. He was born in Culpepper County, Va., Oct. 8, 1764. He lived for a time in Nicholas County, Va., where he was drafted in 1780 under Capt James Tutt, he thought, although he was not sure that was the name. He paid a substitute, William Noll, $500 in Continental money and a new rifle to take his place. He died in Blount County after 1840.

LATON SMITH

Laton Smith applied for revolutionary pension while living in Bledsoe County, Tenn., Feb. 11, 1833. He was born in 1756 near the sea shore in either Kent or Sussex County, Maryland. He resided in Washington County, Va., when he enlisted in the spring of 1775. He served under Captains William Cocke, John Shelby, Lewis, Andrew Colville and James Montgomery and Colonels Shelby and Christie. Six or seven years after the Revolution he moved to Greene County, Tenn., where he lived for several years. He then moved back to Washington County, Va., to Knox County, Tenn., in the part which later became Anderson County, and later to Bledsoe County, Tenn. He died in Bledsoe County, December 12, 1840, leaving children whose names are not given in his pension papers.

GEORGE DAVIDSON SHERRILL

George Davidson Sherrill applied for revolutionary pension while living in Tennessee. He was born in North Carolina in September or October 1762. He enlisted in Capt. Robert Patton's Company and enlisted again when he substituted for Jacob Peake in Col. Charles McDowell's Regiment of Horse. He volunteered again, after he had moved to what is now Tennessee, in Col. John Sevier's Mounted Volunteers and served in the battle of King's Mountain. He volunteered again to go against the Cherokees under Col. Sevier and Maj. Jonathan Tipton. He marched to Highwassee.

Note: George Davidson Sherrill was a son of Samuel Sherrill and brother of Catherine Sherrill, "Bonny Kate," who married Col. John Sevier as his second wife.

SAMUEL STEELE

Samuel Steele applied for revolutionary pension while living in Monroe County, Tenn., Sept 18, 1832. He was born in 1760. He enlisted in April or May 1781 in Virginia troops while he was living in Augusta County, some of his officers being Capt. Samuel McCutcheon, Capt. Francis Long, Col. William Bowyer, Col. McCrary, Col. Hubbert. He was in the battle of Hotwater. He moved to Tennessee after the Revolution. He died in Monroe County, April 6, 1845. His widow, Hannah Harrison Steele, applied for widow's pension while living in Jefferson County, Ala., Aug. 6, 1855, when she was 78 years of age, therefore born 1777. The marriage took place in Blount County, Tenn., May 19, 1817.

SOME TENNESSEE HEROES

OF THE

REVOLUTION

Compiled From Pension Statements

PAMPHLET NO. III

TENNESSEE HEROES OF THE REVOLUTION
SOME PENSIONERS WHO LIVED IN
THE VOLUNTEER STATE

CAPTAIN JAMES BLACKBURN

James Blackburn applied for Revolutionary pension while he resided in Anderson County, Tennessee, in April, 1818. He was 59 years of age which places his birth in 1859. In May, 1778, he entered the service as a Captain in Belinsky's Company, or the Independent Company of Cavalry in Colonel Pulaski's Dragoons. He went in 1779 to Charleston after the defeat at Savannah where Belinsky's company was cut to pieces. He was shot through both feet and cut through the body with a sword. He lay for a long time in a hospital.

SAMUEL BLAIR

Samuel Blair applied for revolutionary pension while living in McMinn County, Tennessee, in March, 1831, aged 75, therefore born 1756. While he was visiting relatives in Burke County, N. C., in the latter part of 1779 he enlisted for six months under Captain William Johnson. In May, 1780, Colonel McDowell sent orders to Captain Johnson for all soldiers that could be furnished horses to march to Burke County Court House and proceed against a party of Tories collected at Ramsour's Mill. He marched as ordered and was placed under Captain Bowman in Colonel Bernard's Regiment in the battle of Ramsour's Mill. Captain Bowman was killed in the engagement. Samuel Blair received his discharge from Captain Johnson and re-enlisted in July, 1780, in Burke County, as a substitute for William Smith, serving under Captain Clark in Colonel Williams' Regiment. He was in the battles of King's Mountain and Cowpens. He was discharged in March, 1781. He re-enlisted and served from July. 1781, to August, 1782, when he was discharged at Chatham Court House. He was in Captain Zabner Mask's, Company and Colonel Roger Griffin's Regiment. After he left the service he returned to Virginia and lived in Shenandoah and Botetourt Counties. He moved to McMinn County, Tennessee in 1829.

JOSIAH BRANDON

Josiah Brandon applied for revolutionary pension while living in Lincoln County, Tennessee, in October, 1832. He resided during the Revolution in Burke County, North Carolina. His father was a Tory, who served with the King's troops in the battle of King's Mountain and was killed in that battle. Josiah Brandon was captured by men under Colonel Joseph McDowell who, when he heard the boy's statement, released him, realizing that the boy had been under age. Josiah Brandon then immediately entered the service of the American troops. George Davidson testified to this action saying that "Josiah Brandon immediately enlisted under my uncle. Captain Samuel Davidson. No censure was ever imputed to him because of his part in the battle of King's Mountain." This last statement is not wholly true as a complaint was made to the Pension Department that Brandon served as a Tory. The Pension Department, however, ruled in his favor and his pension was allowed. He served under Captain Samuel Davidson and Capt. Boykin pursuing Tories, and under Capt. Samuel against Indians. He was born June 6, 1761, according to the record in his father's Family Bible which he had in his possession in 1832. He was a minister. He married Rachel Brown, March 8, 1781. She survived him and applied for pension July 7, 1839 while living in Lincoln County, and was then 80 years of age Among their children were Logan V. Brandon and Samuel Brandon. Samuel Brandon testified that he was born in 1790 and that there were four children older than he.

Note:- This is one of the most voluminous pension records owing to the charge that Brandon was a Tory and the extensive investigation which followed.

DUDLEY BROOKE

Dudley Brooke applied for revolutionary pension while living in Robertson County, Tennessee, in 1833. He was born July 3, 1762, in Chesterfield County, Virginia. He enlisted in 1777 in Captain White's company and in 1778 he again enlisted. In 1779 he enlisted under Lieutenant Henry Johnson and Colonel Anthony New. He enlisted again in Captain Richard Philips' company and in 1781 he served seven months in Captain Robert Carey's company, Colonel Combe's Virginia regiment. In 1802 he left Louisa County, Virginia, where he was then living and moved to Robertson County, Tennessee.

Note:- Dudley Brooke's children were Elizabeth, Sarah, Mary, Harry, John, Frances (or John Francis), and Dudley, junior.

LIEUTENANT RICHARD CAMPBELL

Richard Campbell applied for revolutionary pension in 1833 while living in that part of Hickman County, Tennessee, which became Perry County. He resided in Montgomery County, North Carolina, when he re-enlisted within a week in Crawford, Love and Williams' North Carolina regiment. He then served as First Lieutenant in Captain Douglass' company in Colonel Lytle's North Carolina regiment until the close of the war. He died June 30, 1844 in Hickman County. His application referred to his first marriage to Susannah, her maiden name not being given and to his two children by her, Mary Campbell born 1783 and James, born 1785. Richard Campbell married Rachel in October, 1789, in Rockingham County, North Carolina. The widow, Rachel Campbell, secured pension on her application in October, 1849, at which time she was 80 years of age and living in Perry County. In 1852 she mentioned her age as 80 without explanation of the discrepency. Richard and Rachel Campbell had the following children: Hiram, born 1890; Smithy (a daughter) born 1791; John born 1793; Elizabeth born 1795; Richard born 1797; William born 1799; Wiley born 1804; and Tubal born 1806.

PHAROAH COBB

Pharoah Cobb applied for revolutionary pension while living in Hawkins County, Tennessee, in 1833. He was born in September, 1752, in Northampton, County, North Carolina. He moved to the Watauga River settlement which later became Washington County, Tennessee. He enlisted in a company of volunteers and served four months under Captain Jacob Womack against the Cherokee Indians. In 1777 he served three months as a mounted ranger or spy in Captain Thomas Price's company. He served two months under Colonel Isaac Shelby and volunteered again for two tours in the summer of 1780. He volunteered again and served under Colonel Isaac Shelby and was in the battle of Musgrove's Mill.

Note:- He died in Hawkins County in 1841. His will made in 1823 was probated in 1841. He was a son of William Cobb. He married Barsheba Whitehead and their children were Catherine, born 1776, died 1824, married Julius Connor; Richard Caswell, born 1778, died 1811, married Rebecca Buckingham; Arthur, born 1780, died 1818, married Ailsie Massengale; William, born 1783, died 1839, married Isabella Cooper; Barsheba, born 1797, died 1856, married Absolom Kyle.

SPENCER COLEMAN

Spencer Coleman applied for revolutionary pension while living in Monroe County, Tennessee, December 18, 1832. He was then 80 years and 10 months old, and was therefore born about February 15, 1752. He was born in King and Queen County, Virginia. His father, whose name is not given, moved when Spencer Coleman was about two years of age to Stafford County, Virginia, and when he was fifteen years old to Shenandoah County, Virginia. Spencer Coleman married while residing in Shenandoah County when he was about 23 years of age and moved to Seven Mile Ford in Western Virginia and there joined Captain Francis' Company, Colonel William Campbell's Virginia regiment He served three months as a private, guarded the lead mines on New River and marched to Big Glades against the Tories. He served three months under Captain Wilson. He moved to a point near Abingdon, Virginia, and served three months in Colonel Arthur Campbell's Virginia regiment and was out against the Cherokee Indians. Soon after the close of the Revolution he moved to Big Pigeon River, Cocke County, Tennessee, and in 1826 he moved to Monroe County, Tennessee.

WILLIAM CROSS

William Cross applied for Revolutionary service while he resided in Anderson County, Tennessee, in 1833. He was born in Baltimore County, Maryland, about March 5, 1761 or 1762. The names of his parents are not given in the application. He moved to that part of North Carolina which later became Sullivan County, Tennessee, near the Virginia line. He enlisted in September, 1776 in Captain William Hicks' North Carolina Company and served as a drummer boy, against the Cherokee Indians. He was discharged in October, 1777. He enlisted in August 1781, serving as a private in Captain Thomas Wallace's Company, Colonel Isaac Shelby's regiment, against the British and **Tories** and guarding the frontier against Indians. The length of this tour was three months. In 1817 he moved to Knox County, Tennessee, and in a year moved to Anderson County, Tennessee.

JOHN L. DAVIES

John L. Davies applied for revolutionary pension while living in Wilson County, Tennessee, in September, 1832. He was then 68 years of age and therefore born in 1764. He lived in Mecklenburg County, North Carolina, in April, 1780, when he enlisted as a substitute for his father who was "infirm," and served six weeks as a private in Captain John Brownfield's compnay, Colonel Robert Erwin's North Carolina regiment in pursuit of Tories. He enlisted July 29, 1780, and served thirty days in Captain John Brownfield's company and was in the battle of Rocky Mount and Hanging Rock. He enlisted again a few weeks later and served two months in Captain Brownfield's company, Col. Lock's North Carolina regiment. He enlisted in 1780 and served four months in Captain Samuel Hart's company of Cavalry, Colonel Davies' North Carolina regiment. He enlisted February 1, 1781, and served six weeks in Captain John Brownfield's company, Colonel William Polk's North Carolina regiment. In the year 1803 John L. Davies moved from Mecklenburg County, North Carolina, to the "neighborhood of the Big Springs," in Wilson County, Tennessee. In 1832 he referred to his younger brother, William Davies, who was living in Rutherford County, Tennesse.e

GEORGE DIXON

George Dixon applied for revolutionary pension while living in Hawkins County, Tennessee, November 24, 1819, when he was 66 years of age, which places his birth year in 1753. He enlisted in Stafford County, Virginia, and served in Captain Howard's company, Colonel Buford's 3rd Virginia regiment. He was in battle when Colonel Tarleton defeated the Americans in South Carolina and was in several skirmishes also. He was discharged in the fall of 1781 and had served at least eighteen months. In 1820 his wife was about fifty-two years of age. Her name before marriage is not given. Members of his family then living at home were: Thomas, aged 19 years; Daniel, aged 16 years; Stephen, aged 12 years; Evalina, aged 9 years; and George, aged five years.

JOHN DOYLE

John Doyle applied for revolutionary pension while living in Knox County, May 9, 1818, when he was 70 years of age. He was therefore born in 1858. His place of birth and the names of his parents are not given in his application. He enlisted about May 13, 1777, in Baltimore, Maryland, and served in Captain Lynch's company, Colonel Smallwood's regiment. He was in the battles of Brandywine, Paoli, Germantown, and Monmouth. He was discharged about May 13, 1780. He moved to Tennessee and died June 3, 1837. In 1826 he referred to his wife as "some older" than himself. Her name was Evaline Doyle and there was a son, William Doyle.

ENSIGN FELIX EARNEST

Felix Earnest applied for revolutionary pension while living in Greene County, Tennessee. He was born in Frederick County, Virginia, September 20, 1762, and moved while he was young to Washington County, North Carolina, which later became Washington County, Tennessee. He resided there in the fall of 1780 when he enlisted in Captain Williams' company and marched to meet Major Patrick Ferguson. He was in the battle of King's Mountain. In the fall of 1781 he enlisted again under Captain John Smith and Lieutenant John Butler and was in the battle of Boyd's Creek. In the summer of 1782 he enlisted again under Colonel John Sevier and Captain Williams and served against the Cherokees. He died in Green County, Tennessee, February 16, 1842. He married Sarah Oliphant in Greene County, May 15, 1808. She survived him and applied for pension February 3, 1853.

SAMUEL EVERETT

Samuel Everett applied for revolutionary pension while living in Carroll County, Tennessee in December, 1832. He was born April 5, 1763 in Harford County, Maryland. While residing in Harford County he volunteered early in the year 1780 and served in Captain Day's company, Colonel Alexander Cowan's Maryland regiment and guarded the shores of Chesapeake Bay. In the same year he re-enlisted and served in Captain Huchin's company, Colonel Cowan's regiment. In 1781 he enlisted in Captain Jacob Norris' Maryland company but after serving two months was sick and hired a substitute. Later still in 1781 he enlisted in a company of marines commanded by Captain Jesse Bussey and went on board the "Jolly Tar," commanded by Captain Belt. After cruising off Cape Henry for two months, the ship was in an engagement at Hampton Roads with the British Ship "Perseverance," in which they were captured. Samuel Everett was taken to New York as a prisoner and placed in the hold of the British prison ship "Old Jersey," where he remained for twelve months and was then parolled. In 1786 he moved from Maryland to Caswell County, and Orange County, North Carolina. In 1821 he moved to Smith County, Tennessee, and in 1826 he resided in Carroll County, Tennessee.

ROBERT EVERITT

Robert Everitt applied for revolutionary pension while he was living in Blount County, Tennessee, in 1818, when he was aged "sixty-five years and upwards," indicating his birth about 1750. He enlisted at Lexington, Rockbridge County, Virginia, in July 1780, or earlier. He was in Captain Adam Wallace's company, Colonel Hawes' Virginia regiment. He was also in Captain Sigismund Stribling's company under Major Smith Snead. He was in the battle of Guilford Court House under Major Ridley and in the battles of Camden, Ninety-six, and Eutaw Springs and in a number of skirmishes. He was discharged at Salisbury, North Carolina, January 17, 1792, and his discharge was signed by Captain Stribling and Major Snead. Robert Everitt died in May 1827 in Blount County.

He married July 2, 1783, Margaret Lockhart. She was born in 1758 as she was 68 years of age in 1826. She died in Blount County in February 1832 or 1833. Their children were Caty Everitt, born

1789; Agnes Everitt, born 1791; William Everitt, born 1793; Jean Everitt, born 1795; Ann Everitt, born 1797; Margaret Everitt, born 1900; James Everitt, born 1805; John Everitt, born 1805.

Of the foregoing Caty Everitt married Charles Walker in 1808; Agnes or Nancy Everitt married Isaac White in 1813; Jean Everitt married Baron T. McConnell.

ROWLAND FLOWERS

Rowland Flowers applied for revolutionary pension while living in Fentress County, Tennessee, in July, 1834. He was born in 1846 in Buckingham County, Virginia, and was the son of James Flowers. He was reared in Buckingham and Campbell Counties, Virginia. While he was a resident of Buckingham County he enlisted in the spring of 1781 and served three months in Captain Silas Williams' Virginia Company. At the close of this service he enlisted as a substitute for his father in Captain Peter Gearin's company under Major Bois in Virginia troops and was at the Seige of Yorktown and at the surrender of Cornwallis, serving three months. After the war he continued to reside in Virginia until he was 22 years of age when he moved to Overton County, Tennessee. He drew pension in Fentress County, that part which had been in Overton County. He died in Fentress County, September 23, 1837. He married in Buckingham County, Virginia, about December 1, 1782, Ann or Anna Jarot or Garrott, who was born about March 15, 1762. She applied for pension in October, 1838, while residing in Fentress County. She died May 29, 1854. They had twelve children as follows: William, the eldest, born about August 1783; Betsey; James; Rowland, Jr.; Arthur; Rosanna; Maggie; Sally; Polly; Delila and Judy. Judy, the youngest child aged 31 in 1838, married Rodney King and had eight children. In 1834, Anthony Flowers, a younger brother of the soldier, was aged 61 years and lived in Fentress County.

JOHN GIBSON
Of Lincoln County

John Gibson applied for revolutionary pension while living in Lincoln County, Tennessee, in 1833. He was born in Orange County, North Carolina, September 15, 1760. He was an invalid pensioner under the first act passed in North Carolina concerning pensions. He stated in his application that he moved to Davidson County, Tennessee, in 1805, and lived there until 1809 when he moved to Lincoln County, Tennessee. His home was on Cane Creek about five miles from Fayetteville. He died there in 1844.

JOHN GIBSON
Of Wilson County

John Gibson applied for revolutionary pension while residing in Wilson County, Tennessee, in 1818. He was then 60 years of age. He enlisted April 20, 1778 in Montgomery County, Maryland, for three years in Captain Griffith's company, Colonel Howard's 3rd Maryland regiment, General Smallwood's brigade. He also served in Captain William Wilmott's company under Colonels Ramsey and John Gunley. He was discharged in Camden, South Carolina.

In his application he referred to his wife but gave no name, and to a daughter, aged 26 years but gave no name.

DAVID GOENS

David Goens applied for revolutionary pension while residing in Hamilton County, Tennessee, in 1834. He was born in Hanover County, Virginia, November 21, 1751. He enlisted in Halifax County, Virginia, in Captain Rogers' company; he moved after the Revolution to Grayson County, Virginia, then to Wythe County, Virginia, and then to Tennessee where he lived in Grainger County before he moved to Hamilton County in February, 1833. He died before 1840, as his pension was then being paid to his children. He had a brother Laban Goens.

ABRAHAM HANKS

Abraham Hanks applied for revolutionary pension while living in Lincoln County, Tennessee, in October, 1832. He was born April 2, 1759, in Amelia County, Virginia. While residing in Bedford County, Virginia, in August, 1777, he volunteered in Captain John Talbot's company, Colonel David Mason's Virginia regiment. He enlisted in April, 1779, in Captain Holman Rice's company, Colonel Francis Taylor's regiment and guarded British prisoners at Albemarle Barracks. He was discharged May 1, 1781. After the Revolution he resided in Campbell County, Virginia, and moved to Lincoln County, Tennessee, in 1831. He died July 10, 1833, in Lincoln County. He married April 15, 1788, in Campbell County, Virginia, Lucy Jennings. In 1840, she was living in Lincoln County, Tennessee, and was then 70 years of age.

Children are mentioned in the pension record but their names are not given. In 1840, William Pamplin, Sr., a resident of Lincoln County, stated that he married a sister of the widow Lucy Jennings Hanks.

Note:- The name Abraham Hanks is interesting apart from the above data. The fact that this soldier lived in Lincoln County may be considered merely a coincidence as may be also the fact that Lucy was a name in the family of Nancy Hanks who was the mother of President Abraham Lincoln.

ROBERT HANSLEY

Robert Hansley applied for revlutionary pension while living in Hawkins County in 1834. He had resided in the county for about forty years. He volunteered for service in Sullivan County, North Carolina, now Tennessee as a private in Captain George Maxwell's company, Colonel Isaac Shelby's regiment. He was in the battle of King's Mountain after which he went to Salisbury, North Carolina, and he continued to serve for six months. He enlisted again May 1, 1781, serving as a private in a company of Stokes County, North Carolina, militia under Captain William Cloud and Captain Jonathan Hawley. During this enlistment he went to the border of South Carolina against the Indians. This length of service was also six months. He returned to Sullivan County, and enlisted in the spring of 1782, serving under Lieutenant Fulkerson and in Captain Elijah Chisholm's company. He was engaged against the Indians; he was also in Captain John Blair's company at Campbell's Station. His service included in all eighteen months. He was pensioned as Robert Hansley but his pension application includes his name spelled Hinsley and Hensley.

MAJOR PLEASANT HENDERSON

Major Pleasant Henderson applied for revolutionary pension while residing in Carroll County, Tennessee, in 1832. He was born January 9, 1756, in Granville County, North Carolina. He enlisted in 1776 and served in Captain Thomas Satterwhite's company, Colonel John Butler's North Carolina regiment. He volunteered late in the summer or fall of 1778, was appointed lieutenant and served in Captain Richard Taylor's company, Colonel James Saunders' regiment, and in Captain Jamison's company, Colonel Lytle's regiment. He marched to Charleston and then to Savannah in defence of South Carolina and Georgia. He re-enlisted in 1781 and was appointed major in Colonel Malmedy's regiment. He was in the battle of Ramsour's Mill. He moved from Chapel Hill, North Carolina, May 21, 1830, and arrived in Huntingdon, Carroll County, Tennessee, in July. He attended the University of North Carolina and he stated that he had been chief clerk of the House of Commons of North Carolina for many years. He died December 10, 1843, in Huntingdon. His wife predeceased him. He was survived by the following children: Tip S.; Eliza I. Jones; and Alexander M.

Note:- Pleasant Henderson was the son of Samuel and Elizabeth Williams Henderson. He married Sarah Martin, daughter of James and Ruth Rogers Martin. So far as known the children of Major Pleasant Henderson were. Pleasant Jr.; Alexander. Martin who married Elizabeth Earl Johnson; Tip S.; and Eliza I. born 1798 who married in 1820 Hamilton Chamberlain Jones.

DAVID HENRY

David Henry applied for revolutionary pension while residing in Robertson County in 1832. He was born in 1753 in Pittsylvania County, Virginia. He enlisted in 1777 in Captain John Donelson's company, Colonel Evan Shelby's regiment and was in an expedition against the Indians. He enlisted again in 1778 in Captain Thomas Dillard's company in Colonel George Rogers Clark's expedition to Illinois. He was discharged August 29, 1778.

Note:- The children of David Henry were Isaac, Lemuel, Elizabeth and Catherine.

JOEL HICKS

Joel Hicks was born October 21, 1765, in Hanover County, Virginia. During the Revolution he resided in that County. After the Revolution he moved to Albermarle County, Virginia, and about 1809 he moved to Hawkins County, Tennessee. He applied for revolutionary pension October 7, 1833, while residing in Hawkins County and stated that he entered the service in the summer of 1781 and that he served ten months under Captains Ambrose Lipscomb, William Grimes and Major Burk in Virginia troops. He was granted pension but upon an investigation by the United States District Attorney at Rogersville, Tennessee, it was found that he never served as a soldier of the Revolution and his name was taken from the pension roll October 29, 1836. His application does not state whether or not he was married.

Note:- This is believed to be the only case of a false claim among the residents of Tennessee who applied for Revolutionary pension.

JOHN JONES

John Jones applied for revolutionary pension in October, 1832, while residing in Marion County, Tennessee, when he was aged 73 or 74. He was born in Brunswick County, Virginia, about 1758. He moved after the Revolution to Knox County, Tennessee, then to Bledsoe County and then to Marion County, where he died November 23, 1839. He married Mary ——— in March, 1790. She applied for pension in Marion County, March 5, 1844, when she was 77 years of age and was still living in 1851. The children of John and Mary Jones were Thomas, born 1790; Milberry, born 1792; Benjamin, born 1794; (undecipherable) born 1796; Sally born 1798; William born 1810; and Betsey, born November 25, 18——.

BENJAMIN KILBOURN (OR KILBURN)

Benjamin Kilbourn or Kilburn applied for revolutionary pension July 29, 1819, while living in Blount County, Tennessee. He enlisted at Carlisle, Pennsylvania, in the spring of 1776 or 1777 for three years under Captain William Wyley and Colonel Benjamin Flowers and served until 1780, when he was discharged at the Barracks near Carlisle, Pennsylvania, by Captain John Jordan by orders of General Irvine. He was in the battle of Paoli. In 1782 he enlisted for "during the War" at Reading, Pennsylvania, and served under Captain Andrew Walker and Colonel Richard Butler in the 3rd Pennsylvania Continental regiment. He was appointed sergeant and served under Captain Christie in the same regiment. He was discharged at Carlisle, September 30, 1783.

Diana Kilbourne, aged 78, applied for widow's pension October 3, 1842. She resided in Blount County. She declared that she married Benjamin Kilbourn in 1781 or 1782 in Cumberland County, Pennsylvania, and that her name before marriage was Diana Denning; that they moved to Blount County, Tennessee, in 1802 and that her husband died there in June 1828. They had five daughters and two sons. Three daughters and two of the sons were married and the youngest daughter was 15 in 1842. One of the said sons had been six years in the United States Army. In 1842 one daughter, Elizabeth, was aged 61 and the widow of Robert Hooke, aged about 71.

THOMAS KING

Thomas King applied for revolutionary pension August 21, 1832, while living in Sullivan County, Tennessee. He was born March 17, 1754, in Lancaster County, Pennsylvania. He entered the service in Paxton Township, Lancaster County, in August, 1776, and served under Captains James Cranch and James Morrow, and Colonel Thomas Morrow.

In 1777 he moved to what later became Sullivan County, Tennessee, where he enlisted August 1778 and served in Captain John Duncan's North Carolina company. In 1779 he served in Kentucky aiding in building a fort. In 1780 he served two months in Captain Andrew Cowan's company, Colonel Arthur Campbell's North Carolina regiment. He was in a skirmish with Cherokee Indians and burned their towns. In 1781 he served two months as a substitute for William King in Captain Thomas Wallace's company, Colonel Isaac Shelby's regiment.

Thomas King died June 18, 1857, in Sullivan County, Tennessee.

WILLIAM KING

William King applied for revolutionary pension August 20, 1834, while living in Sullivan County, Tennessee. He was born August 1, 1752, in Chester County, Pennsylvania. In October, 1774, he moved from Lancaster County, to the western part of North Carolina (now Tennessee). He entered the service July 1, 1776, and served under Captain James Shelby and Colonel Christy in a North Carolina regiment. Te was in a battle with the Cherokee Indians. He was discharged November 1, 1776. Later in 1776 he enlisted as a spy under General Russell in pursuit of the Cherokees. October 10, 1780, he again enlisted in an expedition under Captain Andrew Cowan, and Colonel Taylor in a North Carolina regiment. He was discharged January, 1781.

JOHN F. MARION

John F. Marion applied for revolutionary pension while living in Bedford County, Tennessee, in 1832. He was born in Lancaster County, Pennsylvania, October 14, 1760. While living in Mecklinburg County, North Carolina, he enlisted in June, 1779, in Captain William Alexander's and Captain Samuel Martin's company, Colonel William Polk's North Carolina regiment. During the battle of Eutaw Springs his horse was killed under him and he was wounded in his right leg. After ten months' service he re-enlisted in Captain James Simons' company, Colonel Wade Hampton's regiment of light horse in which he served eighteen months. After the War he moved to the Moravian settlement in North Carolina where he enlisted in a regiment of North Carolina troops raised for the protection of white settlers in what was then called the Cumberland settlement, now Middle Tennessee. He moved to Williamson County, Tennessee, and later to Bedford County, Tennessee, where he died.

HAL MASSENGALE

Hal Massengale applied for revolutionary pension while living in Sullivan County, Tennessee, in 1834. He was born in Southhampton County, Virginia, in 1758. He moved to what is now Tennessee and while living in Washington County enlisted in Captain Jacob Womack's company. He also served in Captain Roger Topp's company and Captain Dunn's company. He served under Colonels Sevier, Shelby and Cleveland. He was in the battle of Ramsour's Mill. His second wife was Elizabeth Emmert whom he married in Sullivan County in 1814. Hal Massengale died September 23, 1837. His widow, Elizabeth Emmert Massengale, applied for pension while living in Sullivan County in 1854.

MICHAEL MASSENGALE

Michael Massengale while residing in Granger County, Tennessee, in 1833, applied for revolutionary pension. He was born March 1, 1756, in Northhampton County, North Carolina. He moved to the Watauga River in what was afterwards Washington County, Tennessee, and while residing there he volunteered in June, 1776, in Captain Jacob Womack's company. He served from late in 1776 or early 1777 in Captain James Shelby's company; from July, 1780, he served in Captain Bean's company and was in the battle of Musgrove's Mill; from the latter part of 1780 he served in Captain Burnette's company.

SAMUEL MAYES

Samuel Mayes applied for revolutionary pension while residing in Maury County, Tennessee, in 1832. He was born in Sumter County South Carolina, in 1759. He died in Maury County after 1840. He served in the battles of Savannah, Cowpens and King's Mountain. He married twice; his second wife was Mary McCottery. Among his children was Jane Frierson Mayes, born 1807, died 1851, who married James Morrison Arnell.

JOSEPH McCARMICK

Joseph McCormick applied for revolutionary pension while living in Marion County, Tennessee, with his father. He enlisted under Colonel Benjamin Few and Captain James Bowen. He enlisted again under Colonel Elijah Clarke and was in the battle of King's Mountain. He moved from Tennessee to Jackson County, Alabama, by 1835, to reside with his son Joseph R. McCormick, who had a wife and two children. The soldier had another son whose name is not given in his application.

JOSEPH McMILLEN

Joseph McMillen applied for revolutionary pension while living in Knox County, Tennessee, in 1832. He was born in 1743 in Ireland. He landed in Charleston in 1746 and settled in Abbeville District, N. C., where he was residing during the War of the Revolution. He enlisted in the winter of 1777-1778 and served on various tours during four years. He was a light horseman under Captains Robert Anderson, William Harr and Samuel Roseman and Colonel Andrew Pickens in the South Carolina troops. He was in the engagement at Kettle Creek, marched to Savannah and Augusta, was at Juniper Springs and was out against the Indians. He continued to reside in Abbeville District until "sometime before the late War" (the War of 1812). He then moved to Blount County where he remained a number of years. Thence he moved to Monroe County and thence returned to Knox County.

JOHN NELSON

John Nelson applied for revolutionary pension November 18, 1818, in Overton County, Tennessee. He was born in March 1752. He enlisted in Botetourt County, Virginia, later Rockbridge County, in 1776 or 1777. He served twelve months in Captain Thomas Posey's company. When Captain Posey was promoted John Nelson served under Captain James Buckhanon in Colonel Daniel Morgan's regiment. Later he served in the militia. He was in skirmishes at Monmouth and Seony Point He refered in his application to his wife and five children who were living with him in 1818. Mathew and Daniel Nelson, citizens of Knoxville, declared that in 1818 that they were sons of John Nelson. In July 1820 John Nelson, aged 68 in March 1820, wrote to say that his family consisted of wife, Sarah, aged about 60 years, daughter, Rachel, aged about 19 and a son Samuel aged 17.

WILLIAM NELSON

William Nelson applied for revolutionary pension while living in Hawkins County, Tennessee, in 1834. He was born in Prince Edward County, Virginia, in 1747. He moved to Surry County, North Carolina, and while living there he enlisted in July, 1777, in Captain Cox's company, Colonel Williams' North Carolina regiment. He enlisted again in July, 1779, and served two months in Captain Joseph Claud's (Cloud?) company and was in an engagement with Tories. He enlisted again in the fall of 1779 in Captain Claud's company. He moved from Surry County, North Carolina, to Hawkins Court, Tennessee. He died August 9, 1834.

ABNER NORRIS

Abner Norris applied for revolutionary pension while living in White County, Tennessee, October 19, 1733. He was born January 12, 1758, in Lunenburg County, Virginia. He enlisted while residing in Halifax County, Virginia, in 1776, in Captain James Cobb's company. During the Revolution his father's family moved to Guilford County, North Carolina, and Abner Norris enlisted in Captain John McAdoo's company, Colonel Pacely's regiment, North Carolina troops. He enlisted again under Colonel Pacely and was in the engagement at Shallow Ford.

Note:- Abner Norris appears on the printed list as Abner Morris and he so appears in Pamphlet II but the Veterans Administration Bureau gives his name as Abner Norris.

JAMES PEARCE

James Pearce applied for revolutionary pension while living in Sevier County, Tennessee, in 1832. He was born March 24, 1748. While he was a resident of Washington County, North Carolina, later Greene County, Tennessee. James Pearce, by order of Colonel John Sevier, raised a company of volunteers in the summer of 1779 and marched to the French Broad River to prevent the Indians from crossing. He again raised a company of volunteers in the spring of 1780 and marched against the Indians to the Beaver Dam on Lick Creek. Early in the fall of 1780 he and his company volunteered under Colonel Sevier and marched to King's Mountain. Upon his return to his home he received orders from Colonel Sevier to guard the frontier against Indians, marched his company to the French Broad River, had an engagement with the Indians, and burned some of their towns. He died in Sevier County.

He married sometime in the year 1771 in Frederick County, Maryland, Margaret Dungan. At the time of their marriage they were both living in Berkeley County, Virginia. She was born February 4, 1755, and was the daughter of Jeremiah Dungan. In 1779 and 1780 her father and mother were living in Washington County, North Carolina. The widow, Margaret Pearce, died February 20, 1837, in Washington County, Tennessee, at the home of her son-in-law, Thomas Gibson. James and Margaret Pearce had the following children; George, born 1772; Elizabeth, born 1774; John, born 1776; Mary, born 1778; Sarah, born 1780; Rebecca, born 1783; Margaret, born 1785; Solomon, born 1787; James, born 1789; Orpah, born 1791; Jeremiah, born 1793; Thomas, born 1796; and Charlotte, born 1800.

FRANCES QUARLES

Frances Quarles applied for revolutionary pension while living in Knox County, Tennessee, in February, 1833. He was born February 7, 1752, in Goochland County, Virginia. He lived there until he was about sixteen years of age when he moved to Cumberland County. He moved to Prince Edward County and in about two years moved to Pittsylvania County, where he lived during the Revolution. He enlisted early in the war and served eighteen months in Captain Thomas Dillard's company, Colonel Morgan's Virginia regiment. Later he volunteered and served six months in Captain Gabriel Shelton's company, Colonel Buford's regiment, and was in the battle of Buford's Defeat and the battle of Camden. He was at the battle of Guilford Court House but was guarding baggage. He marched to the Siege of Yorktown and was present at the Surrender of Cornwallis.

He lived in Pittsylvania for five years after the Revolution when he moved to Henry County and then to Wythe County and then to Tennessee where he first settled in Jefferson County and then moved to Knox County in 1823.

BAXTER RAGSDALE

Baxter Ragsdale applied for revolutionary pension in 1832 when he was 74 years of age. He was therefore born in 1758. He resided in Lunenburg County, Virginia, when he enlisted. Later he enlisted again in Granville County, North Carolina. He moved to Bedford County, Tennessee. His last pension check was cashed in Nashville in 1837.

JESSE SAMPLE (OR SAMPLEY)

Jesse Sample or Sampley applied for revolutionary pension in Rhea County, Tennessee, in 1833. He was born in 1763 or 1764 in Spartanburg, South Carolina. He moved with his parents to Edgefield District, S. C., and to Richmond County, Georgia, where his father was killed by Tories and his home destroyed. Jesse Sample returned to Edgefield where he enlisted in June 1799. He served in Captain John Carter's company, Colonel LeRoy Hammond's regiment. He enlisted again in 1789 and served in Captain James Withers' company, Colonel Hugh Horry's South Carolina regiment and was in a skirmish on Little Peedee River and in battles of Fort Watson and Fort Motte. He enlisted again in Captain Jacob Wise's South Carolina company. After the Revolution he lived in Edgefield District with his mother. He moved to Georgia, returned to South Carolina, moved to Tennessee where he lived in several East Tennessee Counties. In 1839 he was living Jackson County, Alabama, having removed from Tennessee because his children, whose names are not given, lived there.

CAPTAIN ARTHUR SCOTT

Arthur Scott applied for revolutionary pension while residing in Knox County, Tennessee, in 1832. He was born in January, 1752, in Cumberland County, Virginia, where he enlisted in the spring of 1778 in Captain Charles Fleming's Virginia company. He joined the army under General Washington and was in the battle of Monmouth. He afterwards went to Salem, North Carolina, and to Richmond, Virginia, where he was discharged after one year's service. He then moved to Surry County, North Carolina, and in the spring of 1780 he received a commission as captain of militia; that winter he commanded a company in Colonel Joseph Williams' regiment and was in skirmishes at Cowan's Ford, at the Shallow Ford and Whitsall's Mill, and was in the battle of Guilford Courthouse. He served as captain for three months and returned to Surry County. He resided there until 1807 when he moved to Wythe County, Virginia, and from thence to Knox County, Tenn.

WILLIAM SHANNON

William Shannon applied for revolutionary pension while living in Greene County, Tennessee, in 1833. He was born September 5, 1756, in Chester County, Pennsylvania. While residing in Cumberland County, Pennsylvania, he enlisted in January, 1776 or 1777, in Captain Samuel Duncan's and Captain Ebenezer Brady's Pennsylvania companies. After the Revolution he moved to Washington County, Tennessee, and lived there and in Greene County for many years. He then moved to Grainger County, Tennessee, where he died.

ANDREW SHORTRIDGE

Andrew Shortridge applied for revolutionary pension in August, 1834, while he resided in Fentress County, Tennessee. He was born in Scotland in 1756 and came to America with his parents when he was an infant. He enlisted in Petersburg, Virginia, in 1781 in Captain Gardner's Virginia company. At the close of the tour he re-enlisted in Captain Armistead's company, Colonel Gall's Virginia regiment and served in Albermarle County, Virginia. After the Revolution he lived in Frederick and Russell Counties, Virginia, and then moved to Pulaski County, Kentucky, where he lived 18 years. He moved to Fentress County, Tennessee, in 1827. He died there February 26, 1846. He married about April, 1789, Nancy Garrison at the home of her father in Tazewell, Virginia. She was 15 years of age in August, 1789, four months after her marriage. She applied for a widow's pension in 1853 in Fentress County, where she died. They had ten children.

RALPH SMITH

Ralph Smith applied for revolutionary pension while living in Lincoln County, Tennessee, in October, 1832. He was born August 23, or 24, 1763. He enlisted while living in York District, South Carolina, in 1780 or 1781, and served until July, 1783, with South Carolina troops under Captains Henry White and Jacob Barnett and Lieutenant Colonels Henry White and Jacob Barnett in Colonel Henry Hampton's regiment of Light Dragoons and also under Colonels Mann and Kimball. He moved from South Carolina about 1812 to Lincoln County, Tennessee, where he died November 2, 1853. He married in York District, South Carolina, in the fall of 1788, Elizabeth ———. She survived him and was allowed pension on her application made in Lincoln County, October, 1854, when she was 86 years of age. Joseph, the first child of Ralph and Elizabeth Smith, was born October 10, 1790. They also had the following children: Margaret, Nancy, Thomas, James, Elizabeth, Ralph and John (twins), Susannah and Jonathan.

WILLIAM SMITH

William Smith was pensioned from January 1, 1803, on account of disibility incured during his services in the Revolution. He was on the pension roll in North Carolina. In 1823 he was living in Lincoln County, Tennessee. He stated that he left North Carolina in 1818. He served in the Virginia troops as a sergeant in Captain John Webb's company, Colonel Alexander McClanehan's Virginia regiment. There are no further data given in his pension record.

WILLIAM C. SMITH

William C. Smith applied for revolutionary pension while living in Lincoln County, Tennessee, April 18, 1833. He was born in Mecklenburg County, Virginia, March 4, 1762. He enlisted while living in Wake County, North Carolina, in May, 1779, and served nine months in Captain Bledsoe's company, Colonel Joseph Mabane's regiment, North Carolina troops. He was in the battle of Drowning Creek and was later taken prisoner by the British and Tories. While making his escape he received a gunshot wound in the leg. He enlisted in November, 1780, and served six months in Captain James Frazier's company, Colonel Bledsoe's North Carolina regiment. He enlisted in May, 1781, and served in Captain Hinton's company, Colonel William Hinton's North Carolina regiment, and was in several skirmishes with the Tories. While living in Wilkes County, Georgia, he served six months in Captain Charles Williamson's company under General Clark and was engaged against the Indians in Georgia. From Wilkes County, Georgia, he moved to Pendleton District, South Carolina, where he lived until about 1817 when he moved to Lincoln County, Tennessee.

JOHN SUTTON

John Sutton applied for pension in Rhea County, Tennessee in 1833 when he was 82 years of age. He enlisted in Georgetown District, South Carolina, where he lived in 1775 and was with South Carolina troops under Captains Wise and Speed and Colonel Thompson, and with North Carolina troops under Colonel Lewis when he lived in Richmond County, North Carolina. He was in the Siege of Savannah and in the battle of Eutaw Springs. He moved to Tennessee about 1795 and was living in Meigs County in 1840. He was killed September 5, 1843, about eight miles from Knoxville where he had walked to secure his pension. He married August 24, 1791, Elizabeth Hodges. His wife survived him and applied for pension in Meigs County in 1845 when she was 75 years of age. Their children were: Anne, born 1798; Elizabeth, born 1800; Codilla, born 1803; John Pierce, born 1805; James Kinney, born 1809, and Polly born 1812. The widow's application states that he was "killed for his pension."

PRESSLEY THORNTON

Pressley Thornton applied for revolutionary pension while living in Weakley County, Tennessee. He was born December 25, 1757, in Orange County Virginia. While he resided in Spottsylvania County, Virginia, he enlisted in Virginia troops in Fredericksburg, Virginia. After the Revolution he moved to Wilke's County, Georgia, thence to

Jackson and Clark Counties, Georgia, and thence to Tennessee where he first resided in Wilson and Rutherford Counties. He then settled in Weakley County, Tennessee, where he died October 1, 1852 or October 1, 1853.

JOHN TURNLEY

John Turnley applied for pension while living in Warren County, Tennessee, in 1821, when he was 65 years of age. He resided in Spottsylvania County, Virginia, (where he was born). He enlisted in 1776 in Captains Towles and Avery's companies, Colonels Buckner and Simms' regiments. He was in both battles of Trenton and the battle of Germantown. He was discharged February 13, 1778, at Valley Forge. He served later in Virginia Militia under LaFayette and was in the Siege of Yorktown. He married in October, 1778, Elizabeth ————. He died December 7, 1832, in Cannon County, Tennessee. Elizabeth Turnley survived him and drew pension until June 23, 1850 when she died in Cannon County. Their children were: Edmund, born 1779; Martha, born 1782; Mary, born 1783; Catherine, born 1785; John, born 1787; Nancy, born 1789; Powell, born 1791; Ellet, born 1793, and Temple, born 1795.

CAPTAIN GEORGE WALKER

Captain George Walker applied for revolutionary pension while living in Bledsoe County, Tennessee, in 1832. He enlisted in North Carolina Militia in Burke County, North Carolina, and served in the battle of Ramsour's Mills. He moved to Knox County, Tennessee, in 1796, and to Bledsoe County in 1807. He died in Bledsoe County October 12, 1833. His children were: William; Ephriam; Sarah (who married ———— Matlock); Dicey (who married ———— Howard); Jesse; Charlotte (who married ———— Cherry); and Buckner. His wife predeceased him.

JOHN WEAR

John Wear applied for revolutionary pension while residing in Sullivan County, Tennessee, in March, 1833. He was born January 12, 1741, on Shammony Creek, Bucks County, Pennsylvania. While he was a resident of Greene County, North Carolina, later Tennessee, he served in North Carolina troops as follows: From January 1, 1781, three months in Captain John Sevier's company in pursuit of Tories; from the last of August, 1781, three months in Captain William Tate's company. He was in the Siege of Yorktown and was present at the surrender of Cornwallis. From the latter part of January, 1782, he was four months in Captain Moses Moore's company, and in Captain Samuel Wear's company. John Wear moved to the Mississippi River in 1800 and to Christian County, Kentucky, where he remained only a few months. He then moved to Sevier County, Tennessee.

Note:- This name is frequently spelled Weir. John Wear was a brother of Colonel Samuel Wear. The family emigrated from Pennsylvania to Augusta County, Virginia, when Samuel and John were children and they moved to Washington County, North Carolina, (later Tennessee) during the Revolution. John Wear married in Augusta County, Virginia, Nancy Blackburn, daughter of Benjamin Blackburn. Their children were: Elizabeth, who married James Gray; Phoebe Wear, who married George Matthews; Susan (?) who married ——— Bird; Hugh; George; Benjamin; Margaret, who married John W. Wilson, and Nancy, who married Thomas Alexander.

ALEXANDER WILLIAMS

Alexander Williams applied for revolutionary pension while living in Hawkins County, Tennessee, in 1820. He was then about 82 years of age. He enlisted in North Carolina in April, 1778, in Captain G. Bradley's company, Colonel James Hogan's North Carolina regiment. He was discharged in December, 1779, at the barracks in Philadelphia. He stated in 1820 that his wife was 76 years of age and that they had no children living with them. He died October 8, 1830.

FRANCIS WILLIAMS

Francis Williams applied for revolutionary pension while residing in White County, Tennessee, in 1832. He was born in January, 1752, in Pennsylvania, and moved to Maryland in infancy with his mother, his father then being dead. Their names are not stated in his pension application. While he resided in Hartford County, Maryland, about twenty-five miles from Baltimore, he was a member of small parties in protecting the property of citizens from attacks by the enemy. He then volunteered and served as a private in Captain Bennett Bussey's company in Maryland troops. The company marched from Baltimore to Annapolis and returned to Baltimore and then marched by way of Philadelphia to Fort Washington. He witnessed the battle of White Plains where three members of his company were killed, although the company was not actually engaged in the battle.

He moved from Masyland to what was later Carter County, Tennessee and moved from there to White County, Tennessee, where he died March 1, 1833. His wife predeceased him. Their children were: Mary Connor, born in 1772; James Williams, who in 1861 was 66 years of age and living in White County, Tennessee; and Francis Williams, born 1791.

WILLIAM WILLIAMS

William Williams applied for revolutionary pension while residing in Hawkins County, Tennessee, in 1834. He was born in 1757 in Chester County, Pennsylvania. He enlisted in Montgomery County, Virginia, in March, 1780, and served in Captain Swift's company, Colonel Campbell's regiment. He volunteered again in August, 1780, and was in Captain Brison's company in the same regiment. He was engaged in several tours against the Tories. He volunteered again about the first of the year 1781 in Captain Brison's company. Colonel Williams' regiment and served for one year. After the Revolution he moved from Montgomery County, Virginia, to Tennessee.

ZEBEDEE WILLIAMS

Zebedee Williams applied for revolutionary pension while living at Carthage, Smith County, Tennessee, in 1818. His age is not given nor the place of his birth. He enlisted in May, 1777, in Captain Dempsey Gregory's company, Colonel Shepherd's 10th North Carolina regiment and was later transferred to Captain Howell Tatum's North Carolina company. His term of enlistment, which was three years, expired during the Siege of Charleston but he was imprisoned there during the siege and was not released until some time in 1781.

JOHN WILLIAMSON

John Williamson applied for revolutionary pension while living in Nashville, Davidson County, Tennessee, in August, 1832. He was born October 27, 1759. He enlisted in March, 1778, with John Fuqua while living in Halifax County, Virginia, in the 1st regiment of the Virginia line under Captain Sharp, Major John Purty, Colonel Hays and General Morgan. He enlisted for the duration of the war and continued in service until September, 1781, when he was discharged. He was in the battles of Cowpens, Guilford Court House, and at the Surrender at Yorktown, where he was wounded in the neck. He lost his discharge papers in April, 1828, when his house was burned. He married Cynthia Montgomery in May, 1816. He died in Davidson County, December 18, 1847. Cynthia Montgomery Williamson survived him and died in Davidson County, about 1866.

JOHN WILSON
Of Lincoln County

John Wilson applied for revolutionary pension while residing in Lincoln County, Tennessee, in October, 1832. He was born May 11, 1747, in Augusta County, Virginia. In 1772 he moved to the settlement on the Holston in what is now East Tennessee, where he enlisted in North Carolina troops. He died in Lincoln County.

JOHN WILSON
Of Carter County

John Wilson applied for revolutionary pension while he was living in Carter County, Tennessee, in 1832. He was born in Amelia County, Virginia, in 1755 or 1756. He moved with his family to the section of North Carolina which later became Washington and Carter Counties, Tennessee. He resided in Washington County, then North Carolina, when he enlisted in a North Carolina Company in November, 1779. His brothers, Joseph and William Wilson, volunteered when he did. John Wilson lived in that part of Washington County which was subsequently erected as Carter County and was located there the rest of his life. He married Elizabeth, widow of John Lindsay, September 2, 1837 or 1838. The widow in applying for a pension said that she married him the day he died!

FRANCIS WINSTEAD

Francis Winstead applied for revolutionary pension while living in Hawkins County, Tennessee, in 1832. He was born November 19, 1758, in Northumberland County, Virginia. While residing in that County he volunteered in the fall of 1776 and served at various times under Captains John Crawley and George Eskridge and Colonel Thomas Jones. A great part of the time he was stationed at Cherry Point on the Potomac River to prevent the enemy from landing. He served until some time in 1782. He moved with his family from Northumberland County, Virginia, to Edgecomb County, North Carolina, in 1793. After living there about twelve years he moved to Hawkins County, Tennessee. He was a Baptist minister.

BELFIELD WOOD

Belfield Wood applied for revolutionary pension while living in Fentress County, Tennessee, in August, 1833, when he was 80 years of age. He was born in Orange County, Virginia, and reared there and in Chesterfield County. He moved to Burke County, North Carolina, and was living there in 1776 when he enlisted in Captain Reuben White's company, Colonel Charles McDowell's regiment. In the latter part of 1781 he enlisted in Captain Thomas Kennedy's company, Colonel Locke's regiment. After the Revolution he moved to Pendleton County, South Carolina, where he lived twenty-two years. He then moved to Madison County, Kentucky, thence to Wayne County, Kentucky, where he lived ten years, thence to Fentress County, Tennessee, where died April 6, 1736. His widow, Nancy Kidwell Wood, applied for pension while living in Wayne County, Kentucky, where she lived with her son, Belfield Wood, Jr., in September, 1856. She married Belfield Wood March 15, 1810, in Pendleton County, South Carolina. The ceremony was performed by Henry Burch. Her maiden name was Kidwell. She was born in 1792, and may have been Belfield Wood's second wife as she was about forty years younger than he. After the death of Belfield Wood she married Thomas Millsaps.

ZADOCK WOOD

Zadock Wood applied for revolutionary pension while, living in Bedford County, Tennessee, in May, 1832. He was born in Frederick County, Virginia, March 7, 1766. He resided in Ninety-six District, South Carolina, in 1722 and 1783 when he was drafted into Captain James Tinsley's company, Colonel James Hayes' regiment. He was in engagements at Hamond's Old Store and Ninety-six District under General Pickens. He served against the Cherokee Indians. He was called out again against the Tories, serving under Major Gordon. After the War he moved to Laurens County, South Carolina, where he resided until 1813. He then moved to Wilson County, Tennessee, where he resided six or seven years. He then moved to Bedford County, where he died.

JESSE WOODRUFF

Jesse Woodruff applied for pension in Lincoln County, Tennessee, in 1818. He said that he was formerly of Washingon County, Tennessee, and also formerly of Kentucky. He was born May 20, 1757, in Spottsylvania County, Virginia. He enlisted in Caroline County, Virginia, in 1776 and served in Captains Howes and Sanford's companies, Colonel Spotswoods' Virginia regiment. He was in the battles of Brandywine and Germantown and was discharged in March, 1778, at Valley Forge. He married March 21, 1783, in Washington County, Virginia, Esther Buchanan. She was born June 1, 1765 and was the daughter of Robert and Mary Buchanan. Jesse Woodruff died October 13, 1826, in Lincoln County. His widow applied for pension in 1840 and was living in 1848. In her pension application she referred to the following children: Mary, born 1784; Susana, born 1786; William B., born 1790; Nancy born 1797; Martha, born 1799; and Eliza, born 1805.

RECORDS OF SOME REVOLUTIONARY PENSIONERS WHO DID NOT LIVE IN TENNESSEE BUT WHO HAVE TENNESSEE DESCENDENTS OR SOME OTHER TENNESSEE INTEREST

WILLIAM ALEXANDER
Of Kentucky

William Alexander applied for revolutionary pension while living in Mercer County, Kentucky, in 1821. He was then 68 years of age. His wife was then 62 years of age. He enlisted in Northumberland County, Virginia, in July 1780. His wife was Margaret Bailey before her marriage.

ROBERT ARMSTRONG
Of Illinois

Robert Armstrong, whose widow, Nancy Green Armstrong, applied for pension in May, 1836, in Menard County, Illinois, was born May 28, 11760. The widow made her deposition in the presence of Abraham Lincoln, member of Congress from the District, and his signature appears. When Robert Armstrong was 19 or 20 years of age he lived at Crowder's Creek, North Carolina. He enlisted as a substitute for his father, James Armstrong, in the North Carolina militia and served as various times under Colonel Little and General Ashe. He was in the battle of Briar Creek. Robert Armstrong died in Menard County, September 9, 1834. The widow declared that they married January 22, 1787, and that she was born February 6, 1768. Her application was rejected on the ground of insufficient proof of Robert Armstrong's service.

The application named the following children: James, born 1788, died 1789; Jesse, born 1789; Robert, Jr., born 1792, died 1798; Rhoda, born 1794; Royal, born 1797; Hugh, born 1800; John of Jack, born 1803; Betsey, born 1805; Nancy, born 1809; and Elizabeth, born 1812.

Note:- Royal is also spelled Ryall and Rial in the application. Hugh Armstrong was a lieutenant under Captain Abraham Lincoln in 1832. Jack Armstrong had a wrestling match with Abraham Lincoln. They were friends for almost lifetime.

JOHN E. BILLS
Of Virginia

John E. Bills was born in 1763 in Hampshire County, Virginia. While residing in Hampshire County he enlisted in the fall of 1779 and served in Captain Henry Enoch's Virginia company. Captain Enoch was an uncle of the soldier. He was on duty up and down the Ohio River. He enlisted again in 1782 and served in Captain Joseph Berry's Virginia Company guarding prisoners at Winchester Barracks. He applied for pension in 1833, when he was residing in Hardy County, Va., a division of Hampshire County. He died July 9, 1852, at his residence in Wood County, Va. He married July 2, 1818, in Hardy County, Va., Mary Reel. The widow was allowed pension on her application in 1853, when she was a resident of Wood County where she had then lived about seven years. She was then between 65 and 70 years of age.

CALEB BROWN
Of New Hampshire

Caleb Brown applied for revolutionary pension while residing in Merrimack County, Pennsylvania, in 1831. He was born August 4, 1859. The place of his birth and the name of his mother are not given in his application. His father was Richard Brown who was a member of the Committee of Safety for Hampton Falls, New Hampshire, durinig the Revolution. Caleb Brown enlisted in Hampton Falls about June 1, 1777, in Captain Joseph Parson s company, Colonel Senter's New Hampshire regiment, and was discharged January 1, 1778. He enlisted again in July, 1778, and served in General Sullivan's Rhode Island Expedition. In the summer of 1779 he went to Massachusetts and enlisted in Captain Lewis Jenkins' Massachusetts company. In April 1780, he enlisted in Captain Robinson's company, Colonel George Reid's New Hampshire regiment, and was transferred to Captain Samuel Cherry's company in the same regiment.

Note:- The History of Hampton Falls, New Hampshire, shows the marriage of Richard Brown to Rachel Snow, August, 1757.

SPENCER CALVERT
Of Kentucky

Spencer Calvert applied for revolutionary pension in Caldwell County, Kentucky, in May, 1833. He was then 72 years of age and therefore born in 1761. He served in the Revolution from Prince William County, Virginia, under Captain Valentine Peyton. In 1780 he served again. He had a brother, Raleigh Calvert, in the 3rd Virginia regiment. He died about 1838.

JACOB CAMPBELL
Of New York

Jacob Campbell applied for revolutionary pension while he was living in Otsego County, New York. He was born February 4, 1762, in Windham County, Connecticut. He enlisted March 16, 1778, in Captain Philip Traffan's company, Colonels Barter and John Topham's Rhode Island regiment. He was in the battle of Rhode Island and continued in service for one year and then reenlisted. He was discharged at Newport, 1781, on account of sickness. After the Revolution he resided in several counties in New York including: Dutchess, Columbia, Chenango and Otsego. His wife was named Martha.

JOHN COLBERT
Of Virginia

John Colbert (Calvert or Colvert) applied for revolutionary pension while living in Frederick County, Virginia, in October, 1827. He was then 62 years of age and was therefore born in 1765. He enlisted near Winchester, Virginia, in May, 1781, as a Dragoon in the troop of Captain Arnold Vaughluson in the Virginia Line. He served until May, 1783, when he was discharged. He was a native of Fredecick County. He moved to Pennsylvania after the death of his first wife. He returned to Frederick County, where he died October 20, 1838. He married again while living in Frederick County.

SAMUEL DAVIS
Of Alabama

Samuel Davis applied for revolutionary pension while living in Madison County, Alabama, in 1832. He was born December 25, 1755, in Augusta County, Virginia. He enlisted while living in Washington County, Virginia, in 1776, in Captain Robert Craig's company, Colonel Christie's regiment. During 1777 and 1778 he served under Captain Matthew Willoughby. He enlisted again in March 1779 in Captain Josiah Harland's company, Colonel Benjamin Logan's regiment. He enlisted again in November 1780 and served in Captain Joseph Black's Company, Colonel Arthur Campbell's regiment. He was in several battles with the Indians. He stated that his father was killed by Indians.

WILLIAM DAVIS
Of Alabama

William Davis applied for revolutionary pension while residing in Jackson County, Alabama. He was born in Hanover County, Virginia, in 1753. During the Revolution he resided in Albemarle County, Virginia, and enlisted from that county in the company of Captain Nicholas Davis in 1776 under General LaFayette. He served several tours, the third tour as a substitute for ——— Steele. He was acquainted in Albermarle County with Colonel James Lewis who resided later in Franklin County, Tennessee. A letter from Colonel Lewis stated that he and William Davis were boys in the same neighborhood in Albemarle County, Virginia. William Davis stated that he moved from Virginia to Kentucky and thence to Alabama.

Note:- The history of Albemarle County, Virginia, gives the location of Colonel James Leuis's residence as a boy. It was on the western part of the present University of Virginia site.

LEWIS DAY
Of Ohio

Lewis Day was born July 19, 1754, in West Springfield, Hampshire County, Massachusetts. He was a minute man in the fall of 1774 while residing in West Springfield and on April 20, 1775 he marched to Roxberry and there enlisted in Captain Enoch Chapin's company, Colonel Timothy Danielson's Massachusetts regiment. He enlisted again in 1776 in Captain Samuel Flower's company, Colonel Woodbridge's Massachusetts regiment. He moved in 1778 to Granby, Hartford County, Connecticut, and in 1800 he moved with his family to the "Northwestern Territory." He applied for pension August 27, 1832 while he was a resident of Deerfield, Portage County, Ohio.

JAMES DYSERT
Of Kentucky

James Dysert applied for revolutionary pension while living in Rockcastle County, Kentucky. He served as a Captain in the Revolution and was pensioned because of a disability incurred during his service.

JOHN FREEMAN
Of Virginia

John Freeman applied for revolutionary pension while living in Culpepper County, Virginia, in March, 1825, when he was 69 years of age. He was therefore born in 1756. He served as a private in the 1st Virginia regiment. He married Phoebe Ostin February 27, 1791. He died March 27, 1844. The widow, Phoebe Ostin Freeman, applied for pension in Culpeper County, August 22, 1844, when she was 79 years old.

ANTHONY GLEAN
Of New York

Anthony Glean applied for revolutionary pension in 1829 while living in New York. He was born in New York City January 12, 1751. He signed his affidavit before Walter Boone, Mayor of New York City. It was attested by Abraham Leggett and John McComb. He served on the "Lady Washington" in 1777. He mentioned his father's house in Pleasant Valley, Dutchess County, New York. He lived in New York City when he entered the service. He died May 1, 1842, leaving children: John, Oliver and Hannah Glean; and grandchildren: Augustus and Margaret (children of Anthony Glean, Jr., deceased).

SAMUEL GWINN
Of Virginia

Samuel Gwinn applied for revolutionary pension while living in Greenbriar County, Virginia, in March, 1835. He was born in Augusta County, Virginia, in 1752. He was in the battle of Point Pleasant in 1775 and served at various times as a scout and spy on the frontier of Vrginia during the Revolution. He was allowed pension but in March 1835 he was dropped from the roll as upon re-examination of his claim his service was not considered military service in an embodied corps in the Revolution as was required by the pension law.

BENJAMIN HARRIS
Of Georgia

Benjamin Harris applied for revolutionary pension while living in Walton County, Georgia, in 1832. He was born January 29, 1761. He enlisted while he lived in Duplin County, Georgia, under Captain Rhodes, Colonel Little, Major Blount, and Lieutenant H——— Holmes. He married Bethena Odom August 23, 1785. John Holly, a justice of the peace of Sampson County, Georgia, performed the ceremony Benjamin Harris died December 30, 1840, in Walton County, Georgia.

BURDITT HARRISON
Of Virginia

Burditt Harrison applied for revolutionary pension while living in Madison County, Virginia, in October, 1733. He was then 75 years of age. He enlisted in 1779 under Captain William Kirtly. His own statement is as follows: "In the early part of the year 1779 I came from the County of King George to the County of Culpeper (that part which is now Madison) to visit a brother. I fell in with William Kirtly, then a captain in the regiment at the Albamarle Barracks commanded by Colonel Frank Taylor. I remained at the Barracks with Captain Kirtly and Captain Porter. I was honorably discharged after two years."

JAMES HOUSTON
Of North Carolina

James Houston applied for revolutionary pension in 1832 while living in Rowan County, North Carolina. He stated that he was born in January 1751. He enlisted in the summer of 1776 in Captain Young's company in General Rutherford's North Carolina troops. He also served three months in 1776 under Captain Young in Colonel Martin's regiment. In the summer of 1780 he enlisted again under Captain Higgins in North Carolina troops. In the fall of 1781 he enlisted under Captain Bell and Colonel Graham. He was in the Cherokee Expedition.

JAMES HOUSTON
Of Iredell County, North Carolina

James Houston's widow, Asenath Brevard Houston applied for pension while living in Iredell County, North Carolina, in 1840. She was born December 26, 1755. James Houston was born June 22, 1757. He served in 1777-1778 as Captain of a North Carolina company in Colonel William Park's regiment. He served in a tour which expired the day before the surrender of Charleston. He was discharged May 11, 1780. In 1780 he was captain of a company in Colonel Francis Locke's regiment. He was in the battle of Ramsour's Mill and was wounded in the thigh. In 1781 he was in an expedition to Guilford County, N.C.

He was pensioned in 1806 on account of disability resulting from his wound. The marriage of James Houston to Asenath Brevard took place September 29, 1775, in Rowan County. They lived in Mecklenburg County. James Houston died June 13, 1819, in Iredell County. The widow died June 13, 1843. Their children were William Houston; Sarah Houston, married ———McKee; Edward R. Houston; Mary C. Houston, married ——— Torrance; J. B., Richard, and George Houston.

JOHN W. HOWE
Of Kentucky

John W. Howe applied for revolutionary pension while living in Greenup County, Kentucky, in June, 1833, when he was 80 years of age. He was therefore born in 1753. He died April 30, 1835. His widow, Mary Ann Howe, applied for widow's pension, March 16, 1841, aged 75 years. She was therefore born in 1766. They were married in Montgomery County, Virginia, September 19, 1782. Their children were: Joseph, born 1783; Rebeckah, born 1785; Elinor, born 1787; Sarah, born 1789; William, born 1791; Daniel Lynham, born 1793, and John Nelson, born 1795.

WILLIAM JAMESON
Of Kentucky

William Jameson applied for revolutionary pension while living in Bath County, Kentucky, in October, 1832, when he was 73 years of age. He was born in Prince William County, Virginia, in 1759. He served under Lieutenant William Farrow of Prince William County Virginia. He had a brother John Jameson.

Note:- Descendants state that John and William Jameson were sons of Robert Jameson of Prince William County, Virginia.

LIEUTENANT WILLIAM STORKE JETT
Of Virginia

William Storke Jett applied for revolutionary pension while living in Westmorland County, Virginia, in September, 1832. He was born September 27, 1763, in King George, County, now Westmorland County, near the town of Leeds and was the son of Thomas Jett. In September, 1779, he enlisted in the militia of Westmorland County and served until January 31, 1781, when he was recommended by the Court of Westmorland County to the Governor of Virginia for promotion. He received the commission of a first lieutenant and served in that capacity until the close of the war. Charles C. Jett, executor of the will of William S. Jett, was the only son and only heir

THOMAS JOHNSON
Of Virginia

Thomas Johnson applied for revolutionary pension while living in Augusta County, Virginia, January, 1834. He was born March 28, 1761, in Louisa County, Virginia. He enlisted while living in Louisa County, in Virginia troops, in 1777 under Captain John Cox and Colonel Winslow. In 1779 he enlisted again under Captain Benjamin Timberlake and Colonel Taylor. In 1780 he enlisted again under captain Richard Philips and Colonel Harrison.

JOHN KEY
Of Virginia

John Key applied for revolutionary pension while living in Lunenberg County, Virginia, in 1825. He served in Captain Boyer's company as a substitute for Christopher Carlton in the First Virginia regiment commanded by Colonel Campbell. He was wounded in the battle of Eutaw Springs. He stated that he had a wife and children. After his death his widow applied for pension about 1832. The widow, Fathey Lester Key, stated that she married John Key in Lunenberg County in 1808 and that she had 15 children, the youngest child was 22 years of age in 1850.

Note:- It is probable that Fathey Lester Key was a second wife.

LIEUTENANT TANDY KEY
Of Virginia

Tandy Key applied for revolutionary pension while living in Fluvanna County, Virginia, in 1834. He enlisted in August or September, 1777, in militia from Buckingham County under Captain John Bates; he was lieutenant of the company. Charles Dibrell who was later Colonel Dibrell of Davidson County, Tennessee, was ensign.

WILLIAM B. KEY
Of Georgia

William B. Key applied for revolutionary pension while living in Elbert County, Georgia, in 1833. He was born October 2, 1759, in Fluvanna County, Virginia, and while a resident of that county in 1776 he enlisted and served two months in Captain Knapper's company, Colonel Cavil's regiment. He enlisted again in 1781 and served four months. He moved to Georgia after the Revolution.

KOHN KINTER
Of Pennsylvania

John Kinter applied for revolutionary pension while living in Indiana County, Pennsylvania, in 1833. He was born May 15, 1755. His birth was recorded in German in his father's Bible which he gave to Conrad Shuey, the husband of his niece. John Kinter enlisted in 1777 in Lancaster County, Pennsylvania, in Captain James Clark's company. He served again in 1778 and 1779 and in 1780 he went into service as a substitute for his brother, Peter Kinter, who had been drafted. He died April 29, 1836. His widow, Isabella Findley Kinter, applied for pension in 1836 when she was 82 years of age and therefore born in 1754. She was married to John Kinter in August, 1782, in Lancaster County by Rev. Enterly. They had nine children among them John Kinter and Peter Kinter. The widow lived until after 1852.

AMBROSE LIPSCOMB
Of Virginia

Ambrose Lipscomb applied for revolutionary pension while living in Randolph County, Virginia, in June, 1833. He was then 81 years of age and was therefore born in 1752. He died May 18, 1841. He married December 23, 1785 Winny ———. She survived her husband and applied for widow's pension in Randolph County in May, 1846, when she was 75 years of age. She was therefore born in 1768. They had the following children: Lucy, born 1768; Richard, born 1788; James born 1793; John, born 1795; Levi, born 1798; Henry, born 1799; Fielding, born 1802: Evan, born 1805.

JOHN McCUTCHEON
Of Virginia

John McCutcheon applied for revolutionary pension when he was living in Little Calf Pasture, Augusta County, Virginia, in 1832. He was born August 13, 1750, in Little Calf Pasture, Augusta County. He served in the Revolution under Captain Andrew Lockbridge, Lieutenante and Ensigns John Wachel, William Kinkead and Sampson Mathews and Major Alexander Robertson.

GEORGE MILLS
Of Virginia

George Mills applied for revolutionary pension while living in Prince Williams County, Virginia, in August, 1832. He was born in 1756. He served as a private in Captain Valentine Peyton's company, Virginia Militia March 9, 1785. He died May 27, 1836. He married Lydia Cooksey or Calvert, probably Lydia Calvert Cooksey, as she was the was the widow of Obediah Cooksey, according to one affidavit. The children of George and Lydia Mills were John Dyson, born 1785; Catherine, born 1789, who married ———— Russell; and Anne, born 1795, who married John Woodward.

JOHN NELSON
Of Virginia

John Nelson's widow, Nancy (Ann) Nelson, applied for pension in November, 1837 when she was living in Mecklenburg County, Virginia. She was 74 years of age and therefore born in 1763. The year and place of John Nelson's birth are not shown but he "was the son of Secretary Nelson of York." In June, 1776, he was appointed captain of a company and he served in Colonel Bland's 1st Cavalry regiment. He was taken ill while on an expedition from Morristown, New Jersey, into Pennsylvania and resigned his commission on account of his health. In 1779 he raised a company of volunteer horsemen and soon afterwards he was appointed major of the Virginia State Cavalry. He served in the South under Baron DeKalb and General Gates. He returned to Virginia and served under Generals Muhlenberg and Lafayette. He was in the seige of Yorktown and continued in the service until February 14 1782. He married July 25, 1781, Nancy or Ann Carter of Williamsburg. They were married in the chapel of the College of William and Mary. He died February 18, 1827. His will was dated June 6, 1826, and he appointed as his executors his sons, John Nelson of Mecklenburg County, Virginia; Thomas Nelson and Robert Nelson.

The children of John Nelson and Nancy Carter Nelson were: Thomas Maudit, born 1782; John, born 1784; Lucy, born 1785; Robert, born 1787; Hugh born 1788 died 1730; Nancy Carter, born 1790, married E. Kennon, died 1831; William, born 1792; Mary, born 1794, died 1795; Nathaniel, born 1798; and Sarah, born 1802. William Nelson, the fifth son, had a daughter Anna Matilda, who was born in 1817.

It is shown in the application that "Secretary Nelson of York" had another son, Thomas, who married Sally Carey, eldest daughter of Wilson Miles Carey. She died soon after the birth of her son Carey Nelson.

JOHN PORTER
Of Kentucky

John Porter applied for revolutionary pension in Butler County, Kentucky, in 1832, when he was 73 years of age. He was therefore born in 1759. He died September 24, 1833. His widow, Rosamond Porter, applied for pension in 1854 aged 87. She was therefore born in 1767. They were married in November, 1832. She was then a widow, Rosamond Brady.

LIEUTENANT WILLIAM PORTER
Of Kentucky

William Porter applied for revolutionary pension while living in Caldwell County, Kentucky, in 1820, when he was 64 years of age. He was therefore born in 1756. He served as a lieutenant during the Revolution. He died January 8, 1821. His widow, Sally Porter, applied for pension in 1838 aged 75 and she was therefore born in 1763. She was Sally Johnson before her marriage which took place June 20, 1782. She died August 25, 1843. Their children were: William C.; Sally, married ———— McLin; Elizabeth D. married ———— Campbell; and Horatio D. Porter. William C. Porter and Sally McLin were living in 1856. Elizabeth Campbell and Horatio Porter died in 1854.

PHILLIP M. RUSSELL
Of Pennsylvania

Phillip M. Russell applied for revolutionary pension while living in Philadelphia County, Pennsylvania, in 1717. He entered the service November 14, 1777 and was attached to the 2nd Virginia Regiment. He was discharged October 8, 1778, on account of deafness resulting from camp fever. He married Esther ———— in Philadelphia, Penn., November 1, 1776. After the revolution they moved to Richmond, Virginia, to reside. Phillip M. Russell died August 11, 1830 when he was ninety years of age. His widow, Esther Russell, drew a pension. She died July 26, 1846, aged 89 years. They had thirteen children, the names given in the pension statements being: Samuel, born August 16, 1780; Moses Milton who served as an officer in the War of 1812 and had one son, Edmund J.; Rachel, born about 1797; Sarah, born about 1804; and Rebecca, born about 1795, who married David Nathans and in 1825 was a widow with two children. There was a grandson, Waring Russell, whose parents' names are not given.

BENJAMIN STROTHER
Of Virginia

Benjamin Strother applied for revolutionary pension while living in Jefferson County, Virginia, in March, 1852. He served as a midshipman in the Virginia State Navy. A land bounty was given in 1834 to his children, namely: Catherine, who married ———— Crane; Margaret, who married ———— Moore; Mary, who married ———— Duffield; John; and the two children of a deceased daughter Elizabeth who married Benjamin Pendleton.

Note:- The children of Elizabeth Strother Pendleton were Benjamin S. Pendleton, James W. Pendleton, and Catherine Pendleton who married John Bailey Nicklin.

BENJAMIN STROTHER
of Prince William County, Virginia

Benjamin Strother applied for pension while living in Prince William County, Virginia, in 1818. He was 63 years of age and was therefore born about 1755. He died December 25, 1833. He married Sarah ─────────. Their children were. John; Larkin; Benjamin F.; James; William; George; Jemima; Elizabeth who married ───────── Lealcck; Catherine; Mary who married ───────── Arrington; Nancy who married Hawkins; and Charlotte who married William Brown.

Note:- William Strother in the list of children married Margaret Kern.

WILLIAM TIPTON
of Kentucky

William Tipton applied for pension while living in Montgomery County, Kentucky, in 1832. He was born in Baltimore County, Maryland, January 1, 1754. He moved from Maryland to Virginia and was living in Fredrick County, Virginia, when he enlisted. After the Revolution he moved to Montgomery County, Kentucky.

JESSE WITT
of Goochland County, Virginia

Jesse Witt applied for revolutionary pension while living in Goochland County, Virginia, in August, 1818. He was then fifty-two years of age and therefore born in 1766. He served as a private soldier under Colonel Samuel Hawes. He married Elizabeth ───────── who was forty-four years of age in 1820. In that year they had the following children: Polly, aged 17 years; Elizabeth aged 15 years; Samuel aged 7 years; Henna aged 5 years; Susannah aged 3 years; and Thomas aged one year and a half.

JESSE WITT
of Bedford County, Virginia

Jesse Witt applied for revolutionary pension while living in Bedford County, Virginia, in August, 1832. He was born May 11, 1862. He served two years and a half in the 14th Regiment of the Virginia Line. He enlisted March 1, 1777. He was in the battles of Brandywine and Germantown and was discharged September 10, 1779 on account of disability. He died February 3, 1842. He married May 6, 1788, Alice Brown who survived him and applied for pension Marci 5,1843. She was born in 1763 and died July 9, 1844. Her marriage bond, dated May 6, 1786, is attested by Henry Brown, Jr., and Samuel Brown.

Note:- The children of Jesse Witt and Alice Brown Witt were: Lettice; Elizabeth; Alice; Daniel; Milly; Jesse; Burgess. The son Jesse was a preacher.

SOME TENNESSEE HEROES

OF THE

REVOLUTION

Compiled From Pension Statements

PAMPHLET NO. IV

TENNESSEE HEROES OF THE REVOLUTION
SOME PENSIONERS WHO LIVED IN
THE VOLUNTEER STATE

FRANCIS ARNOLD

Francis Arnold applied for revolutionary pension while living in White County, Tennessee, September 12, 1818. He died in that county, February 5, 1830 or 1831, both years being given in the widow's application papers. He was born in January, 1758, in Spottsylvania County, Virginia. He enlisted in Newmarket, Spottsylvania County, early in 1777, and served in Captains Quarles and Long's companies, Colonels Charles Dabney and William Brent's Second Virginia regiment. He was discharged sometime in 1780 after three years' service. In 1796 he resided in Pendleton District, S. C., and after 1810 he moved to what later became White County, Tennessee.

He married August 5, 1790, in Greenville District, S. C., Elizabeth Parker who was born December 23, 1775. She survived him and applied for pension in 1840 while residing in White County. In 1851 she lived with her son, Peter Arnold, in Coffee County. She died prior to March, 1853.

Francis and Elizabeth Arnold had fourteen children, among them: William, born 1791; Peter, the seventh child, born 1803; Colbird, a son, the eighth child, born 1807; Samuel, born 1811; Hayes, whose birth is not given, and others who are mentioned although names and birth dates are not given in the widow's application paper.

AMOS BALCH

Amos Balch applied for revolutionary pension while living in Bedford County, Tennessee. He was born in 1758 in Baltimore County, Maryland. He moved to North Carolina and enlisted in Mechlenburg County in 1779 in Captain Richard Simmon's company. He was attached to the regular cavalry under General Washington. He was in the battle of Camden. He died in Bedford County, Tennessee, in 1835. He married Ann Patton.

Note: Among his children: James Calvin Balch married Eliza Jane Hazlett and John Balch married Sarah Cook.

WALTER BEATTY

Walter Beatty applied for revolutionary pension while living in Hawkins County, Tennessee, August 26, 1818, when he was sixty-six years of age. He was born in 1752. The place of his birth is not mentioned in his application. He enlisted in September, 1775, in Cumberland County, Pennsylvania, in Captain Robert Adams' company, Colonel Irvine's regiment, Pennsylvania militia. He went on the expedition to

Canada and while there he was in the battle of Three Rivers, June 8, 1776, and also in some skirmishes. He was discharged at Fort George on account of ill health, October 25, 1776. He subsequently served in frequent tours in the militia. He married sometime in the year 1772 in Cumberland County, Pennsylvania, Mary Miller. The widow survived him and in March 1838, when she was eighty-four years of age and living in Hawkins County, she applied for pension. She was born in 1757. Her brother, Robert Miller, was living in Wythe County, Virginia, in 1838. In 1840 she was living with John Hicks, probably a a son-in-law.

JOHN BEARDEN

John Bearden applied for revolutionary pension while living in Bedford County, Tennessee. His name appears on the 1832 list. He was born in Spottsylvania County, Virginia, in 1744. He served in a company of Rangers from Spartanburg, South Carolina and was in the battle of Ninety-six. He moved to Tennessee in 1842 and settled in Bedford County where he died.

LIEUTENANT GEORGE DAWSON BLACKMORE

George Dawson Blackmore applied for revolutionary pension while living in Sumner County, Tennessee. He was born near Hagerstown, Md., in February, 1762. He moved to Virginia and was living there when he enlisted in the 2nd Virginia regiment. He was commissioned lieutenant in February 1781. He was taken prisoner at Charleston. He moved to Sumner County about 1784 with the Bledsoe family. He was a captain in the Indian wars and served as captain in the Nickajack expedition. He died in Sumner County, September 30, 1835.

Note: George Dawson Blackmore married Elizabeth Neely, daughter of Captain Alexander Neely and Elizabeth Montgomery Neely (whose sister, Catherine, was the wife of Colonel Isaac Bledsoe). They had ten children, 6 daughters and 4 sons: Polly (d. y.), Margaret (d. y.), Elizabeth (d. unm.), Rachel (m. James Carlton), Catherine Montgomery, (m. Josephus C. Guild), Emaline (m. James Hadley), Charles Neely, George Dawson, Jr., (d unm), James H., and William Montgomery Blackmore (m. Rachel Jackson Barry, daughter of Redmond Dillion Barry).

PETER BRAKEBILL

Peter Brakebill applied for revolutionary pension while living in Monroe County, Tennessee. Later he moved to Blount County, Tennssee, where he drew pension until his death in 1844. His widow Catherine Brakebill applied for pension while living in Blount County June 3, 1844, and died July 12, 1844.

Note: Among the children were: Peter, Jr., and John, who married Annie B. Thomas.

JOSEPH BROWN

Joseph Brown applied for revolutonary pension while living in Knox County, Tennessee, in 1832. He was born in Ireland in 1895 and came to America when he was young. He settled in Pennsylvania where he enlisted later in the Pennsylvania militia. After the Revolution he moved to Washington County, North Carolina, now Tennessee, where he was living by 1748. He married Margaret Griffin and Mary Harbison. He died in Knox County, Tennessee, in 1843.

LIEUTENANT MORGAN BROWN

Morgan Brown applied for pension while living in Davidson County, Tennessee. He was born in Anson County North Carolina, January 13, 1758. He served as a Lieutenant in South Carolina service in the battles of Brandywine and Germantown under Baron de Kalb. He moved to Tennessee after the Revolution. He married 1784, Elilabeth Little, born 1765, died 1829. Morgan Brown died after 1832 when he was drawing pension in Davidson County.

Note: Among his children were: Morgan W. who married Tnn Maria Childress; Catherine Stuart who married Judge William Arthur Cook; Elizabeth Little who married Samuel Vance; and William Little Brown.

ELISHA BURKE (OR BERKE)

Elisha Burke or Berke applied for revolutionary pension while living in Marion County, Tennessee, in 1825. Ht was born in 1755. He enlisted while living in Mechienburg County, North Carolina, under Colonel Little and Captain Moort. In 1825 he had two children, Alfred Cameron Burke, aged sixteen years and Keziah Burke aged fourteen years.

Note: In 1835 when he was eighty years of agt he married a second wife. She killed him and was arrested, tried, convicted and sento the penitentiary.

WILLIAM BURNETT

William Burnttt (the name in the pension claim is Burnitt) applied for revolutionary pension while living in Rutherford County, Tennessee, August 27, 1832, at which time he was seventp-three years of age. He was born in King and Queen County, Virginia, in 1759. While residing in Mecklenburg County, Virginia he enlisted and served three months in Captain Thomas Ship's company, in Colonel Munford's regiment. He enlisted again in January, 1781, in Captain Charles Davis' company, Colonel Dick's regiment and was in an engagement in Portsmouth. Later in 1781 he served three months in Captain Jeffrits' company and was in the siege of Yorktown. He was discharged soon after the surrender of Lord Cornwallis. All his service was with Virginia troops.

He moved from Mecklenburg County, Virginia, to Rutherford County, Tennessee, some time after the close of the Revolution.

GEORGE CALDWELL

George Caldwell applied for revolutionary pension while living in Blount County, Tennessee. He was born in Prince Edward County, Virginia, February 15, 1760. He died in Blount County, May 20, 1836. He served in the Virginia line and was in active service as a scout for three years. He left no widow or other surviving heir except John Caldwell, the heir-at-law.

JOHN CARMICHAEL

John Carmichael applied for revolutionary pension while living in Cocke County, Tennessee. He was born August 7, 1757, in Chester County, Pennsplvania, and was taken soon afterwards by his parents to Lancaster County, Pennsylvania, where he resided during the Revolution. He enlisted September 15, 1777, and served two months in Captain David Mitchell's company, Colonel James Watson's Pennsylvania regiment. He also served in Captain Evans' company. February 15, 1779, he enlisted again and served in Captains Schaffner and Hubley's companies. He enlisted again June 15, 1780. when he served in Captains Huble, George Bush and John Alexander's companys Colonel Harmer's Pennsylvania regiment. He was discharged December 23, 1780, near Morristown. During this service he was in a skirmish at block house a few miles above New York.

He moved after the Revolution from Lancaster County, Pennsylvania, to Cumberland County where he resided for ten years. He then moved to Berkeley County, Virginia, where he lived for five years and to Montgomery County, Virginia, where he lived for fifteen years. He then moved to Cocke County, Tennessee.

August 31, 1832, when he applied for pension he had resided in Cocke County, Tennessee, for seventeen years. In May, 1836, he was a resident of Carroll County, Georgia, where he had gone to reside with his children. His address was Tallapoosa, Georgia, and he was then called John Carmichael, Sr.

ROBERT CARUTHERS

Robert Caruthers applied for revolutionary pension while residing in Bedford County, Tennessee, February 9, 1833. He was born February 14, 1750;, in Lancaster County, Pennsylvania. From about 1722 he lived in Mecklenburg, North Carolina, where he enlisted about June 1, 1780, in Captain John Brumfield's company, Colonel Robert Erwin's regiment. He was in the battle of Hanging Rock and in an engagement next day at Flat Rock. Later he served in Captain Porter's company of the same regiment. He next joined Colonel Davie's regiment. of mounted gunmen. About 1791 he moved to the Tennessee country to what is now Davidson County. Six years later he moved to Williamson County and about 1831 he was living in Bedford County, Tennessee. He is referred to in the record as Robert Caruthers. senior. A James Caruthers living in Nashville, Tennessee, is mentioned in 1837 without indicaton of relationship. The soldier's signature was Robert Carothers but he was pensioned as Robert Caruthers and he is the only Robert Caruthers in the revolutionary war records

RICHARD CAVETT

Richard Cavett applied for revolutionary pension August 19, 1820, while living in Madison County, Alabama. He stated that he was then 70 years old and that he was born in 1765 on the headwaters of the James River in what was later Botetourt County, Virginia. While he was still a child his father, Moses Cavett, and his family moved to Sullivan County, (now in Tennessee) and that his father was in the battle of King's Mountain under Colonel Shelby. He stated that he, Richard, wanted to go to the King's Mountain battle and that he went to Colonel Shelby's quarters and begged to go but that his father, Moses Cavett, made him stay at home to protect the forts and the families. He was then only 15 years of age. He did join the service and fought in the Indian warfare on the frontier for two years during the Revolution. He continued in the service for eight years fighting Indians, making a period of ten years in all. He moved after that to Roane County, Tennessee, where he lived for 16 years. He then moved to Madison County Alabama.

Note: It is mentioned in Ramsey's Annals of Tennessee that some of the mountain men who assembled at Sycamore Shoals hoping to start on the march that resulted in the battle of King's Mountain were required to stay at home to protect the women and children.

DANIEL CHUMLEY

Daniel Chumley applied for revolutionary pension while living in Wilson County, Tennessee, June 25, 1833, when he was about seventy-four years of age. This places his birth, which is not given in his pension application, about the year 1759. He lived in Halifax County, Virginia when he enlisted in Captain Triplett's company, Colonel Grayson's regiment. He was in the battle of Monmouth after which he was transferred to Captain Mitchell's company and marched to Charleston, South Carolina. He was at the surrender of Charleston. He served altogether about three years.

CAPTAIN HENRY CONWAY

Captain Henry Conway served in the 10th Regiment Virginia line. His widow Sarah Conway applied for a pension based on his revolutionary service. He was commissioned captain March 10, 1777. He had in all seven years service. The widow stated that they were married in Pittsylvania County, Virginia, July 25, 1769 and that he died in Greene County, Tennessee, September 10, 1812.

Note: Three of their children married into the Sevier family. Elizabeth Conway married John Sevier, Jr. in July, 1788 when he was twenty-two years of age and she presumably about the same age. Nancy Conway married James Sevier, a brother of John Sevier, Jr and also a son of Governor John Sevier. Susannah Sevier married John Sevier, son of Colonel Valentine Sevier (brother of Governor John Sevier).

ROBERT CRAIGHEAD

Robert Craighead applied for revolutionary pension while residing in Knox County, Tennessee. He was allowed pension from January 31, 1818. After the fall of Charleston many North Carolina citizens volunteered for service to oppose threatened invasion of the state. Robert Craighead was one of the volunteers. He joined the army at Lansford (which was later in Chester County, South Carolina) under Major William R. Davie and General Sumter, on the evening before the battle of Hanging Rock. In that action he was severely wounded in the right shoulder, which became stiff and almost totally disabled. His pension was given in recognition of the disability. Although he is called Captain, there is no definite proof that he was an officer. After the Revolution he resided in Mecklenburg County, N. C., and later moved to Tennessee, where he died May 7, 1821. On April 3, 1821, he certified that he had lived in Knox County, Tennessee, for twenty years.

ANDREW CRESWELL

Andrew Creswell applied for revolutionary pension while living in Sevier County, Tennessee, August 2, 1832, when he was seventy-four years and six months old. He was therefore born in February, 1758. He enlisted in 1776 in Washington County, Virginia and served in Captain Colville's company, Colonel Arthur Campbell's regiment. Afterward he served several tours during the next four or five summers and was engaged against the Indians on the headwaters of Clinch River, once under Colonel Evan Shelby and once or twice under Lieutenant Newell. He enlisted in September, 1780, and served in Captain Dysart's company, Colonel William Campbell's regiment and was in the battle of King's Mountain. In 1781 he served again in Colonel William Campbell's regiment and was in the battle of Guilford Court House. There are no family data in his statement and he does not give the place of his birth. He died July 1, 1838.

JEREMIAH DIAL

Jeremiah Dial applied for revolutionary service while living in Bedford County, Tennessee, in 1832, when he was 76 years of age. He was born in 1756. He enlisted when he was living in South Carolina and served throughout the revolution in S. C. troops. He moved to Tennessee after the Revolution and settled in Bedford County. He married December 13, 1789, Nancp Anna McDaniel, who survived him. She was born in 1763 and died in 1848.

CHARLES DIBRELL

Charles Dibrell applied for revolutionary pension while living in Davidson County, in 1832. He was born in Virginia in 1757. He served in North Carolina militia and was in the battle of Yorktown under General LaFayette. He married Martha Burton. He died in Union City, Tennessee in 1840.

PAUL DISMUKES

Paul Dismukes applied for revolutionary pension while living in Jackson County, Tennessee, in 1834. He was born in 1762. He enlisted at the age of sixteen in Spottsylvania County, Virginia, and was in the battles of Camden and Yorktown. He married Sarah Richardson. He died in Davidson County, Tennessee, in 1838.

GEORGE DOHERTY

George Doherty applied for revolutionary pension while living in Jefferson County, Tennessee. He was born in Virginia in 1749 and died in Jefferson County, May 27, 1833. He enlisted in Virginia troops in Greenbury, Virginia. During the Revolution he moved to Washington County, North Carolina, (now Tennessee). In 1779 he was engaged against the Cherokee and in 1780 he served in the battle of King's Mountain under Colonel John Sevier.

Note: He was the son of Major George Doherty and Elizabeth Williams Doherty whose brother was George Williams. He was a member of the first county court of Greene County, Tennessee, in 1783; he was a leader in the State of Franklin movement. He was Colonel of a regiment of militia in Caswell County, State of Franklin. In 1785 he moved to a site west of the present Dandridge, Tennessee and was a member of the Jefferson County Court. He was a member of the North Carolina Convention of 1789. He was Lieutenant Commandant for Jefferson County. He was a member of the first Territorial Assembly in Tennessee and the first Constitutional Convention in Tennessee. He was a member of the first Tennessee Senate and served in the Assembly several terms. He served in the Expedition to Natchez in 1803. In the Creek War he was a Brigadier General of an East Tennessee brigade. He was in the battle of the Horseshoe. He was given a grant of 2,000 acres by North Carolina for service in the Revolution. He married twice, first Priscilla Goforth and second Sally Randal, December 3, 1823. His will in Jefferson County signed January 15, 1833, mentions his wife, Sally; his sons, George, William and James Tennessee; and his daughters, Jenny, Dorcas Inman, Prescilla Morrow, Rachel Leath: his granddaughter Sally, daughter of his son George; his grandson George, son of James T.; his grandson George, son of George; The children mentioned were all by his first wife. George married Nancy McDowell, Dorcas married Benjamin, Priscilla married David Morrow, Rachel married Joseph Leath.

LIEUTENANT RICHARD FENNER

Richard Fenner's widow, Ann McKinney Geddy Fenner, applied for pension for the revolutionary service of her husband, while she was living in Madison County, Tennessee. He served as a lieutenant in North Carolina Troops and received for his service a grant of land which he located in the Tennessee country. He was taken prisoner at Charleston in 1780 when his brother, Robert, was also made prisoner. They were both original members of the N. C., Society of Cincinnati. Richard Fenner married Ann McKinney Geddy in 1788. She was born in 1770 and died in 1852. Richard Fenner died in Jackson, Madison

County in 1828. Among their children were: Ann M., born 1790, who married Thomas Henderson; Dr. Robert who married Anne Jones; Matilda who married Lewis Coorpender; and Mary, who married Julius Johnson.

PETER FINN

Peter Finn applied for pension while living in Sumner County, Tennessee. After 1832 he moved to Kentucky and later moved to Illinois. He was born in Baltimore County, M., July 2, 1751. He died in Marion County, Illinois in 1837. He first enlisted in Maryland troops but by 1779 he had moved to Washington County, N. C., now Tennessee, where he enlisted under Captain Valentine Sevier.

JOHN FITE

John Fite applied for revolutionary pension while living in Smith County. His name appears on the 1832 list as a resident of Smith County and in the 1840 Census as of De Kalb County. He was born in Sussex County, N. J., in 1758 and was the son of Johannes and Catherine Fite. He enlisted in Essex County and served in the N. J. line. He married Martha Haslet. He died in 1848. He had a younger brother Leonard Fite who also served in the Revolution.

LEONARD FITE

Leonard Fite applied for revolutionary pension while living in Smith County, Tennessee. His name appears on the 1832 list as a resident of Smith County and in the 1840 Census as of De Kalb County. He was born in 1760 in Sussex County, N. J., son of Johannes and Catherine Fite. He enlisted in Essex County, N. J., and served in the N. J., line. He married in 1781 Margaret (Peggy) Cross, born 1761, died 1842. He died in 1842 in De Kalb County, Tennessee.

JOHN GIBBS

John Gibbs applied for revolutionary pension while living in Bedford County, Tennessee, in November, 1832. He was born in 1756 in Pittsylvania County, Virginia. His parents died when he was very young and at the age of fifteen years he became an apprentice in Halifax County, Virginia. He volunteered in the spring or summer of 1777 and served three months in Virginia troops under Colonel Peter Rodgers in the defense of Portsmouth. In September, 1778, he went into Granville County, N. C., where he enlisted in Captains Farrar and High's companies in Colonels Henry Dixon and Lytle's North Carolina troops and was in an engagement near Charleston, S. C. He was in the battle of Stone Ferry and was discharged at the expiration of nine months. He returned to Virginia, enlisted in the spring of 1781 in Captain Bird Wall's comyany and was in the battle of Cuilford Court House. He enlisted again in Captain Long's Virginia company and was in the battle of Yorktown.

He moved after the Revolution from Virginia to North Carolina, then to York County, South Carolina; then again to the Yadkin River, North Carolina; then to Kentucky; and to Bedford County, Tennessee.

About November, 1842, he moved to Breathitt County, Kentucky, where he died October 18, 1848.

He married January 22, 1782 or 1783, in Guilford County, North Carolina, Hannah, whose maiden name is not given in the pension application. Hannah Gibbs, the soldier's widow, applied for pension March 29, 1850, in Morgan County, Kentucky, where she then resided. She gave her age as ninety-five which places her birth in 1755, and was survived by the following children: John Gibbs; Sally Gibbs Woods, and Nathan Gibbs, born October 12, 1793, whose residence in 1850 was West Liberty, Kentucky.

ROBERT GUTHRIE

Robert Guthrie applied for revolutionary pension while living in Williamson County, Tennessee, in September, 1832. He was born October 24, 1757. While residing in Waxhaw Settlement, South Carolina, in 1776 he enlisted and served under Captain James Adams in a South Carolina regiment. In 1778 he served in Captain Montgomery's company, Colonel Joseph Kershaw's South Carolina regiment. He enlisted in May, 1780, in Captain Coffee's company, Colonel Kershaw's regiment and was in the battle of Rocky Mount.

After the Revolution he lived in Camden District, S. C., until 1788 when he moved to Kentucky. He lived in Lincoln County, then in Mercer County eight or nine years and then moved to Tennessee, Williamson County, where he died April 13, 1839.

He married March 9, 1780, Mary Taylor, born December 2, 1760. They were members of the "Congregation" in Waxhaw Settlement.

Mary Taylor Guthrie survived the soldier and applied for widow's pension August 1, 1842, while she was residing in Henry County, Tennessee. She died January 5, 1845.

She gave the names and dates of birth of the following children: Elizabeth Guthrie, 1783; William Ferguson Guthrie, 1785; James Guthrie, 1790; Robert Taylor Guthrie, 1793; David Houston Guthrie, 1796; Jacob Finley Guthrie, 1803.

The birth of Adam Guthrie, October 1, 1769, is given in the pension paper but his relationship is not shown.

WILLIAM HALL

William Hall lived in Tennessee, where he moved after the Revolution, until 1815 when he moved to Madison County, Illinois. He was born in Lancaster County, Pennsylvania. He enlisted in April, 1779, at Long Cave, South Carolina, taking the place of his uncle, William Hall, Sr., and was in the battles of Guilford Court House, Ramsour's Mills and Eutaw Springs. He applied for pension in Madison County, Illinois, where he died May 13, 1846.

CAPTAIN SAMUEL HANDLY

Captain Samuel Handly applied for revolutionary pension while living in Franklin County, Tennessee, September 7, 1832. He was born in Pennsylvania in 1752. When he was young he moved to Augusta County, Virginia, that section which later became Rockbridge County. He resided in Wythe County, Virginia, when he served as follows: In the summer of 1776, three months as orderly sergeant in Captain

John Campbell's Virginia company and was in the battle of Long Island on the Holston; in the fall of 1776, three months in Colonel Christian's Virginia regiment, against Cherokee Indians; three months as an ensign in service against Cherokees; three months as ensign against Chickamauga Indians in Colonel Evan Shelby's regiment; three months as Indian Spy on frontier; from October, 1780, four months in Colonel John Sevier's North Carolina regiment and was in battles of King's Mountain and Boyd's Creek and at burning of Hiwassee Town; two months as Captain in Colonel John Sevier's regiment.

After the close of the war he moved to Washington County, N. C., later Tennessee, then to Blount County, Tennessee, and in 1809 to Franklin County, where he died, November 24, 1840. He was a member of the Convention which formed the Constitution of Tennessee.

Note: Although the above transcript states that he moved to Washington County, North Carolina, after the War, he was already a resident of that section when he enlisted in the North Carolina regiment of Colonel John Sevier in 1780. The transcript also makes no mention of an attack of 56 Cherokees on the company of which he was captain in 1793. Lieut. Leeper and two others of the company were killed and Captain Handly was captured. He suffered untold hardships and torment but his courage and stoicism gained the admiration of the Indians and they adopted him into their tribe. He was finally released. His story is one of the most dramatic in Tennessee's annals.

He married Susan Cowan. Among their children were Samuel, Jr., and William Claiborne Handly who married Nancy Reeves. When he died he was living in Winchester, Tennessee.

LABAN HARTLEY

Laban Hartley applied for revolutionary pension while living in Williamson County, Tennessee. His name appears on the 1840 list. He was born in Scotland in 1742 and lived to be one hundred years of age, dying in Union City, Tennessee in 1842. He was in the battle of Briar Creek. He married Sarah Feagley who predeceased him. In his old age he lived with Lycurgus McCall.

GEORGE HAYNES

George Haynes applied for pension in 1818 while he was living in Carter County, Tennessee. He was born in Winchester, Virginia, and served in the Virginia line. He was in the battle of Guilford Court House.

Note: He married Margaret McInturff. Among their twelve children, (nine sons and three daughters) were: David who married Rhoda Taylor; John, James, George, Jr., Joseph, Jonathan, William, Christopher and Aaron.

LIEUTENANT ROBERT HAYS

Lieutenant Robert Hays applied for revolutionary pension while living in Davidson County, Tennessee, July 11, 1818. The date and place of his birth are not given in his pension papers. He entered the service in the fall of 1776 or the spring of 1777 and served as ensign in Captain Thomas Polk's Fourth North Carolina regiment. In January, 1778, he was transferred to Colonel Thomas Clark's First North Carolina regiment, with the rank of second lieutenant. At the time of his application he was called Colonel Robert Hays.

Note: He was an original member of the Society of Cincinnati, in North Carolina. He died in Haysboro, Tennessee. He married Jane Donaldson. His title of Colonel was gained in the Indian Wars and militia service in Tennessee.

JARED HOTCHKISS

Jared Hotchkiss applied for revolutioary pension while living in Roane County, Tennessee. He was born in New Haven, Connecticut and served in the Connecticut line. He lived in Roane County and later in Loudon County, where he died in 1838.

Note: He married Betsy Knight who was born in Virginia and died in Loudon County in 1842. They had six children, among: C. M. Hotchkiss, born 1802, who married in 1838 Sallie Ann Wyley, daughter of Harris and Artemus Taylor Wyley.

GEORGE HUFACRE

George Hufacre (Huffaker and other forms) applied for revolutionary pension while living in Knox County, Tennessee. He was born in Pennsylvania August 7, 1757. He served in Virginia troops and was with Shelby in the battle of King's Mountain. He was also in the battle of Long Island. After the Revolution he moved to Knox County, Tennessee, where he lived for more than forty years.

Note: George Huffaker's obituary is in the Knoxville Gazette (Tennessee) Register of November 8, 1838. He moved to Tennessee before 1798. He gave Dr. Ramsey an account of the battle of Long Island. He served in the Indian Wars after the Revolution and in 1792 he was in command of the guard at Henry's Station.

BENJAMIN HUGHES

Benjamin Hughes applied for revolutionary pension in Campbell County, Virginia. He was transferred to Smith County, Tennessee, and drew pension there until his death, in 1838. He was born in Hanover County, Virginia, and was the son of Henry and Margaret Hughes. He enlisted in Virginia troops at the age of 16 and was in the battles of Brandywine, Malvern Hill, Charles City Court House, and the Siege of Yorktown. After the War he moved to Bedford County, Va., and in 1805 to Campbell County, Virginia. He moved to Smith County, Tennessee, in 1835.

Note: He married .... Tucker, daughter of Littleberry Tucker, of Hanover County, Virginia. She survived the soldier and continued to reside in Smith County. Their children were: Littleberry, Margaret, Alice, Katherine and Tabitha.

LIEUTENANT PETER HUBBARD

Peter Hubbard applied for revolutionary pension while living in Montgomery County, Tennessee. He was born in South Carolina and served in the South Carolina line under Captain Samuel Wise and Captain John Carraway Smith and Colonel William Thompson. He was in the battle of Sullivan's Island. He moved to Tennessee after the Revolution and lived several years in Montgomery County. He moved to Bond County, Illinois, where he died.

SAMUEL ISAACS

Samuel Isaacs applied for revolutionary pension while living in Lincoln County, Tennessee, in 1832. He was born in Frederick County, Virginia, in 1759. He served in South Carolina troops under Francis Marion. He married Mary Wallace and died in Lincoln County, Tennessee, in 1845.

THOMAS IVES

Thomas Ives applied for revolutionary pension while living in Knox County, Tennessee. He was born in 1756. His name is on the 1818 list in Knox County. Before 1831 he had moved to Roane County, where he also drew pension. He served in Captain Drury Ragsdale's company, 1st Viirginia Artilery. He enlisted July 17, 1777. He applied for a bounty land from Virginia. He married four times. His fourth wife was Polly McNite or McNaught. They were married in Roane County, January 10, 1831, when he was 75 years of age and she 65 years of age.

JACOB KEEBLER, JR.

Jacob Keebler, Jr., was born October 22, 1775, in New Castle, Del., according to the pension application of his widow Mary Young Keebler in Blount County, in 1849. He died in Washington County. He was the son of Jaob and Catherine Keebler. Jacob, Jr., married March 11, 1785, Mary Young who survived him. She was born in Chester County, Penn., September 17, 1765, and was the daughter of James and Barbara Young. The soldier had nine children, among them: Sarah, born in Philadelphia, Penn.; Samuel, born in Washington County, Tennessee, 1804; and James, born about 1795 who married Sarah Hawes.

JAMES LANDRUM

James Landrum applied for revolutionary pension while living in Greene County, September 4, 1832. He was then seventy years of age and therefore born in 1762. He entered service in 1780 in Amherst County, Virginia, under his father, Captain Younger Landrum. Later he enlisted again under his father in Amherst County and marched against Lord Cornwallis. He was in the battle of Guilford Court House. He states that he "casually lost his discharge, if ever his father, Captain Landrum gave him a written discharge." He was a minister of the Gospel and moved after the war to Greene County, where he died January 15, 1840, according to declaration of his widow, Mary Landrum, who applied for pension November 4, 1843. She was then seventy-seven years of age and therefore born in 1767. She states that she was married to James Landrum December 22, 1788.

Note: James Landrum's father and brother, Captain Younger Landrum and Younger Landrum, Jr., moved also to Greene County, Tennessee, and there died. Younger Landrum, Jr., married Joanna Goode Sevier, a niece of Governor John Sevier.

THOMAS LANDRUM

Thomas Landrum applied for revolutionary pension while living in Knox County, July 3, 1833. He was born in Chatham County, N. C., August 27, 1759. He was living in Montgomery County, N. C., in August, 1776, when he was drafted into service against the Cherokee Indians. He was discharged in October and thereafter he served several tours. He lived in North Carolina four or five years after the Revolution and then moved to Richmond County, Georgia, where he lived for two years. He then moved to Greene County, Tennessee, and thence to Knox County, where he drew pension for several years.

WETHERAL LATIMER

Wetheral Latimer applied for revolutionary pension while living in Carroll County, Tennessee. He was born in 1857 in New London, Connecticut. He was the son of Jonathan Latimer and Lucretia Griswold Latimer. He served in Colonel Jonathan Latimer's regiment Massachusetts troops in Burgoyne's Campaign. He married Abigail Fitch. He moved to Tennessee after the Revolution. Later before the 1840 census was published he had moved to Pope City, Arkansas, where he died.

JONATHAN LONG

Jonathan Long applied for revolutionary pension while he was a resident of Hawkins County, Tennessee, October 1, 1833. His name appears as Lang in the Census of Pensioners of 1840, but this is an error as the name is Long in the pension papers. He was born October 16, 1758, in York County, Pennsylvania. While a resident of Franklin County, Pennsylvania, he enlisted in September, 1779, and served three months as a private in Captain John Orbisson's company, Colonel Johnson's Pennsylvania regiment and was in a skirmish with Indians in Woodcock Valley. He enlisted again in August, 1780, and served three months in Captain Smith's company in the same regiment and was in a battle with six or seven hundred Indians. Moving to Frederick County, Maryland, he enlisted in 1781 and served nine months in Captain Clickett's Maryland company and was in the Siege of Yorktown where he received a wound in the ankle. He was discharged November 10, 1781.

After the Revolution he moved to Virginia and then to Hawkins County, Tennessee, where he died February 4, 1841. He married in September or October, 1783, in Frederick County, Maryland. Nancy, whose family name is not given in the pension papers. She applied for pension in July 1845, while she was a resident of Hawkins County Their children were: John. born 1784, David, born 1786; James W. born 1788; Sally, born 1790; Nancy, born 1797 and Mary born 1800.

JOHN LUSK

John Lusk applied for revolutionary pension while living in McMinnville, Warren County, Tennessee, February 20. 1820. He was born November 5, 1734, on Staten Island, N. Y. The names of his parents are not given. He enlisted in the spring of 1775 in Captain Joseph Morris' company, Colonel Winant's New Jersey regiment and was in the Siege of Quebec. Early in 1776 he enlisted again and served in Captain Daniel Piatt's and Captain William Piatt's companies, Colonel Ogden's First New Jersey regiment. While helping to build Fort Washngton he was wounded by a piece of timber falling on him. He was wounded in the right thigh at the battle of Brandywine and in the left leg in the battle of Monmouth. He was at the surrender of Cornwallis. He was discharged in the latter part of 1783.

Note: Above is a brief statement of John Lusk's revolutionary service. After his discharge he re-enlisted and continued in the United States Army until he was eighty years of age. He is called the greatest private soldier who ever lived. He was in literally scores of engagements and campaigns and only once in his more than fifty years of service was assigned to garrison duty for a short period.

JOSIAH MARTIN

Josiah Martin applied for revolutionary pension while living in Bedford County, Tennessee in 1832 when he was 77 years old. He was, therefore, born in 1755. He stated that his home was in the shadow of King's Mountain but that he was not in that battle owing to a thigh wound accidently received from a spear in the hands of a comrad. He was in the battle of Ramsour's Mill. He served in Captain Barber's company, Colonel McDowell's regiment He married Mary McCleary, daughter of Robert and Abigail McCleary of Mechlenburg, North Carolina. She survived him and drew a pension. She stated that they were married May 28, 1783, in her father's home. Their children were: Abigail, born 1790; Robert, born 1793; Clarissa, born 1796; Marilla born 1799; Polly McDowell, born 1806; and Matilda born 1808.

JAMES LUTTRELL

James Luttrell applied for revolutionary pension which was not allowed because he had served only six months. At the date of his application more than six months' service was required. Later when that requirement was abated he did not again apply. He was born February 12, 1755, in Westmoreland County, Virginia. and was the son of Richard Luttrell who was also a soldier of the Revolution. James Luttrell served in Virginia troops under Captains James Dillard and Charles Christian and Colonels Peter Rose and Charles Lynch. He married Elizabeth Witt, daughter of Abner Witt. Their children were: William, Nancy, James Churchill, Martha, Lewis, Abner, Elizabeth. Sarah, Rhoda and Robert. He died in Knoxville. Tennessee, in 1848.

MATTHEW MARTIN, SR.

Matthew Martin, Sr., applied for revolutionary pension while living in Bedford County, Tennessee, in 1831. He was born in 1763 in Charlotte County, Virginia, and died in Bedford County, in 1846. He served in the Virginia line and was the youngest of eight brothers who served. He served under his brother, George Martin. He married Mary (or Sallie) Clay.

RICHARD MATLOCK

Richard Matlock or Medlock applied for revolutionary pension while residing in Hawkins County, Tennessee, October 4, 1833. He was born in the month of April, 1761, in Granville County, North Carolina. The names of his parents are not given in his application but he states that his father was living in the lower end of Burke County, N. C., during the Revolution. Richard Matlock or Medlock volunteered in Burke County, N. C., April 1, 1779, and served as a private three months in Captain John Montgomery's company, Colonel Joseph McDowell's North Carolina regiment guarding the frontiers from Indians and Tories. He was stationed a part of the time at "Turkey Cove" on the Catawaba River. He served from July 15, 1779, to October 15, 1779, in Captain Henry Reed's company, Colonel Holmes' regiment, in pursuit of Tories and took many prisoners. He served from November 1, 1779, until February 1, 1780, in Captain Reed's company, Colonel Holmes' regiment. He served from January 20, 1781, to the latter part of April, 1781, in Captain Alexander Irvin's company and was in the battle on the Catawaba River in which General Davidson was killed after which he served under General Pope and marched to the Moravian towns. He served from August 1, 1781, to November 1, 1781, in Captain William Nail's company, Colonel McDowell's regiment, in pursuit of Indians on the North Fork of the Catawba River. He married May 10, 1804, in Hawkins County, Mary Weddel, (Weddell, Waddell). He died November 4, 1847, in Hawkins County. His widow Mary Matlock, Medlock, applied for pension April 24, 1854, when she was seventy-four years, two months and fifteen days of age and therefore born in 1780. At the time of her application she lived in Jackson County, Indiana. George W. Medlock (Matlock) made affidavit in 1854 that he knew the soldier and his wife but no relationship is shown in the papers. Notley Thomas, the soldier's brother-in-law is mentioned in 1833. John Weddel (Weddell, Waddell) moved from Tennessee to Indiana in 1814 and was living in Jackson County in 1854.

WILLIAM MAY

Of Sumner County

William May applied for revolutionary pension while living in Sumner County, Tennessee. His name is on the 1832 list and in the 1840 Census. He was born in Wake County, North Carolina, about 1758. He enlisted in Wake County and served in North Carolina troops. He moved to Sumner County, Tennessee, in 1806. He married Susanna ...... December 25, 1786. She survived his death, January 5, 1843, and applied for pension September 4, 1843, giving her age as 75 years. She was therefore born in 1768. Their children were: Caty, born 1788; Nancy, born 1790; Ailey, born 1792; Thomas, born 1794; Mary, born 1796; and William Jr. born after 1796.

Note: Another William May served in Virginia troops and drew pension in McMinn County, Tennessee.

ISRAEL McBEE

Israel McBee applied for revolutionary pension while living in Grainger County before 1832. He was born in 1756 in Pittsylvania County, Virginia. His family moved to Washington County, and in 1778 his father sent him to Pittsylvania County to visit relatives. He enlisted there August 9, 1778, in Virginia troops and was in active service until he was taken prisoner in Buford's Defeat, May 29, 1780, after which he was paroled. He drew pension in Grainger County until after the Census of 1840. When Union County was formed his home was in that county. He married Nancy Hale.

Note: Israel McBee died in Union County in January, 1860. Among his children was Rachel, born 1786 who married John Huddleston, son of David and Sallie Easley Huddleston.

JOHN McCROSKEY

John McCrosky applied for revolutionary pension while living in Sevier County. He was born in Virginia September 26, 1757. He moved with his family to North Carolina and served in Captain William Beattie's company, North Carolina regiment. He was in the Chickamauga Expedition and the battle of King's Mountain. He had a brother, Robert McCroskey, who was also in the Revolution.

Note: He married Ann ...., born August 15, 1766, died March 13, 1829. He died in Blount County, August 15, 1843. They are buried in Eusebia Cemetery, Blount County. Among their children were: Mary, Robert and John Jr.

ROBERT McFARLAND

Robert McFarland applied for revolutionary pension while living in Jefferson County. His name is on the 1832 list. He was born in Virginia, in 1759. His family removed to North Carolina, to the section which became Tennessee. He enlisted in the North Carolina militia. Later he served in the Indian wars.

Note: He married first, Jenny McNutt, the first white child born south of the French Broad river, the daughter of George McNutt. In 1805 he married Mary Neal Cox, widow of ...... Cox, and daughter of Benjamin Neal. Captain McFarland died in Jefferson County in 1834. His fourteen children were: James, John, Jane, Elizabeth, Margreat, Sarah, Polly, Katie, Rachel, Robert, Jr., Malinda, Benjamin F., Dorcas and Keturah. These names are taken from his will, probated in Jefferson County, September 16, 1836.

JOHN McINTYRE

John McIntyre or John McEntire, the name is spelled both ways, in his application, applied for revolutionary pension while he was living in Anderson County, Tennessee, April 18, 1818. In 1820 he referred to his wife as aged sixty-eight years but he did not give her name.

He enlisted October 11, 1777, and served in Captain Adam Wallace's Captain Mallory's companies and in Colonel William Heth's Third Virginia regiment. He was in the Siege of Charleston in May 1780, when he was wounded in the leg, arm and side and taken prisoner. He was held on board a British Warship for fourteen months. He was then released at Jamestown, Virginia. He returned to his home from which he had then been absent about five years. He moved to Tennessee after the Revolution.

WILLIAM McKELVEY

William McKelvey applied for revolutionary pension while living in Rutherford County, Tennessee, when he was 80 years of age. His name is on the 1832 list. He was born about 1744 in Ireland and came to America when he was young. He was the son of William McKelvey. He enlisted in South Carolina in Captain Baldwin's company, Colonel Andrew Pickens' regiment, South Carolina Infantry.

Note: He died in Rutherford County in 1834. He married Mary Mason.

LIEUTENANT DANIEL McKIE

Daniel McKie applied for revolutionary pension while living in Maury County, Tennessee. He was born in Lunenburg County, Virginia, in 1759. He enlisted in Captain Joseph Wynn's company, Virginia troops, and was appointed second lieutenant. He was in the battle of Stone River. He married, in South Carolina, Frances Hernden but her application for a pension after his death was not allowed as she could not prove the marriage. Among their children were Nathaniel Green McKie, who married Mary Rogers; and B. F. McKie, born 1811, died 1852, who married twice, his second wife being Sally Horton. Daniel McKie, the revolutionary soldier, died in Maury County, Tennessee in 1839.

ROBERT MCMINN

Robert McMinn applied for revolutionary pension while living in Hawkins County, Tennessee, September 3, 1833. He was born January 12, 1764, in Chester County, Penn., and moved when he was a few years of age with his father, to Frederick County Maryland.

While he resided in Frederick County he enlisted in Colonel Price's Maryland Regiment. He enlisted sometime in September 1781 and served six months in Captain Cobble's company under Major Miller. He guarded prisoners taken when Cornwallis surrendered. His pension application does not mention wife or children but does refer to a sister who lived in Virginia, although her name is not given.

SAMUEL McSPADDEN

Samuel McSpadden applied for revolutionary pension while living in Jefferson County, Tennessee, and his name is on the 1832 list and in the 1840 Census. He was born in Virginia and died in Jefferson County, Tennessee, in 1844. He served in Captain Campbell's company, Colonel Dickerson's Virginia regiment.

Note: In 1840 he was living with T. N. McSpadden. He married twice, first Sally Keys, who died in 1798.

WILLIAM MITCHELL

William Mitchell applied for revolutionary pension while living in Rutherford County, Tennessee. His name is on the 1832 list and in the 1840 Census. He was born about 1763 in North Carolina. He served in North Carolina troops and was in the battles of Cowpens, Guilford Court House and King's Mountain.

Note: He died in Rutherford County, in 1850. He married Elizabeth Currey, born 1773, died 1828. Among their children was Addison, born 1811, died 1862, who married Mary Ann Hodges.

CAPTAIN ELIJAH MOORE

Elijah Moore's widow, Susan Mitchell Moore, applied for revolutionary pension while living in Sumner County, Tennessee. He was a lieutenant in 1779 and a captain in 1781, in North Carolina troops. He was born in Granville County, N. C., in 1753. He died in 1800 or 1806 in Sumner County. He married Susan Mitchell in 1781. She was born 1765, died 1839, and was the daughter of David Mitchell.

JOHN MOORE

John Moore applied for revolutionary pension while living in Bedford County, Tennessee. His name is on the 1832 list and in the 1840 Census. He was born about 1761. He served in Captain Robert Gillespie's company, North Carolina troops.

Note: He was in the Tennessee country by 1783 as his name is on the Greene County Tax list in that year. He moved from Greene County to what was then West Tennessee, where he died in 1842. He is buried in Mount Moriah Church Cemetery, between Shelbyville and Wartrace, Tennessee. He married Eleanor Marbrey. Their son, John Moore married Nancy Yell.

THOMAS MOORE

Thomas Moore applied for pension while living in Rhea County, when he was 103 years of age. He was born in Granville County, North Carolina, about 1725. He served in North Carolina troops and was in the battle of Cowpens where he lost a thumb. He was also in the battles of Gate's Defeat, Guilford Court House, Eutaw Springs and King's Mountain.

LIEUTENANT COLONEL WILLIAM MOORE

William Moore applied for revolutionary pension while living in Smith County. His name is on the 1832 list. He was born in North Carolina about 1751. He served as Lieutenant Colonel of an Orange County, North Carolina regiment.

Note: He died in Smith County in December 1823. Among his children was Jane, who married Charles Carter.

BENJAMIN MORGAN

Benjamin Morgan applied for revolutionary pension in Davidson County. His name is on the 1832 list and in the 1840 Census. He was born about 1762 in Faquier County, Virginia. He served in Captain Hank Read's company, Colonel Pendleton's Virginia regiment.

Note: He died in Davidson County in 1841. He married in 1782 Elizabeth Kemper. Among their children was John Morgan who married Ann W. Norman.

LESTER MORRIS

Lester Morris applied for revolutionary pension while living in Giles County Tennessee. His name is on the 1832 list and in the 1840 Census. He was born about 1759 in Brunswick County, Virginia, and enlisted in Virginia troops. He served in the battles of Savannah and Charleston and was wounded and captured in the battle of Charleston. From about the year 1840 he made his home with his son-in-law, Thomas A. Westmoreland.

Note: He died in Giles County in 1853. He married Frances Brown. Among their children were Susan, who married Philip Pipkin; and Elizabeth, who married Thomas A. Westmoreland.

WILLIAM MURPHEY

William Murphey applied for revolutionary pension while living in Greene County, Tennessee. He was born in 1759. He enlisted in Bedford County, Virginia, Militia in 1776. He served in Colonel Christian's regiment in the Cherokee Expedition. He substituted for William Cannon in Captain Robert Sevier's company. He was appointed ensign in 1779 and served in Georgia. In 1782 he served against Indians under Captain Wood of Greene County, Tennessee. He was discharged in Greene County.

Noe: He died in Greene County November 2, 1833. He had a half brother. David Murphey, born 1769. William Murphey married Rachel ...., born November 15, 1764, died January 26, 1782. Their son, John Murphey, was born 1782.

EDWARD NUNNELEE

Edward Nunnelee applied for revolutionary pension while living in Hickman County, September 10, 1832, at which time he was seventy-six years of age. He died at his home in that county April 19, 1836. He lived with his parents in Virginia at the time of his enlistment. Their names are not given, nor the place or time of his birth, but he was evidently born in 1756. He entered the service in 1775, as a private in Captain Faulkner's company, under Colonels Eppes and Isaac Read, in Virginia troops.

His father died during the first year of service. He returned to his mother's home and enlisted again in Captain Thomas Boyer's company, and was in the battles of Guilford Court House, Camden, Friday's Fort, Eutaw Springs and the Siege of Ninety-six.

He was discharged January 6, 1782, having served eighteen months. He moved to Tennessee before 1817, at which time he was residing in Hickman County.

He married June 8, 1817 (1819 and 1820 are also given) in Hickman County, Mary Ann Sunderland, a widow. She was the widow of Nathaniel Sunderland. Her maiden name was Reeves. She was born June 26, 1800. She drew pension for the service and death of Nathaniel Sunderland, in the War of 1812, applying for that pension March 2, 1853.

She drew pension for the service of Edward Nunnalee in the Revolution. Her application for that pension was made November 7, 1853. She also received bounty land for the service of each husband. She died near Centerville, Tenn., November 10, 1882.

Note: This is the only pension record I have seen in which a widow drew pension for two husbands. It is interesting also that her first husband served in 1812 and her second husband in the Revolution.

JOHN PERKINS

John Perkins applied for revolutionary pension while living in Hardin County, Tennessee. He was born in Halifax, Va., May 11, 1765. His father died when he was very young and he took the name of his mother's second husband, Thomas Carson. He enlisted in April, 1781, under that name, but he received his pension under his own name, John Perkins. He served with Captain James Turner in the Siege of Ninety-six. He moved to Caswell County, N. C., in 1782 and served with Captain Elijah Moore and Captain Rhodes and was discharged at Ten Mile House near Charleston. When his step-father died in 1782 he began to be called by his own name. He married Frances ....

ZEBULON SMITH

Zebulon Smith applied for revolutionary pension while residing in Sullivan County, September 24, 1832, when he was "aged seventy-four past." The date and place of his birth and the names of his parents are not given in his pension application. He enlisted while a resident of Sullivan County, then in Virginia and served as a private in Virginia and North Carolina troops. In the fall of 1778 he was three months in Captain Wallace's company in Colonel Isaac Shelby's regiment; in the fall of 1778 he was three months in Captain Jonathan Webb's company in Colonel Shelby's regiment; in the spring of 1780 he was three months in Captain William Asher's company and was a substitute for Solomon Smith (no relationship indicated); in the fall of 1780 he was three months again in Captain Webb's company in Colonel Shelby's regiment; in the fall of 1781 he was three months in Captain Wallace's or Captain Topp's company in Colonel Shelby's regiment; immediately afterward he enlisted and served one year in Captain McKelvey's company in Colonel Moore's regiment; from the fall of 1782 he served three months in Captain John Scott's company in Colonel John Sevier's regiment.

DAVID TATE

David Tate applied for revolutionary pension while living in Grainger County. He was born about 1757 in Augusta County, Virginia. He was the son of David and Catherine Thornton Tate. He enlisted in Botetourt County. Virginia, while living in that County,, in 1780 and served until 1782. He served under Captain Ballard Smith and Captain Thomas Boyer and Colonels Buford and Campbell. He was in the battle of Ninety-six and Eutaw Springs. He married Comfort Knox, August 18, 1784, in Botetourt County.

Note: David Tate died August 7, 1838. in Grainger County. His wife, born 1767 in Virginia, died in Grainger County, 1841. They are buried at Shiloh Church, near Rutledge, Tennessee. Their children were: Edward, born 1785; Lucy Moody, born 1792; Margaret; David, Jr., John Knox, Samuel Baker, Elisha: William Thornton. Harvey and Milton.

DANIEL TAYLOR

Daniel Taylor applied for revolutionary pension while living in Grainger County, Tennessee. He was born in Cumberland County, Virginia, August 13, 1761 and was the son of James and Nancy Ann Owen Taylor. He enlisted in Virginia troops and served in the battle of Shallow Ford on the Yadkin. He married Jane Rowland, in Henry County. Virginia, in 1780.

Note: Daniel Taylor died in Grainger County, November 25, 1834. Jane Rowland Taylor, born in Virginia in 1761 died in Grainger County in 1843. They moved to Grainger County about the close of 1795. They had thirteen children: George, born 1781; Morgan, born 1782; Kaziah, born 1784; Grinefield, born 1785;" Desdemona, born 1788; Elizabeth, bobrn 1790; Mourning, born 1791; Daniel, Jr., born 1793; Hughes Owen, born 1796; James, born 1798; Nancy, born 1793; Jane, born 1802; and William, born 1805.

ALEXANDER TRENT

Alexander Trent applied for revolutionary pension while living in Hawkins County, Tennessee. He was born March 29, 1759, in Chesterfield County. Virginia. He enlisted while living in Bedford County. Virginia. in the spring of 1779, in Captain Terrill's Company,

Virginia Troops and was in the Siege of Savannah, after which he was discharged having served the time of his enlistment. He enlisted again and served in Captain Thomas McConnell's company. He enlisted again and served in Captain Thomas Read's company, Colonel William Davis' regiment. After the Revolution he lived in Virginia and moved to Tennessee. He died in Hawkins County, May 17, 1841.

He married sometime in 1792 in Grayson County, Virginia, Jane Burton. They were married by Rev. Vincent Jones, a Baptist minister. She survived her husband and in 1843 she was 78 years of age. She was born in 1765 and died in 1843.

SAMUEL VANCE

Samuel Vance applied for revolutionary pension while living in Greene County, September 4, 1832, when he was seventy-eight years of age. He was therefore born in 1754 although the date and place of his birth are not given in his application. He volunteered in Washington County, Virginia, in 1774 and served eight weeks against Shawnee Indians under Captain Evan Shelby and General Lewis and during this enlistment he was in the battle of Point Pleasant. He enlisted again May 4 or 5, 1777 and served one month in Captain James Montgomery's Virginia company; he then served under Lieutenant George Brooks in Colonel Martin's Virginia regiment. He served two weeks as a guard at Captain Shelby's house and from three to five months in Captain Andrew Colville's company, Colonel William Campbell's Virginia regiment. He was in the battle of King's Mountain during this enlistment. He served one month in Colonel John Sevier's North Carolina regiment and was in the battle of Big Hiwassee. He died in Greene County September 1, 1838, leaving a widow whose name is not given in the pension papers.

THOMAS VERNON

Thomas Vernon applied for revolutionary pension while living in Monroe County. He enlisted in Virginia troops under Captain Joseph Michaux and Colonel Charles Lewis. He was transferred to Captain Nathan Reed's company. He was in the battles of Brandywine, Germantown, Stony Point and Monmouth. He was born in 1754 in Virginia. He died in Monroe County, Tennessee, in 1841. He married Nannie Hicks.

JOHN WALKER

Of Blount County

John Walker applied for revolutionary pension while living in Blount County. He was born in Ireland in 1747 and died in 1837 in Blount County, Tennessee. He served in N. C., troops. When he came from Ireland he lived for a time in Pennsylvania where his son, David, was born in 1781. He married Mary Johnston, born in 1758, died November 12 1845, who applied for pension in Blount County in 1844. She was a sister of Joseph Johnston. Among their children were David, born in Pennsylvania in 1781; died Blount County, Tennessee, in 1864, who married Jane Johnston.

JOHN WALKER

Of Roane County

John Walker applied for pension in Roane County, Tennessee. He enlisted in the 3rd regiment, Virginia Rragoons, August 11, 1777, for a three years' term. He was in the battle of Monmouth and the Siege of Charleston. He married March 12, 1782, Jane Boyd who died July 24, 1836. They had ten children among them John B. Walker.

MESHACH WILLIS

Meshach Willis applied for revolutionary pension while he was living in Maury County, April 23, 1818. The date and place of his birth and the names of his parents are not given in his pension application. He enlisted February 3, 1777, and served as a sergeant in Captains Jesse Walton and Edward Wood's companies in Colonel Stirk's (Stark?) Georgia regiment. He was discharged February 3, 1780. There are no data in his pension record regarding his family but in 1818 he signed his application as 'Meshach Willis, senior.

SAMUEL WILLIAMS

Samuel Williams applied for pension in Wilson County, Tennessee. He was born in Gates County, N. C., in 1762. He died in Wilson County, after 1840. He enlisted while living in North Carolina in 1776 under Captain West Harris and was an orderly sergeant under Captain James Alston and was later a cornet. He served until the close of the War, after which he moved to the section which became Wilson County, Tennessee. He married Ruth Davidson.

WILLOUGHBY WILLIAMS

Willoughby Williams died June 6, 1802, in Rutledge, Tennessee, while enroute to Davidson County. The date of birth and the names of his parents are not shown in the pension papers of his widow. While he was a resident of Dobbs County, North Carolina, he enlisted in 1776, as a private in Colonel Abraham Shepherd's regiment, and served in all about seven years. He was in the battle of Cowpens, where he was wounded in the right leg. He married, January 1, 1786, Nancy Glasgow, daughter of James Glasgow, Secretary of State of North Carolina. They were married in James Glasgow's home.

Willoughby Williams served as a member of the North Carolina Legislature from Dobbs County, in 1790. Hi swidow, Nancy Glasgow Williams, married August 4, 1806, in Kingston, Tennessee, Joseph McMinn, Governor of Tennessee, who died at the home of his stepson, J. G. Williams, in Calhoun at the Cherokee Agency.

Nancy Glasgow Williams McMinn was allowed pension on account of the services of her first husband, Willoughby Williams. She applied for pension March 8, 1848, when she was a resident of Davidson County, Tennessee, and was then seventy-seven years old, and therefore born in 1771. She died June 27, 1857. She had no children by her second marriage. By her first marriage she had six children: one son was J. G. Williams. The sixth child, Willoughby Williams, Jr., born 14, 1798, was living in Nashville in 1851. The widow, Nancy McMinn, was living in Wilson County in 1840.

BURGES WITT

Burgess (Bergis) Witt applied for revolutionary pension while living in McMinn County, Tennessee, in 1818. He was born in 1765 in Virginia. He was the son of Hezekiah Witt. He enlisted in North Carolina troops in 1781 under Captain William Little and Colonel Archibald Little. He married Elizabeth Mayo. Their children were: Hezekiah, Valentine, Mary Burgess, William and Ephraim.

Note. Burgess Witt died in Monroe County, Tennessee, December 16, 1843.

CALEB WITT

Caleb Witt's widow, Miriam Horner Witt, daughter of Charles Horner, applied for pension while living in Jefferson County, Tennessee, November 30, 1844, because of her husband's service. She was born in 1768, and died in 1844. She married Caleb Witt September 2, 1784, in Washington County, Tennessee. Caleb Witt who was a Baptist preacher, was born in Halifax County, Virginia, September 2, 1762. He died in Jefferson County, Tennessee. He died near Russellville, Tennessee, and is buried in old Bent Creek Cemetery. He enlisted in Halifax County, Virginia, under Captain James Hill and Colonel Campbell. He served also under Colonel Henry Conway, and was present at the Surrender of Cornwallis. He received bounty land from Virginia for his service.

RECORDS OF SOME REVOLUTIONARY PENSIONERS WHO DID NOT LIVE IN TENNESSEE BUT WHO HAVE TENNESSEE DESCENDANTS OR SOME OTHER TENNESSEE INTEREST

WILLIAM ALEXANDER

Of North Carolina

William Alexander applied for revolutionary pension in Wilkes County, North Carolina, October 30, 1832, when he was eighty years of age. He was born in Cumberland County, Virginia, April 15, 1752. He served in Virginia troops as a private.

JAMES ARMSTRONG

Of South Carolina

James Armstrong, whose name appears on the list of invalid pensioners of Abbyville District, South Carolina, was a private, service unknown. His pension commenced November 15, 1811, at $60 per annum and was increased to $96 per annum on April 24, 1816. There are no other data on file in regard to the soldier owing to the destruction of papers in pension claims when the British burned the City of Washington in 1814.

SYLVESTER BUGBEE

Of Vermont

Sylvester Bugbee applied for revolutionary pension while living in Orange County, Vermont, District of Bradford. He was born June 12, 1760. He died after 1833 and before 1843. He enlisted April 1, 1778, before he was eighteen years of age, in Captain Solomon Cushman's company. Colonel Timothy Bedel's New Hampshire regiment. He was discharged at the end of his tour and enlisted again in the spring of 1780 in a company commanded by Captain Jesse Safford. Colonel Benjamin Wait commanded the regiment. He married Jemima ——— September, 1793. She was born in 1766. She survived her husband and applied for a widow's pension June 24, 1843. They had two sons, one had died by 1843 but in that year one of the sons, Stephen Bugbee, who was born September 2, 1800, was living in Newbury, Vermont.

JOHN CAMPBELL

Of Ohio

John Campbell applied for revolutionary pension while residing in Cuyahoga County, Ohio, in 1832. He was born May 11, 1762, in Blanford, Hampshire County, Masachusetts. While he was a resident of New York he enlisted and served in New York troops as follows: one month, August, 1778, in Captain Van Alstyne's company, Colonel John Harper's regiment; from September, 1779, six weeks in Captain Mc-Gonegal's company, Colonel Beebe's regiment; from March, 1780, in Captain Walter Vrooman's company, Colonel John Harper's regiment. He was transferred in May, 1780, to Captain Titus' company. Colonel Weissenfel's regiment, in which he served nine months and fifteen days; from March, 1781, he served nine months in Captain Holt Dunham's company, Colonel McKinstry's regiment; from January, 1782, until the latter part of 1782, he was in Captain Job Wright's company, Colonel Marinus Willett's regiment. In 1792 he moved to Bainbridge, Chenango, County, New York; in 1808 he moved to Marcellus, Onondaga County, New York; and in 1823 he moved to Cuyahoga County, Ohio. In December, 1845, he had moved to Orangeville, Wyoming County, New York, to live with a son.

TIMOTHY CORN

Of Kentucky

Timothy Corn applied for revolutionary pension while living in Mercer County, Kentucky, September 1, 1834. He was then 74 years of age and so born in 1760. The place of his birth is not given in his pension application but in March, 1870, his father and family emigrated from Redstone, Pa., to the mouth of Bear Grass Creek near the Falls of the Ohio. In the same month they took refuge in the Fort on account of Indian attacks. They remained in the Fort until December and Timothy Corn served as a guard under Captain Richard Chenoweth and Colonel Linn, commandant of the Fort. In December Timothy and his father left the Fort and went to Mercer County, Kentucky, in the neighborhood of McGary's Fort. Timothy enlisted there in the spring of 1781. He enlisted again and in the fall of 1782 and served for another short time. Meanwhile he had service in scouting trips and he states in his application that his entire service included "upwards of sixteen months." All his service was under Colonel George Rogers Clark in Virginia troops.

He married in Harrodsburg, Mercer County Kentucky, Mrs. Elizabeth Yeast. The marriage bond is dated June 23, 1831. As he was then 71 years of age it is probable that the marriage was his second as well as his wife's second. After the death of Timothy Corn the widow stated that her son was married in April after her marriage to Timothy Corn in the previous July. This son was probably named Yeast, although his name is not given in her pension application.

WILLIAM EYL

Of Virginia

William Ely applied for revolutionary pension while living in Lee County, Virginia, March 31, 1819. He was born March 25, 1753. He does not give the place of his birth in his application papers. He enlisted in Bedford County, Virginia, February 15, 1799, and served as a private in Captains Woodson and Lawson's companies, Colonel Abraham Buford's Virginia regiment. He was in the battle called Buford's Defeat, where he received a saber wound in the head and shoulder and where he was taken prisoner. He was released on parole in a few days. In 1820 he makes reference to his wife but does not give her name, and refers to his son, John afe about eighteen years.

JAMES HIXSON

Of Virginia

James Hixson applied for revolutionary pension while living in Loudoun County, Virginia, in October, 1832. He died in that county in 1833. He was born in 1763, in New Jersey, and moved in 1772 with his parents to prince William County, Virginia. He enlisted in Prince William County in August 1780, and marched in Captain Farrow's company to Dumfries and Fredericksburg, where he was placed in Captain Berry's company. Later he served under Captain Loveless and Captain Marshall. In December, 1780, he enlisted in Lee's Legion. He was in the battles of Guilford Court House, Fort Watson, Fort Motte, Fort Granby, Fort Galphin, Augusta and the Siege of Ninety-Six. He served until the close of the war. He stated in his pension application that his name was borne on the rolls of Lee's Legion as

William Hixson. He married December 19, 1822, in Fauquier County, Virginia, Mary Hampton. She was his third wife but he does not give the names of his other wives. She applied for pension in Fauquier County, in 1853, when she was sixty-three years of age. She was therefore born in 1780. She died July 16, 1856. Seven children survived James Hixson but their names are not stated in the application. David Hixson testified in Loudoun County, Va., in 1832, and Benjamin Hixson in Loudoun County in 1853, but their relationship to the family is not given.

P. Augustus Klipstein, son-in-law of the widow, Mary Hampton Hixson was living in Salem, Faupuier County, in 1853.

LIEUTENANT ROBERT HANNA
Of South Carolina

Robert Hanna applied for revolutionary pension while living in York District, South Carolina, October 16, 1832. He was born April 1, 1761, eight miles east of Charlotte in Mecklenburg County, North Carolina. He moved to York District, South Carolina, where he was living in June, 1775, when he enlisted under Colonel Neel against the Cherokee Indians. He enlisted again in 1778 in Captain Robert McFee's company, Colonel Neel's regiment. He enlisted again in 1779 and served in Captain Richard Sadler's company, Colonel Neel's regiment. In 1780 he was captured by the British and imprisoned at Camden, S. C., for eight weeks when he was released on parole. He broke his parole, volunteered again and served at various times until the evacuation of Charleston, S. C.

He was appointed lieutenant under Major William Hanna and Colinel William Bratton of South Carolina troops and was in the battles of Fish Dam Ford, Blackstocks, Fridays Fort, Quarter House and Biggin's Church.

He was a ruling elder in the Bethesda congregation, Presbyterian Church, York District. He died March 25, 1841, in York District. He married, date not stated, Mary ...... who was born March 23, 1761. She died before the soldier died. Their children were: Charles Moore, born 1784; Jane Black, born 1786; James, born 1788; Rosenny Berry and Violet Moore, (twins) born 1790; Mary Berry, born 1792; William, born 1794; Robert Cunningham and Betsey Cunningham, (twins) born 1796; Alexander born 1799; Patsey, born 1802; Pagey, born 1804, and Thomas M. C., born 1806.

The following children were living when the soldier died: Dr. Charles M. Hanna, Violet Hanna McCorkle, William Hanna, Margaret Hanna Stafford (probably Patsey), Thomas Hanna and Jane Black Hanna McCorkle.

In 1848 the soldier's sister, Deborah Hanna Watson, aged 81 years stated that she had three brothers in the Revolution, William, Robert and James. William was a Captain and major; Robert was a lieutenant and quartermaster and was imprisoned at Camden but their father, James Hanna, secured his release.

Note: This pension application gives an unusual amount of family information.

JOHN LATHAM
Of Virginia

John Lathab applied for revolutionary pension while living in Harrison County, Virginia. He was born in Stafford County, Virginia, in 1764. He enlisted in that county and served in the Virginia Continental line from 1781 to March 1782 and from the summer of 1783 to November, 1783, under Colonel Haws, Captain William Ballard, Captain Thomas Mountjoy, Captain Fitzpatrick and Captain Johnson. He was in the battle of Yorktown. He married Winifred St. Clair.

Note: He died in Harrison County, now West Virginia, in 1835. His children were: John, James, William, Sarah, St. Clair, Peter, Travis, Bley and two other sons and two daughters.

ZELA RENO
Of Kentucky

Zela Reno (the name also appears Zely Reno) applied for revolutionary pension while living in Harrison County, Kentucky, February 13. 1833. He was born April 3, 1757, in Prince William County, Virginia. He enlisted in Prince William County, Virginia troops in the minute service uniformed in "a purple hunting shirt marked in the breast in large letters 'Libberty or Death' with Macaroni hat and bucktail" under Captain Cuthbert Harrison and Colonel Jesse Ewell. He enlisted again under Captain Henry Hoe or Hough, Colonel Jesse Ewell's regiment. He enlisted again in Captain Simon Hancock's company, Colonel Mathews' regiment.

After the Revolution he lived in Prince William and Loudoun Counties, Virginia, until 1784 when he moved to Fayette County, Kentucky, where he resided for some years. He then lived in Harrison and Bourbon Counties, Kentucky. He died January 30 or 31, 1837.

He married August 3, 1775, at her father's residence in Fauquier County, Virginia, Mary, the daughter of Charles Chinn. She applied for pension in 1838 when she was eighty-four years of age and a resident of Bourbon County, Virginia. There are no references to children.

THOMAS PORTER
Of Virginia

Thomas Porter applied for revolutionary pension in Louisa County, Virginia, November 12, 1833. He was then 82 years of age and therefore born in 1751. He was a brother of Lieutenant William Porter who drew pension in Caldwell County, Kentucky. One Thomas Porter, Captain of Virginia Rangers, died in Wilkes County, Georgia.

MARTIN PRUITT

Martin Pruitt applied for revolutionary pension while living in Madison County, Illinois, in September, 1832 when he was 84 years of age. He was therefore born 1748. He enlisted while living in Washington County, Virginia, in Captain William Campbell's company as a spy and served for two years. When Captain Campbell was promoted to be a Colonel, Martin Pruitt served in Captain William Edmiston's company. He was in the battle of King's Mountain. No family data are included in his pension application. He died February 4, 1841.

ABRAHAM RANDOLPH

Of Alabama

Abraham Randolph applied for revolutionary pension while living in Lawrence County, Alabama, in January, 1832. He was born in 1762. He enlisted in Caswell County, North Carolina, in 1780 in the company of Captain James Willson, and Lieutenant Walter Tate. Other officers in his brigade were General Butler, Colonel William Moore and Major Elijah Moore. He was discharged after his tour of service and re-enlisted the army in 1781 again under General Butler. He lived in North Carolina for ten or twelve years after the Revolution and then moved to South Carolina where he resided for twenty-five or twenty-six years after which he moved to Lawrence County, Alabama.

JOHN SMOOT

Of Kentucky

John Smoot applied for revolutionary pension while living in Hardin County, Kentucky, in September, 1832. He was born May 11, 1755. He enlisted in 1775 and served under Colonel Daniel Morgan until July 1776. He enlisted again when he was living in Frederick County, Virginia, and served until the fall of 1780. In the fall of 1781 he enlisted again and was at the surrender of Yorktown.

JOHN WEIR

Of Vermont

John Weir applied for revolutionary pension while residing in Putney, Westminster District, Windham County, Vermont, in 1833. John Weir was born in Londonderry, New Hampshire, August 24, 1757. While residing in Hampstead, New Hampshire. he volunteered in April, 1775, in Captain French's New Hampshire company and was discharged in June, 1775. He enlisted again in June, 1777, in Captain Roger Gilmore's New Hampshire company and was discharged in August, 1777. He re-enlisted in August, 1777, in Captain Daniel Rand's company, Colonel Benjamin Bellows' company New Hampshire regiment. He was discharged in October 1777. He volunteered again in 1780 or 1781 in Captain Levi Hooper's New Hampshire company. After the Revolution he moved from New Hampshire to Grafton, Vermont, and later lived in Windham county, Vermont. He died June 5, 1837, in Putney, Vermont. He married December 2, 1784, at Westmorland, Cheshire County, New Hampshire, Rebecca Livingston, who was born in October, 1762. She survived him and applied for pension in September, 1838. She died December 29, 1852.

JOHN WILSON

Of Alabama

John Wilson applied for revolutionary pension while living in B.bb County, Alabama, in 1832 when he was 72 years of age. He was born December 20, 1760, in Mecklenburg County, North Carolina. He resided in Mecklenburg County when he entered the service in August, 1780, under Major Davis of the Waxaw Settlement. Some of his other officers were Captains Nathaniel Martin and Giles, General Sumpter, Colonel Hill and General Greene. He knew General Washington who was taken prisoner at Eutaw Springs, General Sumpter and Colonel Lee. He was in the battles of Gate's Defeat, Hanging Rock and Eutaw Springs. After the Revolution he moved to Georgia, then returned to Mecklenburg County, North Carolina, and then moved to Bibb County, Alabama where he continued to reside.

JOHN WILSON

Of North Carolina, Duplin County

John Wilson's widow, Elizabeth Wilson, applied for pension because of the revolutionary service of her husband, when she lived in Duplin County, North Carolina, in July, 1839, and was then 66 years of age. She stated that her husband served under Captain Shuffield. Enclosed is a paper with the following names and dates, (presumably the children of her marriage to John Wilson): Daniel Wilson, born 1793; Alexander Wilson, born 1795; James Wilson, born 1798; Rebecca Wilson, born 1802; Catherine Wilson, born 1804; David Wilson, born 1806; Thomas Wilson, born (......); Elizabeth Wilson, born 1813; Mary Wilson, born 1814; Sarah Jane Wilson, born 1818; and Morgan Wilson, born 18.....

JOHN WILSON

Of North Carolina, Johnston County

John Wilson's only child, Betty Wilson, applied for pension based on her father's revolutionary service, while living in Johnston County, North Carolina, July 30, 1855. John Wilson's widow, Patty Wilson, survived him but was deceased in 1855. Betty Wilson, the applicant, referred to her uncle William Wilson and his wife, Elizabeth Wilson, She stated that John Wilson was a soldier in Captain Walsh's Eighth regiment; that he entered the service January 1, 1777, for three years; and that he was a corporal in 1778. The mariage of John Wilson and Patty Davis took place September 14, 1785. The claim was rejected.

JOHN WILSON

Of South Carolina

John Wilson applied for revolutionary pension while living in Pendleton District, South Carolina, in 1833, when he was aged 77 years. He was born in Pennsylvania in 1755. He moved with his father's family to North Carolina and was living at Guilford Court House when he enlisted in the serfice. He served three tours, volunteering first, then being drafted, and volunteering again for the third tour. He was in the battle of Brier Creek. About four years after the War he moved from Guilford Court House, North Carolina, to Pendleton District, South Carolina, where he continued to reside.

AIRES WITT
Of Kentucky

Aires Witt applied for revolutionary pension while living in Whitley County, Kentucky. He was born in 1761 in Halifax County, Virginia. He enlisted in April, 1780, in North Carolina Troops in Guilford County, North Carolina, under Captain Beshears and Colonel Porterfield and in 1781 he enlisted under Captain Miner Smith and Colonel James Martin. He was in the battles of Hanging Rock, Camden, Drowning Creek, White Swamp, and Brick House.

Note: He died December 15, 1840 in Whitley County, Kentucky. His children were Samuel and William Witt.

ELISHA WITT
Of Kentucky

Elisha Witt applied for revolutionary pension while living in Estill County, Kentucky. He was born September 18, 1759, in Albemarle County, Virginia. He enlisted in Amherst County, Virginia, and served in Virginia troops in the years 1776, 1777, 1778, 1779, 1780, 1781, under Captains Richard Ballenger, John Jacobs, John Biggs and William Harris, and Colonels Hugh Row, Francis Tadlor and John Pope. He was at the Siege of Yorktown and at the Surrender of Cornwallis. He married July 17, 1781, Phebe Dodd.

Note: He died December 16, 1835, in Estill County, Kentucky. His children were William, Annie, Charles, Abner, Elisha, Nathan, Rachel, David, John and Silas.

ROBERT WITT
Of Kentucky

Robert Witt applied for revolutionary pension while living in Logan County, Kentucky. He was born in Bedford County, Virginia, April 24, 1765. He enlisted in that county April 24, 1780 and served until 1783 under Captain John Baley and Colonel George Rogers Clark in Virginia troops. He married Nancy Reese.

Note: He died March 31, 1849. His children were William, Martha, Sarah Rhoda and Rebecca.

Some Tennessee Heroes

of the

Revolution

PAMPHLET NO. V

ELIJAH ALEXANDER

Elijah Alexander applied for revolutionary pension while living in Maury County, Tennessee, September 11, 1832. He was then 72 years of age. He stated that he was born in Mechlinburg County, North Carolina, in 1760, as recorded in his father's family Bible. He remained in Mechlinburg County until 1819 when he moved to Maury County, Tennessee. In March, 1780, Colonel Thomas Polk made a demand on nearby companies of men to guard a magazine. With the consent of Elijah Alexander's father Elijah entered the service under Captain Thomas Alexander and served three months. Shortly after that the father, William Alexander, sent Elijah to Maryland. After returning he enlisted again in February, 1781. Smallpox appeared in camp and Moses Alexander, brother of the Governor of North Carolina, died. Elijah Alexander was sent home to be inoculated. He enlisted again and rendezvoused at Charlotte under Colonel Thomas Polk and Captain James Jack in March, 1781.

Sarah Alexander, widow of Elijah Alexander, applied for widow's pension November 21, 1850, while living in Giles County, Tennessee, aged 88 years. She stated that Elijah Alexander died in Giles County, November 11, 1850. She stated that she was married to the soldier at the home of her grandfather, in Mechlinburg County, N.C. in June, 1783, by ——— Giles, a Justice of the Peace. She stated that her late husband's sister, Ruth Clark, living in Iowa, 86 years of age in 1850, was present at the wedding. In 1855 Mrs. Sarah Alexander had removed from Tennessee to Mississippi.

Note:- This is one of the most interesting pension declarations as Elijah's statement is entirely in his own handwriting. The widow stated that they lived together for sixty-six years but no children are mentioned.

LIEUTENANT RICHARD ALLEN

Richard Allen applied for a revolutionary pension while living in Roane County, Tennessee, October 23, 1832, at which time he was seventy-nine years of age. He enlisted in Goochland County, Va., in 1776, in Captain John Flemming's company, Colonel Patrick Henry's Virginia regiment. He served in Colonel Henry's regiment until Patrick Henry was elected Governor of Virginia. Richard Allen then served in Colonel Eppes' First Virginia regiment. He was in the battle of Long Bridge, in Norfolk when it was burned by the British and in several skirmishes during a service of one year. He then re-enlisted for three years. He became ill and went to his father's home in Goochland County, for six months. He was then appointed Lieutenant of a company of Minute Men. He was in several engagements and in the Siege of Yorktown. He received his discharge in October, 1781.

FRANCIS ANTRICAN

Francis Antrican applied for revolutionary pension February 4, 1839, while living in Grainger County, Tennessee. He was then seventy-five years of age and therefore born in 1764. He enlisted at Orange County Court House, North Carolina. He served in the First Regiment North Carolina State Line, under Colonel Henry Dickson. He was in the battle of Eutaw Springs. He was discharged in May, 1782, and immediately re-enlisted. Later he returned to his home which was about fifteen miles from Orange County Court House. After five years he moved to Greene County, Tennessee, near Babb's Mill. In 1793 he joined a company which served under Captain John Casey and Colonel John Sevier, against the Cherokees. His whole service included 32 months and 7 days.

ISAAC ARCHER

Isaac Archer applied for revolutionary pension while living in Sullivan County, Tennessee, September 29, 1818. He enlisted in Captain Adam Wallace's and Captain White's companies in Colonel Davis's Virginia regiment. He was in the battle of Monmouth and in Buford's Defeat. He served three years when he received a discharge. Twelve months later he re-enlisted and served in Captain Thomas's company and Captain Johnston's company in Colonel How's Virginia regiment. In 1820 he was living in Sullivan County when he stated that he was seventy-one years of age the "twelfth day of last January." He was therefore born January 12, 1749. He died May 13, 1824.

JAMES ARMSTRONG

James Armstrong applied for revolutionary pension while residing in Maury County, Tennessee, in 1832. He was then 68 years of age. He entered the service in what was then Camden and is now Sumpter District, S. C., under Captain Robert McCottery. He stated that in the fall of 1780 he joined Captain John Armstrong's company under Francis Marion. He stated that in the spring of 1782 he joined the regular corps of General Marion and Maj. John Bamble and that he was discharged in December, 1782, near Monk's Corner about 32 miles from Charleston. He stated that he was born in Camden District, now Sumpter District, April 6, 1764 and that in 1805 he moved to Tennessee and in 1809 settled in Maury County, Tennessee.

His declaration was attested by Samuel Mayers, William James Frierson and Duncan Crown, clergyman.

On May 1, 1833, James Armstrong filed an amended declaration with further facts as to his war service.

JOHN ARMSTRONG
of Smith County

John Armstrong applied for revolutionary pension while living in Smith County, Tenn., in 1825. He was then 72 years of age and therefore born in 1753. He enlisted in 1777 in N. C., in the company

130

commanded by Captain Alsey High and the regiment commanded by Colonel Archibald Lytle. He received his discharge in December, 1777, in South Carolina. He mentioned his wife Rebecca as then living.

JOHN BANES

John Banes enlisted in Mecklenburg County, Virginia, in 1779. He served five terms of three months each and one term of six months under Captain Peter Bennett, Captain George Ferrington, Colonel William Moore, Colonel Ambrose Ramsey, Colonel Joseph Taylor and Major Joel Lewis. He was in the battle of Camden. After the Revolution he moved to Sumner County, Tenn., and then to Perry County, Ill., where he died September 2, 1840. He drew a pension.

JACOB BEELER OR BEALER

Jacob Beeler, or Bealer, applied for revolutionary pension while living in Sullivan County, Tenn., in 1832, when he was 72 years of age and therefore born in 1750. He entered the service in Virginia troops under command of Captain William Buchanan and was in the battle of Long Island under command of Colonel William Christian. He was associated with Colonel Elijah Robinson and Captain Evan Shelby in the Cherokee Campaign. He was under Captain John Pemberton in the battle of King's Mountain.

WILLIAM BEARD

William Beard applied for revolutionary pension while living in Sumner County, Tennessee, in 1832, when he was 72 years of age. He was born in Pennsylvania in 1761. He entered the service while living in North Carolina, under Captain William Davidson and Major James White. He joined General Thomas Sumter's forces and was taken prisoner at the battle of Fishing Creek. He escaped with John Miller and Duncan McCowan and was given his honorable discharge by General Rutherford. In 1840 he was living with Frank Yourn.

JAMES BEATTY

James Beatty applied for revolutionary pension while living in Rutherford County, Tennessee, in 1832. He was then 79 years of age and therefore born in 1753. He enlisted in North Carolina troops under Captain Jacob Nicholas, General Griffith Rutherford, Lieutenant David Henry, General Andrew Williamson and General Wiliom Davidson. He was engaged in the Snow Campaign in 1775. He served under Colonel Francis Locke in the attack on General McLeod. He served under Colonel James Martin; and under General Griffith Rutherford in the Cherokee Campaign. He served under General Andrew Pickens in General Andrew Williamson's "Black Hole" fight. He was under Colonel Francis Locke, Captain Jacob Nicholas and General Rutherford in a march through South Carolina and Georgia in 1778 and 1779. He was present in General Jorn Ashe's Defeat on Briar Creek, Georgia.

CAPTAIN CHARLES BOWEN

Charles Bowen applied for revolutionary pension while living in Knox County, Tennessee. He served in Virginia Troops under command of his brother, Captain William Bowen, and Captain John Campbell. He served in the battle of King's Mountain under Captain William Edmondson, Colonel William Campbell and Colonel Benjamin Cleveland. His brother, Reece Bowen, was killed in the battle of King's Mountain. Charles Bowen was given a Captain's commission by Governor Beverly Randolph. Captain Bowen moved to Indiana in 1833 and his pension was transferred to that state.

WILLIAM BRADFORD
of Sumner County

William Bradford applied for revolutionary pension while living in Sumner ounty, Tennessee, in 1818. He served in Virginia troops. He was the son of Joseph Bennett Bradford and Mary George Bradford, and was born in Fauquier County, Virginia, August 4, 1761. He served in the battle of Guilford Court House and was taken prisoner in the surrender at Charleston. He was confined on the British ship "Jersey" until peace was declared. He moved to Tennessee after the Revolution and settled in Sumner County, where he died June 3, 1831.

He married three times, first Mary Steele, second, Katherine Morgan and third Nancy Boyles. By his first wife his children were: Katherine, Fielding and Lucy. By his second wife his children were: Cynthia, Daniel Morgan, Francis, Eliza, Emily, Emma Corbett, Joseph Bennett, Susan and Ann L. By his third wife his children were: Robert Boyles, Larkin, Elizabeth, John Holt, Mary Ann, William Montgomery, Rebecca Ellen, Tabitha and Roxanna.

BENJAMIN BRADSHAW

Benjamin Bradshaw applied for revolutionary pension in the East Tennessee Agency in 1834. He was then living in Jefferson County, Tennessee. He is listed in the 1840 Census as eighty-two years of age and he was therefore born about 1758. His birth is given in the pension papers as "in the year 1757 or on May 28, 1758," in Fluvanna County, Virginia. He served as a private in Virginia troops as follows: In the year 1776 or 1777 three months under Captain Richard Napier and Colonel Earnest; late in 1777 four months under Captain Daniel Tilman and Colonel Taylor; in 1781 four months under Captain Daniel Tilman and Colonel Earnest; in 1781 two months under Captain Joseph Haton an Colonel Earnest.

He married in Fluvanna County, Virginia, Fanny Melton, June 22, 1787, according to the family record, which was submitted by the widow. She was born in Fluvanna County. In 1843 she was 74 years of age, which places her birth in 1759. Benjahin Bradshaw died in Jefferson County, January 12, 1841. His widow applied for pension in 1843 and was living in Jefferson County in 1849. They had moved from Fluvanna County, Virginia, after the Revolution, to Montgomery County, Virginia, and later to Jefferson County, Tennessee.

Their children as shown on the family record were Nancy Bradshaw, born 1788; Mary Bradshaw, born 1791; Betsy Bradshaw, born 1793; Patsey Bradshaw, born 1795; Larner Bradshaw, born 1799, and Pierce W. Bradshaw, born 1803.

LITTLETON BROOKS

Littleton Brooks applied for revolutionary pension while living in Hawkins County, Tenn., in 1832. He was then 76 years of age and therefore born in 1756. He entered the service in North Carolina troops in 1776 under Captain James Elliott and Colonel Christian to fight Indians. He served later under Captain Shelby and Colonel John Sevier in the Cherokee Campaigns. He was in the battle of Long Island, under Captain John Cornack and Captain Robert Kyle. He served under Colonel Robert Allison and Colonel Isaac Shelby as a scout. He lived until after 1840 as he is listed in the 1840 Census of Revolutionary Pensioners.

JOSEPH CATHCART

Joseph Cathcart applied for revolutionary pension while living in Monroe County, Tenn., in 1832 when he was 87 years of age. He was born in Ireland about 1745. He enlisted in South Carolina troops under Captain Turner, Colonel John Winn and General Thomas Sumter. He aided in the capture of the British at Caldwell's Place. He was captured by Tories under command of Captain Rogers and sent to Camden to be tried as a spy.

DAVID CHILDRESS

David Childress applied for revolutionary pension while residing in Sullian County, Tenn., August 22, 1818, when he was 59 years of age. He served in the Second Georgia Regiment for three years. He resided in Charlotte County, Va., when he enlisted in 1775. He marched to Georgia under Lieutenant Littlebury Mosby, in Captain John Mosby's company. After three years' service he was captured by the British and put on a British prison ship for eight months. He escaped and reenlisted at Guilford and Eutaw Springs, North Carolina. He had a wife and three children, living with him when he applied for pension, whose names are not given. The son was 17 years of age, the daughters were 14 and 19 years of age.

Note:- David Childress married Lucy Gaines, daughter of Captain James Gaines. One of the daughters, Elizabeth, married William Hulme. The soldier was the son of John Childress of Surry County, North Carolina.

LIEUTENANT JONAS CLARK

Jonas Clark applied for revolutionary pension while living in Madison County, Tenn., in 1832 when he was 75 years of age and therefore born in 1757. He entered the service in North Carolina in 1779 under Captain Richard Simmons and was sent out to intercept Colonel Cruger who was attempting to join the British at Charleston,

He was later placed under command of Capain Nathaniel Martin and was with General Thomas Sumpter in the battle of Hanging Rock. He was in the defeat of General Horatio Gates August 15, 1780, near Camden. General Sumter's troops were in warfare with Lord Cornwallis' forces. Captain Martin was taken prisoner and command of the company devolved upon Lieutenant Robert Walker. Clark served under General Nathaniel Greene in the battle of Guilford Court House. He was appointed lieutenant by Governor Rutledge and was attached to Colonel William Polk's regiment in skirmishes at Friday's Fort and Orangeburg County Court House and in the battle of Eutaw Springs.

JOHN CLEMENTS (CLEMMONS, CLEMANS)

John Clements, or Clemmons, or Clemans, applied for revolutionary pension while living in Jackson County, Tenn., in 1832 when he was 81 years of age. He was living in Augusta County, Va., during the War of the Revolution and served in a Virginia regiment under Captains Wliam Christy, Tate and Long. He was born in Augusta County, Virginia. He moved to Tennessee after the Revolution and settled in Jackson County where he died in 1834. He married in 1779 in Virginia, Elizabeth Echols, who was born in 1778 and died in 1832.

JAMES COOPER

James Cooper applied for revolutionary pension while living in Hawkins County, Tenn., May 1, 1833. He was born in January, 1758, in Chester County, Pennsylvania. He moved while he was a child to Rowan County, North Carolna. He accompanied his father whose name he did not give in the application papers. He entered the service in Rowan County, North Carolina, in 1776, serving three months in Captain David Caldwell's North Carolina company. He moved in 1779 with his father to that part of North Carolina which later became Hawkins County, Tennessee, and volunteered in 1780, serving three months in Captain Solomon White's company, Colonel Isaac Shelby's regiment. In the fall of 1780 he served two months in Captain Joseph Martin's company, Colonel Arthur Campbell's regiment.

ISAAC CRABTREE

Isaac Crabtree applied for revolutionary pension while living in Overton County, Tenn., in 1832 when he was 76 years of age and therefore born in 1756. He entered service in Virginia troops in 1775 under command of Captain Aaron Lewis. Later he enlisted again under Colonel William Christian and served in the Cherokee Campaign. He served as a spy in Colonel Arthur Campbell's regiment. He served with Colonel Daniel Smith in the Indian attack at Glade Hollow Fort. He also served under General William Russell,

PHILLIP DAY

Phillip Day applied for revolutionary pension while living in Smith County, Tenn., August 1832, when he was 70 years of age. Hee entered the service in 1778 in Caswell County, North Carolina,

He died September 9, 1834. His widow Mary Douglas Day applied for pension in Smith County, September 10, 1836, when she was 66 years of age. They were married March 21, 1793. Their children were Sarah Day, born 1794; Thomas B. Day, born 1795; Jenny Day, born 1796; Bethalum Day, born 1789; John D. Day, born 1800; Mary Day, born 1806; Franky Day, born 1807; Franklin B. Day, born 1809; Phillip Day, born 1811; Elizabeth W. Day, born 1813.

The soldier was born April 16, 1762. He married Mary Douglas, daughter of John Douglas. They were both born and reared in Person County, North Carolina.

JACOB GILLESPIE

Jacob Gillespie applied for revolutionary pension while living in Knox County, Tenn., October 4, 1832. He was then 79 years of age and therefore born in 1753. He entered the United States service in June, 1774, when he was drafted nto the militia in Augusta County, Virginia, under Colonel Andrew Lewis, Lieutenant Colonel Charles Lewis, Captain George Moffatt and Lieutenant James Sawyer. He volunteered later under the same officers for another tour. He was in battle at Big Kanawah River, October 10, 1774. Lieutenant Colonel Charles Lewis was killed, also privates William Gragg, William Bell, John Moffatt, the last a brother of Captain Moffatt. He recalled that fourteen privates of his company were killed and wounded including the above mentioned. He volunteered again under Colonel Dickinson in Augusta County. In 1777 or 1778 he resided in Rockingham County and volunteered under Major Nawl and Captain Guy Hamilton. He volunteered again in 1780 under Captain Hamilton and Captain John Rice. He removed from Virginia to Tennessee about 1796.

THOMAS HARRISON

Thomas Harrison applied for revolutionary pension while living in Franklin County, Tenn., in 1833. He was born about 1760 in Maryland. While living in Lincoln County, N. C., he volunteered in Capt. George Smith's company, Colonel George Dixon's regiment. Later he served in Captain William Naile's company, Colonel Charles McDowell's North Carolina regiment.

He moved from North Carolina in 1795 going to Warren County, Kentucky, then to Franklin County, Tenn., thence back to Kentucky, thence to Missouri and from there to Alabama where he resided for two years. He then returned to Franklin County Tennessee, where he remained until his death, November 2, 1839. He married in 1783 or 1784 in Lincoln County, N. C., Nancy Pack. She survived her husband and applied for pension while she was living in Grundy County, formerly a part of Franklin County. She was born about 1762 and died March 10, 1854. They had children, among them: William, born 1786, died by 1851; Johnson, who lived in Madison County, Alabama, in 1846; Susannah, born 1789 who married ——— Sartan; Elijah, born 1794, lived in Grundy County in 1852.

In 1832 Richard Harrison, brother of Thomas Harrison, made affidavit in Franklin County, Tenn., that he served with his brother in one of his tours.

GEORGE HULME

George Mulme applied for revolutionary pension while living in Williamson County, Tenn., in 1832. He was born October 25, 1761, in Amelia County, Virginia. When he was young he moved with his parents to Northhampton County, N. C. His father died about the beginning of the Revolution and he returned with his mother to Amelia County, Virginia. While living in that county he enlisted in 1776 or 1777 and served in Virginia troops under Captains William Jones and William Gerald or Garrell and Colonel Lewis Burwell. He served again in Virginia militia. About the time of the Peace Declaration his mother moved her family to Surrey County, N. C. George Hulme lived in that county and in Wilkes County, N. C., until about 1803 he moved to Williamson County, Tennessee.

A brother, Robert Hulme, is mentioned in the pension papers but no other data are given.

GIDEON JOHNSTON

Gideon Johnston applied for revolutionary pension while living in Williamson County, Tenn., in 1832. He served in the Revolution under Captain John Armstrong, of Surry County, N. C., and Lieutenant Tate, from Guilford County, N. C. He then resided in Guilford County. Captain Armstrong's company joined the 2nd regiment, N. C., Continental troops.

Gideon Johnston stated in his application that he was born November 7, 1754, in Amelia County, Virginia; that he moved to Guilford County. When the County of Rockingham was taken from Guilford County his home was in that section of North Carolina, and he resided there until 1819. He then moved to Davidson County, Tenn., where he lived until 1826, when he moved to Williamson County, Tenn. He filed a second declaration in 1840 stating that he was then a resident of Davidson County, Tennessee.

JOHN JOHNSTON
of Maury County

Martha Johnston, widow of John Johnston, applied for pension because of the revolutionary service of her husband, in 1841 when she resided in Maury County, Tenn. She was then 83 years of age. She stated that she married John Johnston in the summer of 1774 in Baltimore, Md., and that shorly after their marriage they moved to York District, South Carolina, where they resided until after the close of the Revolution. She stated that her husband was in the battles of Hanging Rock and King's Mountain and that he died October 5, 1818. She stated that after the close of the Revolution she and her husband and their children moved to Davidson County, Tenn., and from there to Maury County, Tenn., where she resided from 1807. She stated that she was born in Nottongham County, Maryland, in 1758 and that she was a member of the Methodist Church. They had several children whose names are not given in the application.

JOHN JOHNSTON

John Johnston applied for revolutionary pension while living in Smith County, Tenn., in 1832. He was born August 30, 1752, but the place of his birth and the names of his parents are not shown. He enlisted in January in the "year that Cornwallis was taken," in Cumberland County, Virginia. He served in Captain Joseph Carrington's Virginia Company and served three months when he enlisted in Captain William Meredith's Virginia company in which he served three months. In 1836 his address was Dixon Springs, Sumner County, Tenn. In 1836 the same address is given for a nephew, H. H. Johnston. There are no further family data. John Johnston died February 15, 1837.

DENNIS KELLY

Dennis Kelly applied for revolutionary pension while living in Wilson County, Tenn., in 1831. He was born in 1758, and died in 1834. He enlisted in the army while living in Kent County, Delaware. He was one of the guards at the execution of Major Andre. After the Revolution he moved to Tennessee and lived in Wilson County. He married, 1784, in Delaware, Elizabeth Thompson, who survived him and drew pension in Wilson County.

Note:- Among their children were Frances, who married John Peyton; Rev. John Kelly, born 1802, died 1865, who married Lavinia Campbell; Drusilla, born 1790, died 1862, who married William Johnston (born 1784, died 1826).

JAMES KERR

James Kerr applied for revolutionary pension while living in White County, Tenn. He entered the service as a spy under General Joseph McDowell and was sent to Blackstocks Fort to watch the British. Later he joined Colonel Williams' forces and was sent to reconnoitre Major Patrick Ferguson's position. As a result he gained information it is said which led to the defeat of the British at King's Mountain.

JOSEPH KERR

Joseph Kerr applied for revolutionary pension while living in White County, Tenn., in 1832, when he was 73 years old and therefore born in 1769. He was a cripple exempt from military duty. Nevertheless he volunteered as a spy in the service of General Joseph McDowell and was detailed to watch operations of British at Blackstocks. He was also commissioned to spy upon Major Patrick Ferguson near King'sMountain. Captain Barnett sent him to the camp of the British under General Floyd and Captain Huck.

Note:- It is possible that James and Joseph Kerr were brothers as their service was similar and under the same officers.

WILLIAR LEAY OR LEE

William Leay, or Lee, applied for revolutionary pension while living in Blount County, Tenn., in 1819. His name is shown in the application papers as Leay, Lee and Lea. He came from Ireland to America when he was about thirteen years of age. He was living in Rockbridge County, Virginia, when he entered the service. In the fall of 1775 he volunteered in Captain John Hay's company, Colonel George Matthews' 9th Virginia regiment and was in the battles of Princeton, Germantown, White Marsh, Stillwater, and at the surrender of Burgoyne; he was discharged from service at Valley Forge, Pennsylvania, having served two and one half years. He returned to Virginia. He had previously served in the battle of Point Pleasant.

He resided in Virginia about thirty years. He moved to North Carolina and later moved to Blount County Tennessee, a short time before 1819. He gave his age at that time as between sixty and seventy years. He stated that he had a family but gave no names. In July 1821 he had no family living at home and was himself living with a Mr. Bogle.

THOMAS HOOD

Thomas Hood applied for revolutionary pension while living in White County, Tenn., in 1832 when he was 76 years of age. He was therefore born in 1756. He enlisted in the service in 1777 in Bedford County, Virginia, under Captain Downey. He substituted for Moses Johnson in Captain Isaac Wilson's company. He was associated with Colonel Evan Shelby, Colonel Charles Robertson and Captain John Sevier. He substituted for Adam Hall in Captain James Morrison's company, Colonel Phifer's regiment and served under Captain John Smith and Colonel Holmes in the battle of Ramsour's Mills and in the battle of King's Mountain. Captain John Cleveland and Captain Benjamin Cleveland are mentioned in his pension application.

MOSES LINDSAY

Moses Lindsay (Lindsey) applied for pension for revolutionary service while living in Williamson County, Tenn., August 28, 1832, when he was seventy years of age. He was born in 1762 in Frederick County, Virginia. While living in Newberry, South Carolina, he enlisted in 1776 in Captain Garrett Smith's South Carolina company. He enlisted again in 1777 in the company of Captain John Lindsay, his uncle. He enlisted in June or July, 1780, again in Captain John Lindsay's company, Colonel John Lyle's South Carolina regiment. He served in the battles of Musgrove's Mills, Fish Dam Ford, Blackstocks, and Cowpens. He was in the Siege of Ninety-six from which he went to the Siege of Augusta and while there he was in the battles of Fort Grierson and Eutaw Springs. He served until after peace was declared. He lived in Newberry, South Carolina, until 1810 when he moved to Williamson County, Tennessee.

CAPTAIN SALATHIEL MARTIN

Mary Martin, widow of Salathiel Martin, applied for revolutionary pension while living in Claiborne County, Tenn., in February, 1845. She was then 81 years of age and therefore born in 1764. She stated that her husband was captain in a North Carolina regiment and that he served eighteen months and was in the battles of King's Mountain and Guilford Court House. She married Salathiel Martin April 23, 1782, in Surry County, N. C. The Secretary of North Carolina testified that Salathiel Martin served in the Revolution as a captain of Dragoons.

JAMES McBRIDE

James McBride applied for revolutionary pension while residing in Lincoln County, Tenn., in October, 1832. He was born in August, 1750, in County Down, Ireland, whence he emigrated to America settling first in Lancaster County, Pennsylvania. He moved to Guilford County, North Carolina, in 1771. He lived there until 1780 when he went to the Tennessee country. He resided principally in Williamson County but later lived in Lincoln County. He enlisted in Guilford County, North Carolina, and served under Captain George Davidson and Colonel Francis Nash in the First North Carolina regiment. He was captured by the British but escaped.

WILLIAM McFERRIN

William McFerrin applied for revolutionary pension while living in Tipton County, Tenn., in 1832. He was born agout 1757 and died in 1845. He enlisted in Virginia Troops in Augusta County, Virginia, where he then resided He moved to Tennessee after the Revolution. He married Jane Laughlin. Among their children were: Eleanor, who married Colin Campbell, and Rev. James McFerrin, born 1784, died 1840, who married in 1804 Jane Campbell Berry.
William McFerrin was living with Colin Campbell in 1832.

CAPTAIN DAVID McNABB

Captain David McNabb's widow, Elizabeth McNabb, applied for revolutionary pension, based on his service, while she lived in Meigs County, Tennessee, in 1837, when she was 79 years of age. She died June 20, 1848, in that county. David McNabb entered the service while living in Washington County, North Carolina, in the section which became Carter County, Tenn. He raised a company of militia in Washington County, in June, 1780, and was elected captain. He served in two tours one under Colonel Robinson and one under Colonel John Sevier and was engaged against the Indians. He assisted in the destruction of their towns. He served another tour of three months in 1781 under Colonel John Sevier during which his company marched into South Carolina and assisted in capturing a number of British soldiers. Captain McNabb returned to Washington County and continued to reside there until his death, May 3, 1826.

He married in the year 1778, Elizabeth Taylor. They were married by "Parson Graham in the Stone Meeting House," in Augusta County, Virginia. They moved to Washington County to reside. She stated that her broher, Andrew Taylor, moved from Augusta County, to Washington County and resided near them. Andrew Taylor was 76 years of age in 1837 when he resided in Washington County.

Note:- Captain McNabb's company marched to King's Mountain following the other Mountain men by twenty-four hours, it is said, and reached the site of the battle one hour after it was ended. Andrew Taylor, Elizabeth Taylor McNabb's brother, was a member of the well known Taylor family of Washington County. His father was Isaac Taylor. For this family see the Taylor Family of Tennessee, Lookout Publishing Company.

JOHN McNATT
of Bedford County

John McNatt applied for revolutionary pension in Bedford County, Tenn., November 6, 1832. He was then between 80 and 85 years of age. He was born in Kent County, Delaware, about 1750. He enlisted in Kent County under Captain Nathan Adams and Lieut. Gordon in a regiment called the Delaware Blues. He marched to Dover, Delaware, then to Lewistown, down to the Light House, bac,· to Lewistown, and then against a detachment of Tories. He moved to Tennessee and lived in Lincoln and Bedford Counties.

JOHN McNATT
of Roane County

John McNatt applied for revolutionary pension while living in Roane County, Tenn., July 23 1832, when he was 70 years of age. He served eighteen months in the 5th South Carolina Regiment. He had a brother who was a major in the regiment. He was born January 1, 1763, in Virginia. He enlisted while living in Marlboro County, South Carolina, in 1779 of 1780, and again in 1782. He died in Roane County in 1848 and his widow, Lucretia McNatt, applied for widow's pension. She was then 60 years of age and so born in 1788. She was married to the soldier in March, 1816, in Roane County.

Lucretia McNatt was probably John McNatt's second wife as her marriage to him took place when he was about 54 years of age.

CAPTAIN JOHN MEDEARIS

John Medearis applied for revolutionary pension while he was living in Bedford County. Tenn,, September 19, 1828.

He was the son of John Medearis and Rachel Davis Medearis. He was born in Essex County, Virginia, "between "Rappahannock and Dragon." He entered the service in 1776 and was a captain in North Carolina troops until November 1, 1778, when he was appointed Assistant Deputy Quartermaster General. He continued in service until August 1, 1783.

John Medearis married December 20, 1870, Sarah, the widow of Thomas Bell.

John Medearis died March 21 or 31, 1834. His wife had predeceased him but date and place of death are not given in the pension papers. The following data regarding the children of John Medearis are given: Washington Davis Medearis, born 1783, married Elizabeth S. Woodward; Benjamin Medearis, no data; B. W. H. Medearis, no data; Polly Medearis Smith was the only surviving child in 1854. The names of several grandchildren appear.

PETER MOWREY

Peter Mowrey applied for revolutionary pension in 1833 while living in Knox County, Tenn. He was born September 15, 1760, in Philadelphia County, Pennsylvania, where he lived only a few years and then moved to Augusta County, Virginia. The names of his parents are not given in his pension application. While residing in Augusta County he volunteered in the latter part of the summer or early in the fall of 1780 and served six months as a private in the company of Captain Thomas Smith, Colonel Campbell's regiment

After the Revolution he moved to what is now Tennessee country and lived for a year in Sullivan County and then to Knox County where he drew pension.

LIEUTENANT COLONEL WILLIAM POLK

William Polk applied for revolutionary pension while living in Wake County, North Carolina, in April, 1833. He was born in Mechlenburg County, North Carolina, July 9, 1758. He entered the service in Mechlenburg County. He moved in 1785 to Davidson County, then North Carolina, now Tennessee, where he lived for three years. He returned to Mechlenburg County, where he lived until 1799, when he moved to Wake County. He entered the service in 1775. He received a commission later as Lieutenant Colonel. He was in the battle of Eutaw Springs and in the battle of Brandywine where he was wounded by a musket ball in the cheek. His paper gives full detail for his service. He died January 14, 1834.

RICHARD PORTERFIELD

Richard Porterfield applied for revolutionary pension January 27, 1824, while living in Greene County, Tennessee. He enlisted in March, 1779, in a company commanded by Captain Fulkner, in a Virginia Regiment, commanded by Colonel William Washington. He served in the battle of Camden, where he was wounded. According to his age as given in 1840 he was born about 1758 but he does not give the year of his birth or the place. When he entered the service he was living in Albemarle County, Virginia. He moved to Greene County, Tennessee, by or before 1820. He was married twice. In his application for pension in 1824 he stated that his wife had been dead for about three years and that he had two sons and two daughters. The name of his deceased wife and the names of the children are not given. He moved to Knox County where he married, August 31, 1847, Louisa Bose, born 1816. She survived him, applied for a widow's pension, which was granted, and died in Knox County after 1866.

ABRAHAM SEVIER

Abraham Sevier applied for revolutionary pension while living in Overton County, Tennessee, in 1832. He was born February 14, 1760, in Shenandoah County, Virginia. While he was a resident of Washington County, N. C., later Tennessee, he served with North Carolina troops, as follows: in the summer or fall of 1778, as a spy under Ensign Robert Sevier in service against the Indians; in the spring of 1779 he served three months in Captain Valentine Sevier's company, Colonel Evan Shelby's regiment· he marched to the Cherokee Nation, killed "a few Indians" and took some prisoners; in the summer of 1780 he served three months in Captain Valentine Sevier's company, Colonel Charles McDowell's regiment, and was in two engagements with the British at Moffett's Iron Works; in the fall of 1870 he was in Captain Valentine Sevier's company, Colonel John Sevier's regiment, and was in the battle of King's Mountain; later in 1780, he served a month in Captain Landon Carter's company, Colonel John Sevier's regiment, and was in an engagement with the Indians on Boyd's Creek. In the fall of 1781 he served four months in Captain Valentine Sevier's company.

In the fall of 1782 he served four months in Captain George North and Captain James Richardson's company, under Colonel John Sevier, in pursuit of the Cherokees, and was in the engagement on Lookout Mountain. He died in Overton County, June 18, 1841.

Note:- Abraham Sevier was the son of Valentine Sevier and Joanna Goode Sevier, and was the brother of Captain Robert Sevier, Captain Valentine Sevier, and Colonel John Sevier.

He married Mary Little, and had nine children: Elizabeth, Mary Ann, John (d. in infancy), Jemima Douglass, Joanna Goode, Valentine, Rebecca Richards, Abraham Rutherford and Catherine Sherrill.

It is interesting that he refers to the engagement on Lookout Mountain in the fall of 1782 (September 20). This was during the last campaign of the Revolution, and the engagement was the last battle of the Revolution.

WILLIAM SHARP

William Sharp applied for revolutionary pension while living in Jefferson County, Tenn., January 25, 1830. He was born June 3, 1760. He enlisted in August, 1777, in Virginia, under Captain Mims, Lieut. Francis Mims and Colonel Richard Parker, in the Virginia Continental Line, commanded by General Mullenberg. He was discharged after eighteen months' service, at Middlebrook, N. J. He served in the battles of Monmouth, Guilford Court House and Yorktown. He stated that his first wife died and that his second wife, named Elizabeth, was alive in 1830. By both wives he had sixteen children, ten by the first wife and six by the second wife. In 1830 they were all alive, but one John aged 42 years, William aged 40 years, Elisha aged 38 years, Betsey aged 36 years, Susanna, aged 34 years, David aged 32 years, Peggy aged 30 years, Andrew aged 28 years, Mahala aged 36 years, Casper aged 24 years, children of the first wife were married and settled in different counties and states, none in Jefferson County. By the second wife the living children were: Matilda aged 14 years, "who is a perfect idiot," Sarah aged 12 years, Polly aged 10 years, Rachel aged 8 years and Thomas Jackson aged 6 years. He stated that he had one cow, two beds and furniture, one ax, one pot, one oven, one half dozen knives and forks, one skillet, one table, one half dozen plates, six tin cups, two pails, one hoe.

Elizabeth Sharp, widow of William Sharp, applied for widow's pension in Greene County, February 28, 1853. She married the soldier October 25, 1815, in Greene County. Her maiden name was Elizabeth Massey. William Sharp died December 17, 1842.

Note:- This list of possessions is given here as it forms an illustration of the financial status of hundreds of early pensioners of the revolutionary war. The veterans who applied later under the 1832 Act were not required to declare such absolute need.

WILLIAM SMITH

William Smith applied for revolutionary pension while living in Jefferson County, Tenn., in 1832. He was born in Virginia in 1746. He volunteered under Captain Richard Pollard, Colonel Andrew Williamson, and Major Andrew Pickens. He participated in the Snow Campaign. He aided in the capture and hanging of Tory Captain Linley; he served in the Indian attack at Phillips Fort, Georgia, and served with Colonel William Henderson in the Siege of 96. He died before 1840 as his name is not on the 1840 Census of Revolutionary Pensioners.

MOSES SPENCER

Moses Spencer, also spelled Spenser, applied for revolutionary pension while living in Maury County, Tenn., December 28, 1818. He was born January 16, 1744, but the place of birth and names of his parents are not given. He enlisted February 10, 1778, in Captain James Baytop's company in the Seventh Virginia regiment and later in Colonel William Heth's Virginia regiment. He transferred to Captain Young's company and was in the battle of Monmouth. He received his discharge February 16, 1779. He volunteered for service in the battle of Guilford Court House.

Soon after the close of the Revolution he moved to North Carolina and then moved to South Carolina. From there he moved to Mercer County, Kentucky, then to Barren County, Kentucky, and about the year 1810 to Lawrence County, Tenn., which had meanwhile been erected from Maury County. He died March 27, 1826, in Lawrence or Maury County. He married November 20, 1779, in Henry or Amelia County, Virginia, Elizabeth Tinsley, daughter of Thomas Tinsley, who was present at the marriage. The eldest child of Moses and Elizabeth Spencer was born February 9, 1781. In 1820 Moses Spencer referred to his son Amasa Spencer, and in 1821 he said that his youngest son Amzi, was twenty-three years of age. Other children were: Ellen Blithe (Blythe), Thomas, who in July, 1850, said he was sixty-five years old, Tabitha Woods, the oldest daughter.

The widow, Elizabeth Spencer applied for pension in 1843 when she was a resident of Lawrence County, and eighty years old. She died August 13, 1849, in Lawrence County. Her surviving children in that year were: Thomas, Tabitha Woods and Ellen Blythe.

CONWAY STONE

Conway Stone applied for revolutionary pension November 17, 1832, while he resided in Monroe County, Tenn. He died in Monroe County, November 25, 1834. He was born July 16, 1761, in Granville County, N. C. While he was a resident of Surry County, N. C., he enlisted in 1780 and served three months in Captain David Humphreys' company, Colonel McDowell's regiment. He enlisted again after the battle of Guilford Court House and served three months under the same officers. He moved after the Revolution to Randolph County, N. C., where he resided until 1808 or 1809. He resided there until 1828 when he became a resident of Monroe County.

He married in 1781 in Surry County, N. C., Elizabeth Galaglee or Galagie. She died July 10, 1842, aged about 80 years. Children who survived the mother were: Nancy, married to Fuquay Beasley;

William, Joel, John, Conway, Jr., Barsheba, married to William Hargus; Susan, married to Samuel Gilbreath, and Mary, married to Josiah Roberts. Hannah, who was dead in 1845, had married Henry McCurdy.

JOHN STONE

John Stone applied for revolutionaly pension September 20, 1825, when he was living in Moulton, Lawrence County, Alabama. His pension certificate was not issued, however, until December 13, 1828, when he had returned to Bedford County, Tenn., where he had formerly lived, to be with his children.

He enlisted in Jonestown, Lancaster County, Pennsylvania, in January or February, 1777, in Colonel Richard Hampton's Pennsylvania regiment and was wounded in the battle of Brandywine. He was taken prisoner and was held ten months. He was discharged March 24, 1781, by Captain W. Finney, 6th Pennsylvania regiment.

In his application he referred to his wife, Mary, but did not give her family name not the date of their marriage. He mentioned his daughter Polly Tucker, aged 55 in 1825, and her son Jackson Tucker; a grandson, Earl Baylies, aged two years, whose mother was dead. In 1828 another daughter, Nancy, and her husband, John A Marrs, were living in Shelbyville, Bedford County, Tenn.

JOHN TATE

John Tate applied for pension in 1819 and drew his pension in the Tennessee Agency, (which means in Nashville, Davidson County). On May 22, 1819, according to his pension statement, he was 75 years of age and therefore born in 1744. As he enlisted in August, 1775, in Captain Benjamin Chambers' company, Colonel Hartley's Pennsylvania regiment, he was probably born in Pennsylvania. As he was a Corporal and Sergeant in that first year's service he was a man of character and leadership.

He served one year under Captain Chambers. From 1776, when he reenlisted, he served a year as a sergeant under Captain Daniel Piatt in the First New Jersey regiment, commanded by Lord Stirling, (Colonel William Alexander). He reenlisted under the same officers in the spring of 1778 and was in a skirmish at "Spanktown," in which he was severely wounded in the leg and foot and totally disabled for three months. Subsequently he was attached to the hospital department by Lord Sterling and continued in that service until the close of the Revolutionary war. His service amounted to six years.

In 1819 the pensioner's wife and eight children by his second wife lived with him. The oldest child was then about 19 years of age which indicates his second marriage as taking place about 1799. John Tate, Jr., aged 27 years, veteran's son by his first wife resided in March, 1819, near Carthage, in Smith County, Tennessee.

This indicates the birth of John Tate, Jr., as in 1792. The veteran referred in his pension papers to a son in Kentucky but did not give the name. This suggests that he resided in Kentucky for a period before moving to Tennessee. He moved to Carthage, Smith County, Tenn., in 1818. He was still living in Carthage in 1821. He died August 12, 1835.

ABRAM VAUGHN

Abram Vaughn applied for revolutionary pension while living in Wilson County, Tenn., in 1832. He was born in January, 1764, in Dinwiddie County, Va. He enlisted on Easter Monday in 1779 and served seven months in Captain Peter Wright's company of Artillery in the Virginia regiment of Colonels Harrison and Porterfield. He enlisted again in Captain George Pegram's company in the Third Virginia regiment of Colonels Faulkner and Downman and was discharged in November, 1780. He enlisted again and served four months under Colonel Dick and was discharged in October, 1781. In 1807 he moved from Dinwiddie County, Va., to Wilson County, Tenn., where he lived the rest of his life. He married, April 30, 1832, in Wilson County, Margaret S. Gold. She was born in 1805. She died in Wilson County, July 7, 1855.

Note:- The marriage in 1832 suggests that Margaret Gold was a second wife as Abram Vaughn was then 68 years of age.

STEPHEN WHITE

Stephen White applied for revolutionary pension while living in Rutherford County, Tenn., in 1832. He was born November 25, 1762, in Granville County, N. C. He enlisted while living in Granville County, N. C., in August, 1780, and served in Captain Yancey's company, North Carolina regiment; he enlisted again in December, 1780, and served in Captain Richard Harrison's company, Colonel Joseph Taylor's North Carolina regiment; he enlisted again in April, 1781, and served in Captain William Armstrong's and Captain Langam's North Carolina companies. From the fall of 1781 he served under Edmund Granville, quartermaster at Salisbury, N. C., and was discharged there April 5, 1782. He did not give his parents name in his application papers but he named his stepfather, Zachariah Williams.

In 1784 he moved to Madison County, Ky. In 1805 he moved to Rutherford County, Tenn. He died in Rutherford County, March 9, 1846.

Note:- Stephen White married Hannah Dickinson, June 23, 1814. (She was probably a second wife as he was then 52 years of age).

CALEB WILLIAMS

Caleb Williams applied for revolutionary pension while living in Stewart County, Tenn., in 1832. He stated in his application papers that he was born September 20, 1760, in Dorchester County, Maryland. He was living in Orange County, N. C., when he enlisted for service in May or June, 1780. He served three months in Captain David Scoby's company in Colonel Taylor's North Carolina regiment. He volunteered again in January or February, 1781, and served three months in Captain Harris' North Carolina company. Several years after the close of the Revolution he moved to Crab Orchard, Ky., and one year later he moved to Lincoln County, Ky. Seven or eight years later he moved to Montgomery County, Tenn., and after living there a year he moved to Stewart County, Tenn. He gave no family data in his papers.

JOSHUA ADCOCK
of North Carolina

Joshua Adcock applied for revolutionary pension while living in North Carolina. He enlisted in 1777 in the First and Tenth regiments, North Carolina Continental Line, under Lieutenant John Low. At the time of enlistment he was living in Caswell County, N. C. He was taken prisoner at Charleston.

CAPTAIN WILLIAM ALEXANDER
of North Carolina

Captain William Alexander applied for revolutionary pension while living in Mechlenburg County, N. C. He entered service in that county under Captain Adam Alexander. He was commanded by General Griffith Rutherford in an attack on the Indians. He served under Captain Ezekial Polk in pursuit of the Tory William Cunningham. He served under General Thomas Sumter in the battles of Rocky Mount, Hanging Rock and Gates Defeat. He was associated with Colonel Wade Hampton in the battles of Monk's Corner, Eutaw Springs, and the taking of Friday's Fort.

CAPTAIN RICHARD ALLEN
of North Carolina

Richard Allen, Sr., applied for revolutionary pension in Wilkes County, N. C., September 4, 1832. He was born November 22, 1741, in Baltimore County, Maryland. When he was twenty-one years of age he moved to Frederick County, Va., where he lived for seven years. He moved to Rowan County, now Wilkes County, N. C., in September, 1770. In October or November, 1775, he entered the service as a volunteer in Captain Jesse Walton's company, the first unit which was raised in the county. He was promoted to ensign and then to captain.

WILLIAM ALLEN
of Illinois

William Allen applied for revolutionary pension while living in Illinois, September 18, 1832. He was born in Pennsylvania and while still very young moved from Pennsylvania to Orange County, N. C., where he was living when he volunteered for service in September, 1781. He served under Lieutenant John Campbell and Colonel Archibald Lytle. He was taken prisoner at Hillsboro, N. C., and was kept on board a British prison ship until exchanged, August 11, 1782, after which he returned to his home in Orange County, N. C.

JESSE ALSOBROOK
of North Carolina

Jesse Alsobrook applied for revolutionary pension December 26, 1832. He enlisted in Halifax County, N. C., April 25, 1781, under Captain Robert Raiford, Lieutenant Dudley, Major Armstrong and Colonel Dickson. He served in the battle of Eutaw Springs where two mess mates, John McCoy and John Russell, were killed. Twenty-nine men in the regiment were killed. He served in the North Carolina Continental troops.

WESTWOOD ARMISTED
of North Carolina

Westwood Armistead applied for revolutionary pension while living in Chatham County, N. C., March 5, 1844. He was then 81 years of age and therefore born in 1763. He was drafted in the service in 1781 when he was very young and living in Northhampton County, a short time before the battle of Guilford Court House. He was in that battle and in the battles of Hobkirk's Hill, and Augusta. He served twelve months under his brother, Anthony Armistead, when he was taken prisoner in the battle of Ninety-six. He was put on board a British prison ship, carried to England and landed on the Isle of Jersey where he was very sick. When he recovered he was sent to Spithead where he remained until "peace was made." He was then sent to Havre de Grace in France. The American Consul there let him have some money and a "pas" (passport?). He went to L'Orient and from there on an American ship to Boston where he arrived in May or June, 1783.

JOHN ARMSTRONG

Jane Armstrong, widow of John Armstrong, applied for pension for revolutionary service of her husband. She was living in Lexington, Fayette County, Ky., June 16, 1854, when she made her application. She stated that her name was Jane Patrick before her marriage and that she married John Armstrong August 27, 1827, in Montgomery County, Ky., and that Thomas Boone, a preacher, performed the marriage ceremony. She stated that in 1836 John Armstrong started from Clark County, Ky., to Nashville, Tenn., on business and that she never saw him again. She believed that he died in Tennessee in 1847. The deposition of Allen Armstrong of Clark County, Ky., stated that he was the son of John Armstrong by his third wife, Jane Patrick, and that he had received a letter from relatives near Nashville, Tenn., about 1849, stating that John had died at the house of a man named Mike Emery at the age of nearly 100 years Michael Emery, William M. Emery, and Katherine Armstrong of Henry County, Tennessee, deposed September 8, 1854.

JOHN BALDWIN

John Baldwin applied for revolutionary pension while residing in Ashe County, N. C. He resided in Burke County when he volunteered to fight Cherokee Indians under Colonel Robert Alexander. He was stationed at Edmondston's Fort and served under Major Joseph McDowell in the battle of Cowpens. He was granted a discharge by Major Joseph McDowell.

JOSEPH BURCH
of Kentucky

Joseph Burch applied for revolutionary pension while living in Scott County, Ky. He was born in Albemarle County, Va., June 28, 1763. He served in Virginia troops. He married in Scott County, Ky., July 26, 1838, Anne J. Hawkins. She was born in 1788. She applied for a widow's pension. She was living April 14, 1856.

CAPTAIN ANDREW CARSON
of North Carolina

Andrew Carson applied for revolutionary pension while living in Iredell County, N. C., August 22, 1832. He was born March 1, 1756, in Rowan County, N. C. He volunteered under Captain Joseph Dixson. He served under Captain David Caldwell in the Cherokee Campaign. He was in the battle of Briar's Creek. He served as a ranger and at times commanded a company of volunteers.

Note:- His tombstone states that he was a revolutionary soldier and that he died January 29, 1841.

BENJAMIN CHILDRESS
of Virginia

Benjamin Childress applied for revolutionary pension while living in Albemarle County, Va., April 3, 1850. He was born April 3, 1764, and entered the service when he was 16 years of age, in October, 1780. He served two months under Lieutenant James Montgomery and Robert Wright. He served two months in 1781 under Captain James Pamphlin. He was reduced by disease and Major Harris applied for a furlough for him. Before he recovered the war was over.

ISAAC DADE
of Massachusetts

Isaac Dade applied for revolutionary pension while living in Gloucester, Essex County, Mass., April 3, 1818. He entered the service in January, 1777. He served until September of 1777, when, having received a wound in the neck in the battle of Brandywine, he was obliged to retire on furlough. He was then serving in Captain Gardiner's company, Colonel Lee's Virginia regiment. A year later he entered the Continental Frigate South Carolina, commanded by Captain Gillam and served six months. He was discharged about September 7, 1788. His birth is given as May 10, 1756, in Boston, Mass. He died February 4, 1819, in Gloucester.

His widow, Fanny Dade, applied for widow's pension in Gloucester, August 3, 1838. She was born March 27, 1766, in Virginia. She married Isaac Dade December 22, 1787. She died May 4, 1843.

FRANCIS DAY
of North Carolina

Francis Day's widow, Jane Farmer Day, applied for revolutionary pension March 6, 1843, while she was living in Person County. She was then 78 years of age. She stated that he enlisted at Oxford, Granville County, N. C. He served under her own cousin, Colonel Thomas Farmer in Georgia. He married Jane Farmer in 1787. Francis Day died February 20, 1816. She mentioned a son, John Day.

WILLIAM DAY
of Virginia

William Day applied for revolutionary pension August 21, 1818, while living in Charles City, City County, Va. He was then 57 years of age. He entered the service in September, 1779, and was discharged in Salisbury, North Carolina, in January, 1781. In the year 1820 he stated that his family consisted of a wife aged 59 years, a son who was of age, and two daughters who were of age.

WILLIAM DAY
of South Carolina

William Day applied for revolutionary pension while living in Pendleton District, S. C., October 26, 1820. He was then 64 years of age. He received his discharge from the service at Fredericktown, Maryland. His wife was dead in 1820 but he had sons, Reuben, aged 16, and Lewis, aged 14. No other children were living with him.

JOHN DENNY
of North Carolina

John Denny applied for revolutionary pension while living in Guilford County, N. C., in 1833 when he was 75 years of age and therefore born in 1758. He was born in Ireland and came to America when a child with his parents. They settled first in Chester County, Pennsylvania, and then removed to Guilford County, N. C., where he resided thereafter. He was drafted into the army December, 1779 or 1780. When his tour was over he volunteered under Captain Wilson. In June, 1781, he volunteered again under Captain Robert Bell and marched to join General Greene at Camden. He was in the battle of Eutaw Springs.

JOHN GILLESPIE
of Kentucky

John Gillespie applied for revolutionary pension while living in Todd County, Kentucky, November 13, 1882, when he was 69 years of age. He was born August 12, 1763. He lived in Edgefield County, S. C., and entered the service in April, 1781. He lived in Wilkes County, Georgia two years after the Revolution. He then moved to Fairfield, S. C., where he lived two years and then moved to Clarke County Kentucky, where he lived one year, then to Georgia where he lived for seven years, part of which time he served against the Indians; then to South Carolina where he lived 19 years, then to Todd County, Ky. He married Holly Medford, March 15, 1792, in Spartanburg, S. C. He died May 31, 1835 in Todd County, Ky. Holly Medford Gillespie was the younger sister of Mrs. Francis Walker and lived with her at the time of marriage. Mrs. Walker was 70 years of age in Todd County, July 15, 1843. Holly's name is given in one paper as Hallidith Gillespie. She lived until after December 16, 1870, and was then living near Hopkinsville, Kentucky.

JOHN GILLESPIE
of Pennsylvania

John Gillespie applied for revolutionary pension while living in Chester County, Pennsylvania, May 6, 1818. He was then 70 years of age. He entered the service January 18, 1776. He served six years and six months and was discharged June 17, 1783. His family consisted of a wife, Jane, who was over 60 years of age when he made his pension application in 1818.

WILLIAM GILLESPIE
of Virginia

William Gillespie applied for revolutionary pension September 26, 1832, when he was 77 years of age. He entered the service in 1777 as an Indian spy in Greenbriar County, Virginia. He died October 11, 1837. His widow Margaret Eddy Gillespie, age 74 years, applied for pension June 8, 1841. She married William Gillespie February 21, 1792.

MAJOR JOSEPH GRAHAM
of North Carolina.

Major Joseph Graham applied for revolutionary pension while living in Lincoln County, N. C., in October, 1832. He was born in Chester County, Pennsylvania, October 13, 1759. He removed to Mechlenburg County, N. C., when he was about ten years of age. He stated that he "was present in Charlotte on the 20th day of May, 1775, when the committee of the County of Mechlenburg made the celebrated Declaration of Independence of the British Crown." After 1792 he resided in Lincoln County.

Note:- He died November 12, 1836.

COLONEL WILLIAM GRAHAM
of North Carolina

Colonel William Graham applied for revolutionary pension while living in Rutherford County, N. C., in October, 1832. He was appointed colonel commandant of Tryon County, North Carolina, Militia. He stated that in 1832 he was "old and blind." He was born in Augusta County, Virginia, 1742. When the revolution commenced he was living in Tryon County, N. C.

GEORGE HAMPTON
of Georgia

John Hampton applied for revolutionary pension while living in Jackson County, Georgia. He entered the service in North Carolina in 1778 and participated in General John Ashe's Defeat at Briar Creek, Georgia. He served with General Thomas Sumter's forces in engagements at Ramsour's Mill, King's Mountain, Fishing Creek and Musgrove's Mill. Captain Wade Hampton, General Andrew Pickins, Colonel John Purvis and Captain Williams are mentioned in the application papers.

JAMES HIXSON
of New Jersey

James Hixson applied for revolutionary pension while living in Washington County, Pennsylvania, October 1, 1832, when he stated that he had lived there about thirty years. He was born in 1757 in Hunterdon County, New Jersey. He enlisted while living in Hunterdon County and served from June 1776 for five months in Captain

John Anderson's company, Colonels Johnson and Phillips' regiment and was in the battle of Flatbush; from March, 1777 one month under Captain John Phillips and Colonel Snook; in September, 1777, two weeks under Captain Philip Snook; in September, 1777, two weeks under Captain Phillips; from December, 1777, one month under Captain Hoppack; from February, 1778, two months under Captain John Shank and Colonels Phillips and Jacob Houghton.

CAPTAIN WILLIAM HUTCHINSON
of North Carolina

Captain William Hutcheson applied for revolutionary pension while living in Mecklinburg County, North Carolina. He was born in Augusta County, Virginia, in 1750. He entered the service in Mecklenburg County, North Carolina, in 1774. He served under Colonel Thomas Polk and General Richardson in the Snow Campaign. Later he served as Lieutenant in Captain John Brownfield's company, General Griffith Rutherford's troops. He also served under Colonel Thomas Brandon, Colonel George Alexander, Colonel Adam Alexander, Colonel Phifer and Captain Jack. He served with General Griffith Rutherford in Cherokee Campaign. He was appointed Captain by General Thomas Sumter. He served in the battle of Monk's Corner, South Carolina. He was discharged by Colonel William Henderson during the illness of General Thomas Sumter.

JAMES JONES
of Kentucky

James Jones applied for revolutionary pension while living in Daviess County, Kentucky. He volunteered in 1778 in Rowan County, North Carolina, under Captain William Wilson, Lieutenant John Todd, Ensign Alexander Dobbins, Colonel Francis Locke and Brigadier General Rutherford. During 1780 and 1781 he served seven tours of duty as a minute man against the Tories. He was born in York County, Pennsylvania, in 1760. He moved to Rowan County, N. C. In 1824 he moved to Daviess County, Kentucky.

JOHN LAWRENCE
of Georgia

John Lawrence of Larrance, applied for revolutionary pension in Gwinnett County, Georgia, August 28, 1828. He served as a private in Captain Terry's First Virginia regiment. He was taken prisoner and carried to England as a prisoner of war. He also served under Captain Conway according to the affidavit of William Bryant who served with him in the 14th Regiment Virginia Line. John Lawrence was born in 1737 and died January 19, 1841. He was married to Betheland Smith, September 3, 1788, by Rev. Thomas Douglas, in Pittsylvania County, Virginia. April 4, 1855 she was 84 years old and so born in 1771. She applied for pension May 1, 1843.

COLONEL WILLIAM LENOIR
of North Carolina

William Lenoir applied for revolutionary pension while living in Wilkes County, N. C., in May, 1833. He was born in Brunswick moved to Charleston, S. C., and a short time later to Ninety-Six District, that part which later became Newbery District. In January 1782, he moved to Colonel Earl's Station in Rutherford County and in 1790 he moved to Green River in Buncombe County, N. C. He was still living May 29, 1839. There are no family data in his pension papers.

CAPTAIN JOHN MEBANE
of North Carolina

John Mebane applied for revolutionary pension while living in Chatham County, N. C., 1833. He was then 76 years of age and therefore born in 1757. He entered the service in Orange County North Carolina, in 1779, or 1780, and served in several different tour in North Carolina troops under Captains Douglas, John Williams, William Lytle, Major Crafton, and Colonels Joseph Lewis, John Hogan, Dudley, and Robert Mebane. The last was his brother and arranged an exchange when he, John, was taken prisoner. He served as a private and as a captain.

Note:- Captain John Mebane died September 13, 1837.

JOHN MILLER
of Kentucky

John Miller applied for revolutionary pension in Scott County, Kentucky, June 7, 1832, when he was 67 years of age. He was therefore born in 1765. He lived in Bedford County, Pennsylvania, and resided there during the Revolution. He had a sister, Katherine Miller Osborne, who was 69 years old in 1832. They lived with their father in Bedford County during the Revolution. John Miller moved to Indiana and died there September 10, 1836.

JACOB MOMIE (MOOMEY, MUMY)
of Pennsylvania

Jacob Moomey (Momie Mumy) applied for revolutionary pension while living in Columbia County, Pennsylvania, April 23, 1935, when he was 72 years of age. He entered the service under Captain John Deal in Germantown, Pennsylvania, as a substitute for Henry Switzer in the fall of 1778, as a drummer. He was drafted later in Berks County; drafted again in 1782 in Amity Township, Berks County. He was born in Baltimore, January 1, 1763. He was living at Chestnut Hill, ten miles from Philadelphia when he first entered service and lived afterwards in Berks County until he was 18 years of age. He moved later to Hemlock Township, Columbia County, Pennsylvania.

CHRISTOPHER MUMMY
of Ohio

Christopher Mummy applied for revolutionary pension while living in Morgan County, Ohio, in 1832. He was born April 2, 1753, at Germantown, Pennsylvania. He lived in that part of Virginia which is now called Brooke County, part of which was in Washington County Pennsylvania. He lived in Harrison County, Ohio, for eight years and then moved to Morgan County, Ohio, where he had lived for eight years previous to 1832.

County, Virginia, May 8, 1751. He moved to Surry County, N. C. He volunteered for service in the Revolution and was first commissioned a lieutenant. He became a captain in 1776 and served in the Cherokee Expedition. He served in the battle of King's Mountain where he was wounded in the arm and in the side. A third shot passed through his hair above where it was tied without wounding him. In a letter dated Fort Defiance, May 16, 1833, he says that he was Colonel of Cavalry of the 5th Division North Carolina militia and a major general of said division in 1796.

Note: He died May 6, 1836.

COLONEL JAMES MARTIN
of North Carolina

Colonel James Martin applied for revolutionary pension while living in North Carolina, October 17, 1832. In May, 1774, he moved from New Jersey to Guilford County, N. C. He was appointed Colonel Commandant of Guilford County Militia by Samuel Johnson, President of Congress and afterward Governor of North Carolina. His brother was Colonel Alexander Martin. In June, 1776, he marched with Guilford militia on the Cherokee Expedition. He served continuously against the Indians and Tories.

Note:- He died October 31, 1834.

JOHN MARTIN
of Kentucky

John Martin applied for revolutionary pension while living in Henderson County, Ky. He was drafted into service in Newberg County, South Carolina, under Major Gillam. He served in the battle of Stone Ferry. He was with Colonel Williams in an attack on Tories. He was again with Colonel James Williams in an attack on Tories. In 1779 he served in General Andrew Williamson's Cherokee Campaign.

MOSES MARTIN
of Kentucky

Moses Martin applied for revolutionary pension while living in Pulaski County, Ky. He entered the service in 1776 under Captain Richard Good and Colonel Martin Armstrong. When their troops joined General Griffith Rutherford. Moses Martin served under Colonel Gilliam Christian and Colonel Williams in the Cherokee Campaign.

MATTHEW MAYBIN OR MAYBEN
of North Carolina

Matthew Maybin, Maben or Mayben applied for revolutionary pension while living in Buncombe County, N. C. He was born in County Antrim, Ireland, January 13, 1756. He enlisted in January, 1775, and served eight tours, over two years in all and to the close of the War, in South Carolina troops under Captains Thomas Gordon, William Waddleton, or Waddington, James Lisle, David Dickson or Dixon, Caldwell, Frederick Lipham, and Colonels John Lisle, Jack, Brannam, Philemon Waters, and James Miller. He was in the battles of Rocky Mount, Hanging Rock and Fishing Creek. In 1772 he

JOHN MOMMY (MOOMY)
of Ohio

John Moomy applied for revolutionary pension while living in Pickaway County, Ohio, in 1829. He was then 76 years of age and therefore born in 1753. He enlisted in the service in Maryland in December, 1776. He was captured and made prisoner of war. After his escape he married. His wife was also 76 years of age in 1829.

WILLIAM MOORE
of North Carolina

William Moore applied for revolutionary pension while living in Rowan County, N. C. He entered the service June 22, 1780, under Captain Peter Hardwick, Colonel Francis Locke, and General Griffith Rutherford. Later he served under Captains Thomas Carson, William Cole, Hugh Hall and John Topp. He served in a skirmish against the British and Tories commanded by Colonel Fanning.

THOMAS NORTH
of Virginia

Thomas North applied for revolutionary pension while residing in Charlotte County, Virginia, in 1832. He was born in 1760 in Dinwiddie County, Virginia. He enlisted in July or August, 1776, and served in Captain Josiah Martin's Virginia Company. He served again under Major Jones. He served again under Captain Robert Jennings' and Captain Gideon Spencer's companies, Colonel John Holcomb's regiment. He was at the Siege of Yorktown and the surrender of Cornwallis. No data are given in regard to his family.

ROBERT ROBINSON
of North Carolina

Robert Robinson applied for revolutionary pension while living in Mecklenburg County, N. C. He entered the service under command of Captain John Sharp and Colonel Frederick Hambright. Later he joined General Benjamin Lincoln's troops; and later he was under the command of Captain William Alexander, Colonel Wade Hampton and General Thomas Sumter.

WILLIAM SMITH
of North Carolina

William Smith applied for revolutionary pension while living in Mecklenburg County, N. C. He entered the service under General Griffith Rutherford and Colonel Adam Alexander in the Cherokee Campaign. He served under General Benjamin Lincoln and Captain James Osborn in the Siege of Charleston; and also served with General Thomas Sumter, Colonel William Polk and Captain Thomas Shelby.

GEORGE STROTHER
of Virginia

George Strother applied for revolutionary pension while living in King George County, Va. He enlisted in King George County and served in Virginia militia under Captain Francis Conway and Colonel

Skinner. He served until April 9, 1781, at which time he was injured by a gun shot wound inhis left shoulder and unable to serve longer. He was born in KingGeorge County in 1760 and drew pension in that county. There are no data regarding his family.

ELIZABETH STROTHER
WIDOW OF JAMES STROTHER
of Virginia

Elizabeth Strother, aged 75 years, June 24, 1842, of Virginia, declared that she was the widow of James Strother, who enlisted in 1777. He served for three years in a Virginia regiment under Colonels Morgan and William Brent.

She married James Strother May 8, 1788, in Fairfax County, Virginia. Her name before marriage was Elizabeth Battle Morton and she was the daughter of "Parson" Morton. James Strother died April 27, 1844, leaving the following children: James P. Strother, of Smyth County, Virginia; Jane Strother Ewell, of Russell County, Virginia; and Nancy Whitten Strother, of Tazewell County, Virginia.

James Strother made oath as to his revolutionary service in Russell County, September 4, 1811.

Harry Smith of Russell County declared that he was half brother of James Strother and was aged 68 years July 9, 1842. Peggy Smith declared that she was 66 years of age, July 9, 1842, and that she was a half sister of James Strother.

Mary James Strother, widow of Anthony Strother, and mother of the soldier, James Strother, married for her second husband in 1771, Colonel Henry Smith, in King George County, Virginia, by whom she was tne mother of the affiants, Harry and Peggy Smith. Mary James Strother Smith was born in 1736 and died in 1822. Her first husband, Anthony Strother was born in 1710 and died in 1765. Anthony Strother had another son by his first wife (Betheland Storke Strother). This Benjamin Strother, half brother of the pensioner, was also in revolutionary service, first in the Virginia State Navy and later in the land forces.

JAMES TATE

of North Carolina

James Tate applied for revolutionary pension while living in Surry County, N. C., November 10, 1828, when his age was about 71 years. He lived in Westmoreland County, Va, when he entered the service as a private from February 1778 until March 19, 1779, under Captains Henry Fauntleroy and Bentley and Colonels Richard Parger and Gaskins in the Virginia troops and subsequently in Virginia militia on Garrison duty in the Northern Neck of Virginia until the close of the War. He stated that he was in the battle of Monmouth.

In 1828 his wife was living and a step daughter was living with them but the names are not given.

JOHN TAYLOR
of Virginia

John Taylor was residing in Montgomery County, Virginia, when he applied for revolutionary pension, July 1, 1823, he was then 87 years of age. The date and place of his birth, and the names of his parents are not given in his application.

He enlisted while residing in Fincastle County, which was later Montgomery County, about March 1, 1777. Ht served as a private under Captains James Knox and Woodfall, and unner Colonels Muhlenberg, Bowman, and Neville, in Virginia troops. He was in the battles of Brandywine, Germantown, and Monmouth, and was discharged at the surrender of Cornwallis. He then returned to Montgomery County. He stated that he had never married.

ANDREW WALLACE
of Pennsylvania

Andrew Wallace applied for revolutionary pension while living in Chester County, Ptnnsylvania, in 1833, but his application was executed in Washington, D. C. He was 103 years old and therefore born in 1730. He enlisted in the Revolutionary army in April, 1776, at Turk's Head, Chester County, in Captain Church's company, Colonel Anthony Wayne's regiment. He served in the battles of Three Rivers, Iron Mills, Brandywine, Paoli, Germantown and Monmouth, was in the storming of Stony Point, under Captain Grant of the 9th regiment; he was in the battles of Camden, Cowpens, and Eutaw Springs under Colonel Stuart and in the Siege of Yorktown undtr Captain Davis.

JOHN WILFONG
of North Carolina

John Wilfong applied for revolutionary pension while living in Lincoln County, N. C., in October, 1833. He was born in North Carolina, April 8, 1762. He enlisted in Lincoln County where he was living in 1780. He served in the battle of King's Mountain where he was wounded in the left arm. He returned to his home the next day after the battle. He volunteered again in July, 1781, and was in the battle of Eutaw Springs.

JOHN WILSON
of North Carolina

John Wilson applied for revolutionary pension while living in Cumberland County, N. C., in March, 1830, when he was 73 years of age. He entered the service in Dobbs County, N. C., in 1778. He was discharged in 1782 near Greenville, on Tar River. He stated that he was born in Pitt County, N. C., in 1756. He mentioned his wife and a son.

JOHN WILSON
of Georgia

John Wilson applied for revolutionary pension while living in Greene County, Georgia, August 30, 1832. He was then 77 years of age. He enlisted in 1779 at Petersburg, Virginia. He was taken prisoner May 12, 1780. He married Elizabeth ——— September 2, 1780. They had children but no names are given.

INDEX

SOME TENNESSEE HEROES OF THE REVOLUTION
FIVE PAMPHLETS

	Pamphlet		Pamphlet
Adair, John,	II	Butler, James,	I
Alexander, Dan, of Marion Co.,	I	Butler, Zahariah, Sullivan Co.,	I
Alexander, Dan, of Henderson Co.,	I	Butler, Zachariah, Maury Co.,	1
Alexander, Elijah,	V*'	Caldwell, George,	I
Allen, Richard,	V	Campbell, James, Knox Co.,	I
Allison, Robert,	I	Campbell, James, Carter Co.,	I
Antrican, Francis,	V	Campbell, Jeremiah,	I
Archer, Isaac,	V	Campbell Ensign Joseph,	II
Armstrong, Isaac,	I	Campbell, Richard,	III
Armstrong, John,	V	Campbell, Robert,	I
Armstrong, John, of Smith Co.,	V	Carmichael, John,	IV
Armstrong, Thomas,	I	Carroll, William,	I
Arnold, Francis,	IV	Carter, Landon, Widow of,	I
Balch, Amos,	IV	Carter, Samuel,	II
Banes, John,	V	Caruthers, Robert,	IV
Barnett, Carter,	I	Cathcart, Joseph,	V
Bealer, or Beeler, Jacob,	V	Cavett, Richard,	IV
Beard, William,	V	Chester, John,	II
Bearden, John,	IV	Childress, David,	V
Beatty, James,	V	Chilton, George, (see Shelton),	III
Beatty, Walter,	IV	Chumley, Daniel,	IV
Benson, Spencer,	I	Clark, Jonas,	V
Blackburn, James,	III	Clark, William,	II
Blackmore, George D.,	IV	Clay, William,	II
Blair, Samuel,	III	Clements, John,	V
Boston, Christopher,	I	Cobb, Pharoah,	III
Bowen, Charles,	V	Coleman, Spencer,	III
Bradford, William, Jefferson Co.,	I	Conway, Henry,	
Bradford, William, Sumner Co.,	V	Cooper, Richard,	I
Bradshaw, Benjamin,	V	Cooper, James,	V
Bragg, William,	I	Crabtree, Isaac,	V
Brakebill, Peter,	IV	Craighead, Robert,	IV
Brandon, Josiah,		Crawford, John,	I
Brannon, Thomas,	I	Creswell, Andrew,	IV
Brooke, Dudley,	III	Cross, William,	III
Brooks, Littleton,	V	Crye, William,	I
Brown, Joseph,	IV	Cunningham, John,	I
Brown, Stephen,	I	Cunningham, Valentine,	I
Brown, Morgan,	IV	Curtis, John,	II
Broyles, Daniel,	I	Dalton, John,	II
Burke, (Berke), Elisha,	IV	Davies, John L.,	III
Burnett, William,	IV	Davis, Andrey,	II
		Davis, James,	I

157

	Pamphlet		Pamphlet
Davis, Nicholas,	I	Hall, William,	IV
Davis, Samuel,	I	Handly, Abraham,	III
Davis, Robert,	I	Handly, Capt. Samuel,	IV
Day, John,	II	Hansley, Robert,	III
Day, Phillip,	V	Jackson, Samuel,	II
Dibrell, Charles,	IV	Jackson, William,	II
Dismukes, Paul,	IV	Jennings, William,	II
Lixon, George,	III	Johnston, Gideon,	V
Doherty, George,	IV	Johnston, John,	V
Doss, John,	II	Johnston, John, Maury Co.,	V
Doyle, John,	III	Jones, Darling,	I
Dudley, Guilford,	I	Jones, James,	I
Dyche, Charles,	I	Jones, John,	III
Dyer, John,	II	Keebler, Jacob, Jr.,	IV
Dysart, John,	II	Kelly, Dennis,	V
Ernest, Ensign Felix,	III	Kelly, William,	I
Elliott, William,	II	Kerr, James,	V
Estes, John.	II	Key,, William,	I
Ethridge, John,	II	Kilbourn, Benjamin,	III
Evans, Andrew,	II	King, Thomas,	III
Evans, Joseph,	II	King, William,	III
Evans, Samuel,	II	Landrum, James,	IV
Everett, Samuel,	III	Landrum, Thomas,	IV
Everett, William,	II	Lane, Joseph,	I
Everett, William,	II	Lanham, Abel,	I
Everett, Robert,	III	Latimer, Wetherell,	IV
Ewing, Alexander,	II	Leay, Lee, William,	V
Fain, Ebenezer,	II	Leonard, John,	I
Fenner, Richard,	IV	Lindsay, Moses,	V
Finn, Peter,	IV	Longley, William,	II
Fite, John,	IV	Love, Hezekiah,	I
Fite, Leonard,	IV	Lusk, John,	IV
Flowers, Rowland,	III	Luttrell, James,	IV
Ford, John,	II	Malaby, John,	II
Frazier, Henry,	III	Marion, John F.,	III
Fuller, George,	I	Martin, Josiah,	IV
Gaines, Ambrose,	I	Martin, Robert,	II
Gammon, Harris,	I	Martin, Matthew, Sr.,	IV
Gann, Thomas,	I	Martin, Salathiel,	V
Gibbs, John,	IV	Massengale, Hal,	III
Gibson, John, of Lincoln Co.,	III	Massengale, Michael,	III
Gibson, John, of Wilson Co.,	III	Matlock, Richard,	IV
Gillespie, Jacob,	V	May, William,	II
Goens, David,	III	Mayes, Samuel,	II
Goodman, Henry,	II	McBee, Israel,	IV
Goodwin, David,	II	McBride, James,	V
Graham, William,	II	McCormick, Joseph,	II
Grantham, Richard,	I	McCroskey, John,	IV
Gregory, George,	I	McDonough, Andrew,	II
Guthrie, Robert,	IV	McFarland, Robert,	IV
Hale, Amon,	I	McFerrin, William,	V
Hale, John,	I	McIntyre, John,	IV
Hale, Nathan,	I	McKelvey, William,	IV
Hale, Nicholas,	I		
Hale, William,	II		

	Pamphlet		Pamphlet
McKie, Lieut. Daniel,	IV	Reed, Lovett,	II
McMillan, Joseph,	II	Reid, William Porter,	II
McMinn, Robert,	IV	Richardson, Amos,	II
McNabb, David,	V	Ritchie, Alexander,	I
McNatt, John, Bedford Co.,	V	Roark, Michael,	I
McNatt, John, Roane Co.,	V	Roberts, Edmund,	I
McSpadden, Samuel,	IV	Roberts, William,	I
		Rogers, Jeremiah,	I
		Rogers, Joseph,	I
McVey, Eli,	II	Rogers, William,	I
Medearis, John,	V	Samples, Jesse,	III
Miles, Michael,	II	Scott, Arthur,	III
Metcalf, William,	II	Sevier, Abraham,	V
Miller, Adam,	II	Sevier, James,	I
Miller, James,	I	Sevier, John, Children of,	I
Miller, John H.,	I	Sevier, Maj. Valentine, widow of,	I
Miller, Martin,	I	Shannon, William,	III
Miller, Samuel,	I	Sharp, William,	V
Mitchell, James,	I	Shelton, George,	I
Mitchell, Solomon, Hawkins Co.,	I	Sherrill, George Davidson,	II
Mitchell, Solomon, Sumner Co.,	I	Shortridge, Andrew,	III
Mitchell, William,	IV	Sims, James,	II
Moore, Capt. Elijah,	IV	Smith, Laton,	II
Moore, Thomas,	II	Smith, Ralph,	III
Moore, Thomas,	IV	Smith, Ransom,	I
Moore, William,	IV	Smith, Robert,	I
Morgan, Benjamin,	IV	Smith, William, Loncoln Co.,	III
Morgan, James,	II	Smith, William, Jefferson Co.,	V
Morgan, Valentine,	II	Smith, William C.,	III
Morris, Abner,	II	Smith Zebulon,	IV
Morris, Lester,	IV	Standifer, Benjamin,	II
Mowrey, Peter,	V	Spencer, Moses,	V
Murphey, William,	IV	Steele, Samuel,	II
Narramore, John,	II	Stephenson, Meshack,	II
Nelson, John,	III	Sterling, Robert,	II
Nelson, Moses,	III	Stone, Robert,	II
Norris, Abner,	III	Stone, Conway,	V
Nunnelee, Edward,	IV	Stone, Ezekial,	I
Obar, Robert,	II	Stone, John,	V
Palmer, Thomas,	II	Stone, Solomon,	I
Patterson, Robert,	II	Sutherland, Daniel,	I
Paugh, Young,	II	Sutton, John,	II
Pearce, James,	III	Tate, David,	IV
Pearson, Able,	III	Tate, John,	V
Perkins, John,	IV	Taylor, Andrew,	II
Perry, Jesse,	II	Taylor, Christopher,	I
Poindexter, Chapman,	I	Taylor, Daniel,	IV
Polk, William,	V	Taylor, Isaac,	II
Pollard, Chatten D.,	II	Taylor, James,	I
Porter, Mitchell,	II	Taylor, Leroy,	I
Pryor, Matthew,	II	Tedford, John,	I
Quarles, Francis,	III	Tedford, Robert,	II
Ragsdale, Maxter,	III	Thomas, John,	II
Raines, Capt. John,	II	Thompson, Stephen,	II
Range, James,	I	Thornton, Pressley,	III

	Pamphlet		Pamphlet
Thurman, Charles,	II	White, Stephen,	V
Thurman, Philip,	II	Williams, Alexander,	III
Tipton, Jonathan,	I	Williams, Benjamin,	I
Tipton, William,	I	Williams, Caleb,	V
Town, William,	II	Williams, Francis,	III
Towns, Thomas,	II	Williams, John J.,	II
Trent, Alexander,	IV	Williams, Mathias,	II
Troxal, Jacob,	I	Williams, Samuel,	IV
Turnley, George,	I	Williams, William,	III
Turnley, John,	III	Williams, Zebedee,	III
Tyner, Dempsey,	II	Williams, Williughby,	IV
Vaughn, Abram,	V	Williamson, John,	III
Vance, Samuel,	IV	Willis, Seshack,	IV
Vernon, Thomas,	IV	Wilson, John, Carter Co.,	III
Vickery, Luke,	II	Wilson, John, Lincoln Co.,	III
Walker, John, Blount Co.,	IV	Wilson, Joseph,	II
Walker, John, Roane Co.,	II	Winstead, Francis,	III
Walker, Capt. Samuel, Roane Co.,	II	Witt, Burgess,	IV
Walker, Samuel, Bradley Co.,	II	Witt, Caleb,	IV
Walker, George,	III	Wood, Belfield,	III
Wallen, Elisha,	II	Wood, Zadock,	III
Wear, John,	III	Woodruff, Jesse,	III
Weir, James,	I	Wooten, Turner,	I

VETERANS WHO DID NOT LIVE IN TENNESSEE

In gathering pension records of Tennessee Soldiers of the Revolution records were accumulated of veterans from other states. In order not to lose these valuable data they are included in the Pamphlets.

	Pamphlet		Pamphlet
Adcock, Joshua, N. C.	V	Gwinn, Samuel, Va.,	III
Alexander, William, Ky.,	III	Hampton, John, Ga.,	V
Alexander, William, Wilson Co., N. C.,	IV	Hanna, Robert, S. C.,	IV
		Harris, Benjamin, Ga.,	III
Alexander, William, Mecklinburg Co., N. C.,	V	Harrison, Burditt, Va.,	III
		Hixson, James, Va.,	III
Armstrong, Robert, Ill.,	III	Hixson, James, N. J.,	V
Armstrong, James, Ky.,	V	Houston, James, N. C., Rowan Co.,	III
Armstrong, James, S. C.,	IV		
Allen, Richard, N. C.,	V	Houston, James, N. C., Iredell Co.,	III
Allen, William, Ill.,	V		
Alsobrook, Jesse, N. C.,	V	Howe, John W., Ky.,	III
Armistead, Westwood. N. C.,	V	Hutcheson, William, N. C.,	V
Baldwin, John, N. C.,	V	Jameson, William, N. C.,	III
Bills, John E., Va.,	III	Jett, William Storke, Va.,	III
Brown, Caleb, N. H.,	III	Johnson, Thomas, Va.,	III
Bugbee, Sylvester, Ver(.,	IV	Key, John, Va.,	III
Burch, Joseph, N. C.,	V	Key, Tandy, Va.,	III
Calvert, Spencer, Ky.,	III	Key, William, Ga.,	III
Campbell, James, N. Y.,	III	Kitner, John, Penn.,	III
Campbell, John, Ohio,	IV	Latham, John, Pa.,	III
Carson, Andrew, N. C.,	V	Lawrence, John, Ga.,	V
Childress, Benjamin, Va.,	V	Lenoir, William, N. C.,	V
Colbert, John, Va.,	III	Lipscomb, Ambrose, Va.,	III
Corn, Timothy, Ky.,	IV	Martin, James, N. C.,	V
Dade, Isaac, Mass.,	V	Martin, John, Ky.,	V
Davis, Samuel, Ala.,	III	Martin, Moses, Ky.,	V
Davis, William, Ala.	III	Maybin, Mathew, N. C.,	V
Day, Francis, N. C.,	V	Mabane, John, N. C.,	V
Day, William, S. C.,	V	McCutcheon, John, Va.,	III
Day, William, Va.,	V	Miller, John, Ky.,	V
Denney, John, N. C.	V	Mills, George, Va.,	III
Dysart, James, Ky.,	III	Momie, Jacob, Penn.,	V
Ely, William, Va.,	IV	Mummy, Christopher, Ohio,	V
Freeman, John, Va.,	III	Mommy, John, Ohio,	V
Gillespie, John, Ky.,	V	Moore, William, N. C.,	V
Gillespie, John, Penn.,	V	Nelson, John, Va.,	III
Gillespie, William, Va.,	V	North, Thomas, Va.,	V
Glean, Anthony, N. Y.,	III	Porter, John, Ky.,	III
Graham, Joseph, N. C.,	V	Porter, Thomas, Va.,	IV
Graham, William, N. C.,	V	Porter, William, Ky.,	III

	Pamphlet
Pruitt, Martin, Illinois,	IV
Robinson, Robert, N. C.,	V
Smith, William, N. C.,	V
Smoot, John, Ky.,	IV
Strother, Benjamin, Prince William Co., Va.,	III
Strother, Elizabeth, widow of James, Va.,	V
Strother, George, Va.,	V
Randolph, Abraham, Ala.,	IV
Reno, Zela, Ky.,	IV
Russell, Philip M., Penn.,	III
Tate, John, N. C.,	V
Taylor, John, Va.,	V
Tipton, William, Ky.,	V

	Pamphlet
Wallace, Andrew, Penn.,	V
Weir, John, Vt.,	IV
Wilfong, John, N. C.,	V
Wilson, John, Cumberland Co., N. C.,	V
Wilson, John, Duplin Co., N. C.,	IV
Wilson, John, Johnston Co., N. C.,	IV
Wilson, John, Ala.,	IV
Wilson, John, Ga.,	IV
Wilson, John, S. C.,	IV
Witt, Aires, Ky.,	IV
Witt, Elisha, Ky.,	IV
Witt, Jesse, Bedford Co., Va.,	III
Witt, Jesse, Goochland Co., Va.,	III
Witt, Robert, Ky.,	IV

www.ingramcontent.com/pod-product-compliance
Lightning Source LLC
Chambersburg PA
CBHW060358080526
44583CB00012B/372